PROSTHETIC

MEMORIES

ANIMA: Critical Race Studies Otherwise

A series edited by Mel Y. Chen, Ezekiel J. Dixon-Román,
and Jasbir K. Puar

P R O S T H E T I C
M E M O R I E S

POSTCOLONIAL
FEMINISMS
IN A
MORE-THAN-HUMAN
WORLD

Hyaesin Yoon

DUKE UNIVERSITY PRESS
Durham and London
2025

© 2025 DUKE UNIVERSITY PRESS
All rights reserved
Printed in the United States of America on acid-free paper ∞
Project Editor: Liz Smith
Designed by A. Mattson Gallagher
Typeset in Minion Pro and Real Head Pro by
Westchester Publishing Services

Library of Congress Cataloging-in-Publication Data
Names: Yoon, Hyaesin, [date] author.
Title: Prosthetic memories : postcolonial feminisms in a
more-than-human world / Hyaesin Yoon.
Other titles: ANIMA (Duke University Press)
Description: Durham : Duke University Press, 2025. | Series:
Anima | Includes bibliographical references and index.
Identifiers: LCCN 2024022136 (print)
LCCN 2024022137 (ebook)
ISBN 9781478031246 (paperback)
ISBN 9781478028017 (hardcover)
ISBN 9781478060222 (ebook)
Subjects: LCSH: Memory—Social aspects. | Postcolonialism. |
Feminist theory. | Technology—Social aspects—Korea (South) |
Technology—Social aspects—United States. | Human-animal
relationships—Social aspects. | Human-computer interaction—
Social aspects. | BISAC: POLITICAL SCIENCE / Colonialism &
Post-Colonialism | SOCIAL SCIENCE / Women's Studies
Classification: LCC HM1033 .Y66 2025 (print) | LCC HM1033
(ebook) | DDC 303.48/3—dc23/eng/20240808
LC record available at https://lccn.loc.gov/2024022136
LC ebook record available at https://lccn.loc.gov/2024022137

Cover art: Minouk Lim (b. 1968), *Wind Seal*, 2022. Wood cane,
cuttlebone, epoxy resin, metal plate, 73¾ × 14⅛ × 12⅝ inches
(186 × 36 × 32 cm). Image © the artist and Tina Kim Gallery.
Photo by Dario Lasagni.

Contents

Note to Readers

When there are already published or existing transliterated forms for Korean proper nouns (including the names of artists, directors, and scholars) and for Korean nouns that are well known to English speakers, I use existing familiar forms even if they are inconsistent with formal transliteration systems (for example, Seoul, kimchi, or Hyaesin Yoon).

For Korean names, I generally put the given name first. Exceptions are political figures or celebrities (for example, Kim Young-sam and Kang Won-rae) whose names might already be familiar in their original Korean order.

In all other cases, I follow the McCune-Reischauer system.

All translations of Korean sources are mine unless otherwise noted.

In the bibliography, for authors of sources in Korean language, I put family name first followed by given name without a comma between. For authors with Korean names of sources written in English, I put a comma between the family name and given name.

Acknowledgments

The research project that evolved into *Prosthetic Memories* began when I was a graduate student in the Department of Rhetoric at the University of California, Berkeley. I am grateful for the mentorship of Trinh T. Minh-ha and Charis Thompson, whose intellectual brilliance and professional generosity have offered lasting guidance and inspiration. I feel lucky and thankful for the dear friendship and many discussions I have had with the peers I met there, in particular Mark Minch-de Leon and Keerthi Potluri, who also read and commented on several parts of this book at various stages even after we all graduated.

I am thankful for the Department of Gender and Women's Studies (GWS) at UC Berkeley for generously hosting me as a visiting scholar after the completion of my PhD. It offered me a vibrant academic community wherein I had the pleasure of meeting amazing scholars from all over the world visiting GWS or affiliated with the Beatrice Bain Research Group—in particular, Marcin Smietana, Tomomi Kinukawa, Ingvill Stuvøy, Meltem İnce Yenilmez, Teresa Sacchet, Noémie Merleau-Ponty, Meeta Rani Jha, Doris Leibetseder, Sé Sullivan, Christina Hee Pedersen, Chinyere Oparah, Smadar Lavie, and France Winddance Twine. Intellectual exchanges with them helped me envision how to turn what felt like a mercurial constellation of thoughts into a book that has now become *Prosthetic Memories*. It was during this time that Mel Chen told me about the then-new book series ANIMA (of which they are a coeditor) and encouraged me to make my book a part of it. This conversation meant the world to me and has been a source of strength to keep me dreaming and progressing until today.

At Central European University (CEU), I've received invaluable intellectual and institutional support. I extend my warmest thanks to my wonderful colleagues at the Department of Gender Studies, especially Erzsébet Barát, Francisca de Haan, the late Linda Fischer, Elissa Helms, Nadia Jones-Gailani, Jasmina Lukic, Adriana Qubaiova, Hadley Z. Renkin, Sarah Smith, and Eszter Timár. I wouldn't be the same person without the experience of working with them and supporting each other, especially through the difficult times when the university relocated from Budapest to Vienna due to political pressure, followed by the COVID-19 pandemic. I also thank my former students and now fellow scholars Lieks Hettinga and Ida Hillerup Hansen, who trusted me as their PhD supervisor when I was just beginning my academic career myself and who have provided affective and intellectual refreshments in the process of writing this book. I am grateful for Shreya Bhat, who helped me organize the references and bibliography in my manuscript. My heartfelt thanks to all other former and current students I have been privileged to teach at CEU, who have continually reminded me of the beauty of humanity and of teaching and learning in academia.

A significant part of this book was written during my sabbatical leaves, generously granted by CEU, to stay at the Reproductive Sociology Research Group (ReproSoc) and later at the Center for Gender Studies at the University of Cambridge—I deeply appreciate the warm hospitality from both institutions. I especially acknowledge Sarah Franklin and other members of the ReproSoc for their astute questions and suggestions about this book's early chapter drafts, which deepened my understanding of reproductive and regenerative technologies. I must also mention my flatmates during my stay in Cambridge: Francesco Cecchi, Arantxa González de Heredia, and Elizabeth Gasson. Late-night conversations, laughter, meals, and adventures with them added much joy to the process of writing this book.

I have presented early chapter drafts, fragments, or ideas at various conferences, symposiums, and colloquiums: the Critical Global Studies Institute Colloquium at Sogang University, Seoul (online); the European Society for Literature, Science, and the Arts annual conferences in Athens and Copenhagen; the Yun Posun Memorial Symposium at the University of Edinburgh; the Association for Asian Studies Annual Conference in Washington, DC; the "Power and the Chthulucene" symposium at Uppsala

University; the Society for Literature, Science, and the Arts annual conference at University of Notre Dame; the Colloquium at the Interdisciplinary
Program in Gender Studies at Seoul National University; and the "Funny
Kinds of Love" conference at UC Berkeley. The helpful feedback and encour-
agement from panel members and audiences at these venues were vital for
revising and developing these presentations into the book manuscript. I am
grateful to Nayun Jang, Myojung Bae, Lynn Turner, Youngmi Kim, We Jung
Yi, Ann-Sofie Lönngren, Eun-kyung Bae, and Harlan Weaver for these in-
vitations and organizations.

An earlier version of chapter 2 and a brief section from chapter 1 were
published as "The Biopolitics of Languaging in the Cybernetic Fold" in
Journal of Gender Studies 29, no. 1 (2020) and reproduced as a chapter in
C. L. Quinan and K. Thiele, eds., *Biopolitics, Necropolitics, Cosmopolitics*
(Routledge, 2021). An earlier version of chapter 4 was published as "Disap-
pearing Bitches: Canine Affect and Postcolonial Bioethics" in *Configurations:
A Journal of Literature, Science, and Technology* 24, no. 3 (2016).

I thank Woo Suk Hwang and other scientists at Sooam Biotech Research
Foundation, Seoul, for kindly showing me around the facility and explaining and sharing information about their dog-cloning processes. I also appreciate David (a pseudonym) for generously sharing his experience with
cloning companion dogs and living with them.

Many thanks to Margaret Rhee's brilliant interlocution, which has made
my writing about her poetry even more delightful. I was also touched by
the kindness of Soyo Lee, who generously sent me a copy of her book *Kŏllŏ
chŏmmok sŏninjang* (Ornamental cactus design) by post from Seoul to
Vienna—it provided a wonderful source of inspiration in the final stage of
writing this book. The Berkeley Art Museum and Pacific Film Archive have
kindly allowed me to screen Theresa Hak Kyung Cha's video pieces again
and again and to use a still from one of her videos in this book.

I was fortunate to have as my editor Courtney Berger at Duke University
Press. I am deeply grateful that she saw the potential of this book and guided
me toward its publication with vision, patience, and kindness. I also thank
Duke University Press's anonymous readers, whose incredibly rigorous
and encouraging reports on my manuscript made this book better despite
my shortcomings. Sincere thanks also to all those at Duke University Press
who helped this book appear in the world. Immense thanks to Matthew
Jeremy Ritchie, who has read various stages of the manuscript, offering a
keen pair of eyes to help me seek a style of writing with clarity, sophistica-
tion, and elegance.

I wouldn't have made it this far without the wonderful circle of friends I feel blessed to have. My special thanks to Seunghyun Yang, Jiyeon Kang, Meongwon Choi, and Ju Li for all the conversations, phone calls, travels, and walks together. Also, I am grateful for the animal friends who accompanied me through the ups and downs of writing this book. Sending love to my late dog Jasper and late cat Viola, and to Cielito the cat.

I offer boundless gratitude to my loving family. My brother Seungjun Yoon, sister Haeyoung Yoon, brother-in-law Sunkyu Park, and nephew Ryan Jungmin Park have been both my rocks to stand on and my cheerleaders. Last, this book is dedicated to my late father, Dong-min Yoon, and to my mother, Jung-Mee Wi, whom I owe everything.

Introduction

Prosthetic Memories: Postcolonial Feminisms in a More-Than-Human World explores an emergent mode of collective memory arising from technological assemblages of humans, animals, and machines across and between contemporary South Korea and the United States. It proceeds from the primary stake of embodied memory in an era of advanced biotechnology and informatics: that how we remember is embedded in our entanglements with human and nonhuman others in parasitic/nurturing, exploitive/creative, and unevenly interdependent webs spun beyond human consciousness and control. This book takes up as a postcolonial feminist agenda both the conundrums and the potential that such a state of embodied memory entails, proposing a new approach to prosthetic memory—revising its conventional conception as an artificial supplement to natural (human) memory.

Let me begin with an art project that involves the ancient technology of plant propagation. Seoul-born, Los Angeles–based artist Kang Seung Lee's 2020 work *Untitled (Harvey)* is a 150 × 114 cm graphite drawing of a Christmas cactus in a pot. This drawing is a hyperrealist portrayal of the work of Lee's fellow artist and friend Julie Tolentino, *Archive in Dirt* (2019–). The main component of Tolentino's *Archive in Dirt* is a living plant nicknamed Harvey after Harvey Milk (1930–78), a pioneering openly gay politician and civil rights activist in San Francisco.[1] Harvey was cut from a mother plant that Milk had cultivated at home (cared for by his former roommate after

Milk's assassination), gifted to Tolentino via an archivist friend of hers.[2] *Archive in Dirt* thus expresses how memories of artists and activists outside conventional boundaries are relayed through collective care and affection, to which Lee's drawing is a performative tribute.[3]

During Lee's exhibition at the 2021 New Museum Triennial in New York, *Untitled (Harvey)* was accompanied by a piece named after his friend, *Julie Tolentino (Archive in Dirt)*, featuring a living cactus clipped from Tolentino's Harvey and given to Lee.[4] This new generation of cactus was planted in a pot made of soil from two noted locations: from the garden in Dungeness tended by British filmmaker Derek Jarman (1942–94) as an act of grief and love while he lost close friends to AIDS, until he himself succumbed to AIDS-related complications, and from Topgol Park in Seoul, a historic cruising ground for residents of the city.[5] In this way, Lee's *Julie Tolentino (Archive in Dirt)* also reverberates with Lee's earlier efforts to entangle the memory of Jarman with the (absent) traces of lesser-known Korean LGBT rights and HIV/AIDS awareness activist Joon-Soo Oh (1964–98), who also died from AIDS-related complications in the 1990s.[6] As the tender shoot is cut, calluses, and grows in a new pot, carrying the memories of queer connections tracing back to Harvey Milk, a lesser-known South Korean gay activist's trace is grafted onto the memory of a famous British filmmaker, nurturing and haunting the cactus.

Lee's art illuminates key features of the emergent mode of prosthetic memory this book concerns. Different from the conventional portrayal of prosthetic memory as technologically exteriorized memory that transcends the body, Lee's art illustrates memories that arise at and transpose as they circulate through various interfaces of body-technology (even ones as rudimentary as drawing or a plant propagating but, as I discuss shortly, also more cutting-edge information and biological technologies).[7] Thus, if Lee's *Julie Tolentino (Archive in Dirt)* is "an unexpected living archive," as introduced by the New Museum's official Twitter (now X), it isn't so much a container of memories transplanted from humans as a metonym for the broader matrix of memories—the entanglements of the drawings, the generations of cacti, and the pebbles and soils surrounding the cacti and constituting the pots, as well as the artists, activists, their friends, and the staff at the museum exhibitions who have tended these succulents.[8]

I figure these intra- and interspecies entanglements as *chimeracological*, borrowing Rachel Lee's neologism that merges "the terms 'chimera,' derived from ancient Greek '*Khimaira*,' referring to a hybrid monster composed of several different animal parts, and 'ecological,' a secular subset of the

I.1   A view of Kang Seung Lee's exhibition at the 2021 New Museum Triennial. Lee's *Untitled (Harvey)*, a drawing of Julie Tolentino's *Archive in Dirt (left)*, is accompanied by Lee's *Julie Tolentino (Archive in Dirt)*, featuring a living succulent propagated from Tolentino's Harvey and given to Lee *(right)*. Source: Screen shot from the New Museum Twitter (now X), November 8, 2021.

cosmological."[9] Rachel Lee's usage of *chimeracological* does not refer simply to the medical and pharmaceutical production of chimeric matters, where boundaries between different species and between organisms and technologies blur. It also refers to what biogeneticists and microbiologists have confirmed about interspecies epigenesis and evolution (such as a mammalian embryo's use of cues from intestinal microbes to complete its development) that renders our embodied worldings always chimeric.[10] Thus, the concept of chimeracological highlights both mundane and paranormal milieus that condition the peculiar mode of prosthetic memory that grows more salient in a (post)cybernetic and (epi)genetic postcolonial world.

Thinking of the memories that arise and transpose at these chimeracological junctures, I wonder how then the unexpectedness of *Julie Tolentino (Archive in Dirt)* might denote the inhuman otherness of these memories. Speculation about memories from the perspectives of a cactus stem or a pebble evokes a sense of the unreal (another meaning of *chimeric*), but such a perceived sense of inhuman alterity does not necessarily mark the ontological division between human and other beings. Rather, it indicates the abyss between Western humanism's scientific reason and other senses and knowledge, which unsettles the privilege given to the rational human subject (often saved for the Anglo-European subject) as a reference point of memory.

Kang Seung Lee's work also helps me portray prosthetic memories in line with Rachel Lee's sought-for femi-queer engagements with the affective and material labor of gestating and nurturing other life (wherein female bodies are figured as chimeracological), the significance of which is even greater with the advancement of reproductive and regenerative technologies.[11] Combining a plant's capacity to regenerate with humans' affective care for plants (and for fellow humans connected via the plants) and with the intensive labor put into hyperrealist drawings, Kang Seung Lee's art furthers the political potential of prosthetic memories in a chimeracological world— moving from traumatic memories of necropolitical erasure, displacement, and injury toward the network of care woven through entangled memories.

In my engagement with Lee's art project, I propose a specific mode of prosthetic memory as a working concept for engaging with various body-technology interfaces at the turn of the twenty-first century. This new mode of prosthetic memory emerges in chimeracological milieus that blur body-technology boundaries, entails inhuman otherness beyond the usual human perception and subjectivity, and has potential to generate networks of care and intimacy that counter fragmenting, isolating, and uprooting biopolitical forces. The proposed concept of prosthetic memory is therefore both resonant and dissonant with existing discourses regarding the relationship between human memory and emergent and anticipated technologies at various points in history (from writing to television to artificial intelligence)— and with ideas that the term *prosthetic memory* might initially evoke in the minds of readers. I hope to mobilize such resonances and dissonances to develop a postcolonial feminist mnemonic attuned to the contemporary biopolitical world, where human and nonhuman mind-bodies, alongside their affective forces, are increasingly recruited, modified, assembled, and disposed of in the transnational circuits of biotechnology (BT) and information and communication technology (ICT).

This book engages with prosthetic memories across primarily the United States and South Korea, centering on two clusters of body-technology interfaces around the tongue and the gene. It explores sites of technological intervention into language practices and (epi)genetic materials—such as tongue surgery (purported to improve English pronunciation), human-machine poetry, commercial pet cloning, and human embryonic stem cell research—that unsettle the assumed grounds of embodied memory and provoke a set of questions about postcolonial feminist mnemonics situated in the contemporary transpacific context.

Both the tongue and the gene are archetypal figures of embodied memory, marking the interchanges between body and mind, biological and cultural. The mother tongue is often seen as the root of culture (especially among diasporas and the colonized), and genetic composition is seen as a bearer of biological data (imprinted with individual identity as well as race and species kinship). Artificial mediations into these figures are therefore typically considered in terms of interruption in (or erasure of) cultural and biological memories. However, what if we instead look at them less as natural sites for preexisting identity and origin and more as compound interfaces, where self, lineage, and relation are composed through technological articulations with others? Can we think about the prosthetic memories that emerge from these articulations, accounting for the emergent assemblages of human, animal, and technology that have become both mundane and phantasmal conditions of life? What onto-epistemological and political visions does such an approach to memory challenge or afford for engaging with chimeracological entanglements across gender, race, species, and geopolitical differences in the context of neoliberal globalization?

To answer these questions, *Prosthetic Memories* proceeds from and interweaves three streams of inquiry. First, this book refigures the concept of prosthetic memory, departing from the long-standing suspicion of prosthetic memory as the technological replacement of human (that is, assumably natural) memory in Western philosophical and literary tradition—and also from its mirror image, the transhumanist celebration of prosthetic memory. My aim here isn't to make a general proposition about the relationship between human and technology alternative to these two prevalent approaches; instead, I hope to put into perspective how prosthetic memory, as a concept, has come to reflect and also shape our understanding of (human) memory within specific techno-cultural configurations at the turn of this century. To build a new stage for this conceptual genealogy of prosthetic memory, the first part of this introduction ("Prosthetic Memory: Rearticulating Humanity, Technology, and Memory") reviews the existing discourses on prosthetic memory as an emerging mode of collective consciousness in late nineteenth and twentieth-century modern societies and introduces key changes in the contemporary techno-cultural and biopolitical landscape (the chimeracological milieu) that backdrops my proposal for a renewed figure of prosthetic memory.

Second, the particular mode of prosthetic memory addressed in this book is not only contingent on the cultural deployment of technologies such as tongue surgery, machine poetry, genetic animal cloning, and human stem cell research but also haunted by the "imaginary chorus" that the term *prosthetics* evokes.[12] The next part of this introduction ("Recasting *Prosthetic*: An Intersectional Dialogue") reflects, on one hand, on how discourses about prosthetics often hinge on the metaphoricity of disabled mind-bodies (as the assumed users of assistive technologies) only to disavow their materiality and, on the other, on how gendered, racial, and geopolitical critiques about reproductive and care work (and the interdependency such labor suggests) demand reassessment of the supplementarity underlying the concept of prosthetic memory. This imaginary chorus both guides and haunts my efforts in the following chapters to refigure and engage with prosthetic memories in revising postcolonial feminist mnemonics in the transnational circuits of BT and ICT.

Third, with its revised concept of prosthetic memory, this book aims to advance postcolonial feminist discussions on memory across South Korea and the United States that have been focused on the trauma of Japanese colonialism, the Korean War, and the resultant postcolonial and diasporic experience—expanding the topoi into various body-technology interfaces across the two countries. In doing this, as discussed later in this introduction ("Rethinking Postcolonial Feminist Mnemonics at the Turn of the Twenty-First Century"), this book engages with contemporary feminist approaches to embodied memory as a dynamic site for competing ideas about the relationship between bodily experience and language (and the realm of representation in general). I posit a renewed postcolonial feminist perspective by way of critically revisiting the posthumanist narrative of the turn from the linguistic to the material. Here I take the unresolved tension between these two theoretical branches as a call to reflect on the West's notion of the human and the cognate concepts (such as body, language, and reality) that hover over both approaches despite claims otherwise. In this way, I hope from the chimeracological entanglements to open a space for envisioning a postcolonial mnemonic at the edge of the human and in relation to non-human beings, inviting decolonial and Black critics of the West's notion of the human and its repercussions as forceful interlocutors.[13] This does not mean to conflate the coloniality and postcoloniality of South Korea with the colonial and racial histories in which North America–based and transatlantic decolonial and Black feminist critiques are largely interested. Nonetheless, the historical and conceptual commerce between these two (post)colonial genealogies offers fertile ground to recharge a transnational feminist alliance for reenvisioning how we carry memories of ourselves and others in a chimeracological world. The following parts of the introduction outline the contexts and implications of these three sets of inquiry, followed by chapter overviews.

Prosthetic Memory: Rearticulating Humanity, Technology, and Memory

In its general sense as an artificial supplement to memory, prosthetic memory has been a rich topos for figuring the relationship between human and technology. The ambivalence toward artificial as opposed to natural memory is probably most evident in sci-fi films such as *Blade Runner* (1982), *Total Recall* (1990), and *Her* (2013). It also has a long history in the Western metaphysical tradition, from Plato's hierarchical binary between writing (as a technology that is poisonous to memory) and speech (an effective medicine for living knowledge) in *Phaedrus* to Martin Heidegger's criticism of the typewriter tearing the work of the hand away from writing.[14] Thinkers in this tradition are generally concerned with the double edges of artificial supplementation to memory—that while such technologies extend the capacity of the human mind, they also disempower humans by creating dependence or simply moving beyond our control. This suspicion of artificial (supplementary and alien) memory as opposed to natural (organic and interior) memory is a frequent object of deconstruction by Jacques Derrida, who argues that all memory is supplementary, both familiar and alien to oneself, and therefore prosthetic.[15] For Derrida, the problem of artificiality of memory is the inevitable trace of the other within us that nonetheless cannot be fully incorporated into us (and in this context, let me provisionally define *us* as *humans*). The problem is therefore not something we can opt out of by remaining with natural memory, but rather a reminder of the prostheticity of the self and therefore a demand for hospitality toward the other within us. I take Derrida's critique as guidance for engaging with the moral and political valences of prosthetic memory as I explore a genealogy of how technology of memory has been conceived in relation to its human and posthuman embodiment, from the appearance of electric technology in modern societies to the acceleration of BT and ICT in the contemporary world.

Prosthetic memory is often presented as a conceptual figure for addressing emergent media technologies and their bearing on the relationship between human and technology in modern society. In his influential 1964 book *Understanding Media*, Marshall McLuhan asserts that any medium is an extension of ourselves, and that thanks to electric technology "we have extended our central nervous system itself in a global embrace."[16] McLuhan further anticipates that "rapidly, we approach the final phase of the extensions of man—the technological simulation of consciousness, when the creative process of knowing will be collectively and corporately extended to the whole of human society."[17] However, he suggests that technological extension happens only at the cost of "self-amputation," a body's strategy to countercompensate for the stimulation overload caused by technology.[18] From this perspective, electric technology has made us "numb our central nervous system."[19] Yet according to McLuhan, "this age of unconsciousness and of apathy" has, strikingly, enabled the final awareness of technology as an extension of our physical body and consequently the "social consciousness" of connectedness and responsibility toward the human race.[20] Likewise, while McLuhan does not refer to the term *prosthetics* itself, he approaches electric technology as a sort of prosthetic consciousness with both disabling and enabling power. In this, what McLuhan portrays as the amputating power of electric technology—a numbing of the (individual) human nervous system—turns out to be the very condition and cost for the collective consciousness of our species across the globe.

A few decades after *Understanding Media*, Alison Landsberg reconceptualized "prosthetic memory" as a new form of public memory that emerged through the technologies of mass culture at the beginning of the twentieth century.[21] Looking at cases of immigration to the United States in the 1910s–1920s, African Americans after slavery, and the Holocaust, Landsberg discusses how a person visiting a movie theater or museum might experience "a deeply felt memory of a past event through which he or she did not live" but which nonetheless "has the ability to shape that person's subjectivity and politics."[22] Landsberg argues that while the kinship ties (between parents and children and between individuals and the community) in these three populations had been broken, mass cultural technologies made the memories of disenfranchisement and displacement wearable "by anyone, regardless of skin color, ethnic background, or biology."[23] As such, Landsberg suggests, this kind of mediated, experiential, and commercially exchangeable prosthetic memory in capitalist societies also bears a political possibility of empathy and alliance—suggesting a new mode of public memory beyond the binding politics of identity.[24]

Taking up from Landsberg's discussion, this book explores an emergent mode of prosthetic memory enabled by technological assemblages of bodies and images at the turn of the twenty-first century, and the political possibilities it opens. In this, I am not suggesting a clear discontinuity in the history of technology between the period of Landsberg's discussion and of this book (about one century apart), but I do hope to sketch out the constellation of changes and differences that compel a reconceptualization of prosthetic memory. While Landsberg is concerned primarily with a new form of public memory enabled by the technologies of mass culture in modern American society (such as film, television, and experiential museums), I instead ask how the acceleration of ICT and BT—which increasingly incorporate human and nonhuman lives on a planetary level—might bear upon a mode of collective memory of our time in and between South Korea and the United States.

The historical and techno-cultural specificity of Landsberg's discussion is reflected in her reference to the 1908 silent film *The Thieving Hand* as an illustration of prosthetic memory.[25] This film revolves around a prosthetic arm given to a beggar by a sympathetic passerby—an arm that of its own accord keeps stealing from other people on the street and eventually turns out to have been owned by a one-armed thief. Much as the beggar's prosthetic arm can be worn by someone who is not the original owner, Landsberg's prosthetic memories can be "worn" by different groups of people thanks to the cultural technologies of modern American society. These memories can therefore shape the identity and consciousness of people who do not have firsthand experience in historical disenfranchisement and displacement.

In comparison, the chains of memories in Kang Seung Lee's *Untitled (Harvey)* and *Julie Tolentino (Archive in Dirt)* allow us to think about prosthetic memory somewhat differently. These memories are not carried by an external device separate from an organic body, but are instead embodied by and through different organisms, matters, and media entangled in an unevenly interdependent network. The memories transform rather than simply transfer within the chimeracological milieus, creating a collectivity that is nonetheless different from Landsberg's public based on mass cultural consumption. Such differences also signal how the reconceptualization of prosthetic memory through Lee's art project (rather ironically, given its use of not-so-state-of-the-art technologies such as drawing and grafting) reflects rearticulations among human, technology, and memory alongside changed biopolitical conditions shaped by advancing science and technology and globalizing neoliberal capitalism.

This emergent mode of prosthetic memory invites an up-to-date cartography, akin to what Donna Haraway offered in "A Cyborg Manifesto" to revise socialist feminism addressing the Cold War–driven capitalist world order in the late 1980s.[26] In particular, Haraway's insights into BT's and ICT's bearing on the breached boundaries between human and animal, organism and machine, and physical and nonphysical are particularly relevant—and also merit updates.[27]

First, Haraway's questioning of the boundary between human and nonhuman animals prefigures the interspecies biopolitical matrix of our time. In particular, *Prosthetic Memories* concerns the interspecies biopolitical matrix wherein reproductive technology and regenerative medicine take part in the governance of planetary life by experimenting on and deriving surplus from human, animal, and other forms of living matter.[28] This phenomenon can be approached as what Julie Livingston and Jasbir K. Puar call an "interspecies event," which concerns "relationships *between* different forms of biosocial life and their political effects."[29] An "interspecies" approach compels a critical inquiry that takes nonhuman actors and their roles as "racial and sexual proxies" seriously, and at the same time is cautious about "an unmarked Euro-American focus" and the attendant resuscitation of "'the human' as a transparent category" in much posthumanist thought.[30]

In addition, such an interspecies matrix speaks to humans' often racialized and gendered entanglements with other humans, animals, and plants as a grounds for both the colonial production of knowledge and the subversive potential of other subjugated knowledges—as suggested by Neel Ahuja and Clapperton Chakanetsa Mavhunga, among other critics of Western-centric modern science, technology, and medicine.[31] In this light, the transspecies entanglements I explore in this book—most conspicuously in the connections between the dog meat market, the pet-cloning industry, and human stem cell research—are not only an ontological condition of but also a source of chimeric vision for prosthetic memories to counter what Melinda Cooper calls contemporary biotechnology's delirium of "reinventing life beyond the limit," per neo-imperialist capitalist aphorism.[32]

Second, the infiltration between biological and technological at the epigenetic and molecular turns intensifies the circulation and experience of prosthetic memories without a distinct technological device external to organic bodies. Haraway's figuration of the cyborg as "a hybrid of machine and organism"—illustrated by the origin of the term, a mouse with an implanted osmotic pump that served as an experimental animal model for developing a system to remotely control human astronauts during the Cold War space race—offers only a primordial picture given the subsequent advancement of biomedicine and reproductive technology.[33] Nikolas Rose notes that new biomedical technologies have now entered our genes and brains at the molecular level, through which we have become "neurochemical selves" under the new bioeconomic regime.[34] We also live in a time when what Sarah Franklin calls "transbiology" ("a biology that is not only born and bred, or born and made, but made and born") is increasingly becoming "more the norm than the exception."[35] Reflecting on the advancement of genetic cloning, Luciana Parisi offers a Deleuzean assertion that biodigital technology accelerates bacterial (contagious and parasitic) sex, thereby intensifying the potential for unpredictable mutations of bodies-sexes and for feminine desires detached from the order of sexual reproduction and entropic pleasure.[36] Parisi's radical argument seems more intriguing, considering nanoscience's involvement in cryonics—freezing humans (Walt Disney being perhaps the most famous example) with the prospect of resurrecting them using nanotechnology, which theoretically can reengineer matter atom by atom.[37] These scholars offer insightful observations on the boundary breaches between the biological and the technological, with its potential for engineered and unforeseeable mutation of what we presently consider organisms.

In the following chapters, I want to enrich the ongoing conversation by offering and highlighting geopolitical contours of the boundary breakdown between biological and technological. On one hand, a new mode of prosthetic memory concerns how technological infiltration of biological bodies (such as tongue surgery, pet cloning, and stem cell research) is interlaced with postcolonial imaginaries of life and technology and with ethnoracialized recruitment of biological, intellectual, and affective resources.[38] On the other hand, in response to the shuffling boundaries between organic and mechanical, it reenvisions our racialized relationship with the technological others and their human proxies (such as robots and "robot-like" Asian workers).

This leads to the refiguration of prosthetic memory that can account for the development of Haraway's third boundary event. The actual and virtual breakdown of division between physical and nonphysical has been further amplified by the development of ICT and virtual media, offering a larger picture enfolding the second boundary breakdown discussed above.

The development of transbiology is imbricated in what W. J. T. Mitchell calls "biocybernetics reproduction"—a new mode of (re)production in the late capitalist era when "the assembly line begins to produce, not machines, but living organisms and biologically engineered materials" and "image production moves from the chemical-mechanical technology of traditional photography and cinema to the electronic images of video and camera."[39] From another angle, Paul B. Preciado caricatures the biopolitics of postindustrial society that centers around production of the sexual subject/object in intertwined flows of the biomolecular (pharmaco-) and the semiotic-technical (pornographic).[40] In this era of biomolecular, digital, and high-speed technologies, Preciado argues, we've moved past the disciplinary technologies that control bodies from the outside and are now under the regime of "micro-prosthetics" that surveil and control subjects by infiltrating the body until they become indistinguishable from it.[41] Mitchell's and Preciado's analyses dovetail where they concern the short-circuit between BT and ICT, articulating the collapsing of planes between physiological and semiotic and between body and mind in contemporary techno-cultural capitalism and presaging a new approach to prosthetic memories beyond these divisions.

However, as they are situated respectively in the post-9/11 US context and in the postmodern Anglo-European context, to what extent the analyses of Mitchell and Preciado might bear upon different parts of the world—such as South Korea—is yet to be examined. In rescaling their theories from a transnational perspective, my aim is more than simply adding transpacific geopolitical specificity but also foregrounding the politico-epistemological conditions of the leaky ontologies that these theories postulate. In other words, I hope to put into perspective the propositions about ontological leveling of the material and immaterial (often translated as body and language) by illuminating the biopolitical operations undergirding Western metaphysical views of what constitutes the material/immaterial, body/mind, and (more fundamentally) real/unreal. In the later part of the introduction, I return to the problem of Western-centric metaphysical views, critically interrogating the contemporary posthumanist narrative of the turn from linguistic to material in conversation with decolonial and Black critiques. This perspective underpins the structure of this book, as I explore prosthetic memories around the tongue and the gene as the porous loci at the boundary where the linguistic and the corporeal encounter each other.

Prosthetic Memories proposes a new understanding of its namesake to rearticulate the relationships among humanity, technology, and memory as they attune to these changing techno-cultural and biopolitical conditions on a global scale—and to explore alternative visions. This new mode of prosthetic memory is thus an iteration of rather than a complete rupture from the long genealogy of prosthetic memory (from Plato to Heidegger to McLuhan and to Landsberg), which is both a burden and a possibility for recasting the concept as a postcolonial feminist mnemonic in a more-than-human world.

Recasting *Prosthetic*: An Intersectional Dialogue

As the brief genealogy of prosthetic memory I sketched out above shows, the meanings of *prosthetic* often hinge on differential capacity, disability, debility, and (inter)dependency of mind-bodies in varying forms and intensities. This section examines the political implications of using the term *prosthetic*, whose meaning operates in habitual reference to the normalization of disabled and trans bodies, and further reassesses the social values attached to the concept of supplementarity through the lenses of the division of labor, of the network of care, and of regulation of intimacy within the intra- and interspecies web of ecology and politics. Mapping the intersections of such semiotic-material exchanges, I would like to explore both the problematic and generative potential that my engagement with prosthetic memories entails, in conversation with critical disability studies, trans and queer theories, and postcolonial and decolonial feminisms.

Metaphoric Prosthetics and Disabled Bodies

Per the *Oxford English Dictionary*, the word *prosthetic* is borrowed from Latin *prostheticus*, etymologically tracing back to "Hellenistic Greek προσθετικός, adding, furthering, advancing, giving additional power," and to "ancient Greek πρόσθετος, added, additional." The dictionary lists the definitions as follows:

A. adj.

1. *Grammar*. Of or relating to prosthesis; (of a letter or syllable) that has been prefixed to a word. Now rare.

2. a. *Medicine*. Of or relating to prostheses; of the nature of a prosthesis; employing or caused by a prosthesis.

b. *Esp.* in the performing arts: of, relating to, or designating an object or procedure designed to alter a person's physical appearance temporarily.

3. *Biochemistry.* Designating a non-protein group forming part of or combined with a protein, and often necessary for biological activity.

B. n.

Artificial replacement of a part of the body; (also) an artificial body part or feature worn as theatrical make-up for special effects.[42]

Whether they directly use the term *prosthetic* or not, discourses on technologically mediated memory often mobilize the second (medical) sense of the term. As we have seen, both McLuhan's approach to the impact of electricity (and technology in general) as self-amputation and Landsberg's discussion of modern media in reference to the film *The Thieving Hand* draw on an assistive device for physical disability to illustrate a prospectus on new modes of collective consciousness and memory. Thus, an imaginary chorus evoking the phantasmagoria of disabled mind-bodies using assistive devices hovers over my efforts to reconceptualize prosthetic memory.

It is therefore imperative to engage with scholars in disability studies who offer critical perspectives on the prevalent use of the term *prosthetics* in contemporary theories. Sarah S. Jain criticizes popular tropes of prosthetics in which the medical sense of prosthesis is a metaphor for the technological supplement to some sort of physical insufficiency in general.[43] Jain argues that this kind of trope "both depends on and disavows a very particular model of physical impairment," as it operates by evoking the figure of people with physical disability but glides over their difference from "other not 'whole' bodies" such as racialized, gendered, and aged bodies in need of technological support.[44] In a similar vein, Vivian Sobchack interrogates the trend in the recent humanities and arts wherein prosthetics has become "tropological currency for describing a vague and shifting constellation of relationships among bodies, technologies, and subjectivities."[45] Weary of this kind of metaphorical discourse that has little to do with the material realities of people with disability, Sobchack explores the tension between "*the* prosthetic as a tropological figure and *my* prosthetic as a material but also a phenomenologically lived artifact" in an effort to inform a more embodied sensibility and ethical responsibility in discursive practice.[46]

From a more affirmative perspective, Alison Kafer examines how the cyborg as a feminist figure also mobilizes disability, as illustrated in "A

Cyborg Manifesto" by Haraway: "Perhaps paraplegics and other severely handicapped people can (and sometimes do) have the most intense experiences of complex hybridization," owing to their reliance on machines and prosthetics.[47] While taking issue with the ableist deployment of disability "solely as an illustration of the cyborg condition" in feminist cyborg theories, Kafer nonetheless sees value in pushing these theories closer to the promise of a situated, noninnocent, yet responsible feminism from a disability perspective.[48] In this light, Kafer invites us to rethink the connection between disabled people and cyborgs based on political practices—as in the case of Connie Panzarino, who during Pride marches would attach to her wheelchair a signboard reading "Trached dykes eat pussy without coming up for air."[49] In this way, Panzarino turns the normative idea of adaptive technologies for superhuman abilities into a public announcement of her queer bodily pleasure, subverting through a blasphemous sense of humor the perceived lack of (normative) sexuality associated with a disabled woman.

Critiques from scholars of disability studies show both the political and theoretical stakes of using the concept of prosthetics outside the context of disability. While I recognize the risks discussed above and am indebted to these scholars' insights, I carefully insist on keeping this concept within the repertoire of critical theories even when it isn't necessarily in immediate reference to the experience of people with disability. One gain from loosening the connection between the concept of prosthesis and people with disability is a space to reimagine this concept in light of what Jasbir Puar calls the biopolitics of "debility," which aims at and results in a massive scale of abject bodies that are sustained "in a perpetual state of debilitation precisely through foreclosing the social, cultural, and political translation to disability" as a condition for the incorporation of disability into neoliberal states.[50] Puar's observation allows us to consider various kinds of technological assemblage of mind-body capacities (such as skills, creativity, productivity, reproductivity, regenerativity, and networking) and debilities (such as injuries, illness, exhaustion, wear and tear, isolation, and state of siege) in the neoliberal and postcolonial context. Furthermore, it sheds light on how the biopolitical recuperation and capacitation of subjects in such an uneven landscape of debilitation goes hand in hand with the neoliberal and postcolonial exceptionalization of prosthetic technologies—through which assessments of who is expected to use, who can access, and what counts as prosthetic devices and systems take place.[51]

From this perspective, Black lesbian feminist Audre Lorde's refusal to wear a prosthesis after her mastectomy is not a rejection of assistive devices in general but a refusal to accept the nurse's gaze that sees her visibly single-breasted presence as "a threat to the 'morale' of a breast surgeon's office" and to participate in the silence about how breast cancer disproportionately debilitates poor, Black, and other socially marginal women in the United States.[52] On the other side of the Pacific, the gap between prosthetics that look like "mannequin's limbs" handcrafted in the Garwŏl prosthetics district in Seoul and smart skin for prosthetics that captures senses of touch developed at Seoul National University enfolds postcolonial memories of debilitation—from injuries due to the Korean War and the remaining land mines over the past seventy years to amputations due to "illness characteristic of an advanced society . . . caused by 'eating too well' rather than by bombing and malnutrition."[53] In this vein, we can think of prosthetic memory in relation to debilitating and recuperating technological assemblages imbricated in the planetary and local production, modification, and disposition of mind-bodies.

Some trans-queer theories offer useful insights for navigating the relationship between human and technology without relying on the model of disabled embodiment as if it were naturally prone to technological supplementation, yet nonetheless account for the normalizing distribution of the political, moral, and aesthetic valences of various forms of technological embodiment within specific biopolitical contexts. In "Animal Trans," Myra J. Hird criticizes how discourses around transsex/transgender have been "deeply concerned with authenticity" based on "a distinction between natural and artificial sexual difference," and how this assumed artificiality in turn relies on the idea of "human-made technology."[54] Hird instead proposes a different approach to trans embodiment, drawing upon Lynn Margulis and Dorion Sagan: "Life itself is, and has always been, technological in the very real sense that bacteria, protoctists, and animals incorporate external structural materials into their bodies."[55] Hird's critique helps us to reexamine the notion of the natural (as opposed to artificial) human body as a politically laden human-centric and gendered construct, regarding either concern for authenticity (which trans people lack, according to some discourses) or a celebration of the transgressiveness of artificial bodies (which trans people embody, according to other discourses).

The trans-queer theory of somatechnics offers a further critique on how the social perception and valuation of natural and technological mind-bodies hinges on biopolitical norms of embodiment. The term *somatechnics* highlights "the inextricability of *soma* and *techné*, of the body (as a culturally intelligible construct) and the techniques (*dispositifs* and hard technologies)."⁵⁶ This concept problematizes the common assumption that technology is something added to the already constituted natural body for the use of an already embodied self, and instead highlights how the corporealization of embodiment "takes place through certain highly regulated (situated) somatechnologies."⁵⁷ For example, the discourses around transgender surgery and self-demand amputation illustrate how certain embodiments become legible, identified, and integrated into social fabrics within specific contexts (such as a capitalist validation of malleability and a liberalist claim on the body as property) at the cost of foreclosing or denigrating other modes of embodiment.⁵⁸ Such a somatechnical perspective also informs feminist theorist and critical disability studies scholar Margrit Shildrick's argument for a posthumanist prosthetic imaginary, focusing on how microbiomes and microchimerisms bear on our understanding and experience of the self in the fields of organ and tissue transplantation, stem cell therapy, and surrogacy.⁵⁹ Shildrick argues that these somatechnical phenomena of what she calls "visceral prostheses" (as opposed to "mechanical prostheses") not only deconstruct the autonomous notion of the self but also invite a creative imaginary of human embodiment and its ethics.⁶⁰

In a similar vein, a somatechnical understanding of body-technology articulations (as are imbricated in biopolitical recognition and regulation within a specific social and political economy) informs my use of the term *prosthetics* when not directly related to people with disability. This includes the sites of postcolonial and diasporic memories discussed in this book, such as tongue surgery on Korean children (as neoliberal linguistic subjects), poetry machines for capacitating intimacy across species and racial differences, and pet cloning as a nonnormative apparatus of mourning.

Thus, while Jain's and Sobchack's criticisms of the tropes of prosthesis offer critical insights into the discourse around prosthetics in contemporary scholarship, sticking to the literal (that is, medical) sense of the word as distinct from its metaphorical sense might not be the only resolution. Jain herself explains, citing David Wills, "First introduced into English in 1553 as *a term of rhetoric* meaning 'attached to' or 'setting forth' or, literally, 'adding a syllable to the beginning of a word,' prosthesis did not come to bear the medical sense of the 'replacement of a missing part of the body with an artificial one' until 1704."⁶¹ As above, the current OED also first lists the linguistic (rhetorical) sense of *prosthetic* (as an adjective), followed by the medical sense. My point here is not to argue that the linguistic/rhetorical sense is the primary (literal) meaning or to dismiss the prevalence of references to the medical sense in current discourses on prosthetics in the humanities and social sciences. Rather, by drawing attention to the historicity and plurality of this term, I propose to explore commerce between the meanings and the associated bodies (beyond the dichotomy of the literal and the metaphorical) as a potential site for revalidation and affinity across difference in addition to being a site for the extraction of metaphorical values from people with disability.

Rethinking Supplementarity: Feminist Reflections

To further the discussion on the potential of prosthetic memory in enabling and debilitating assemblages within the transnational circuits of technology, I reexamine one of the key connotations of the term *prosthetic*—supplementarity. Scholars of disability studies have criticized how the trope of prosthetics often assumes disability as a deficit that needs to be supplemented—corrected—by technology, subtending the long-standing disavowal of disabled people's status as fully human subjects. Critics have also discussed how such disavowal relies on the Western liberalist fantasy of the independent and self-sufficient subject, which obscures the supplementary infrastructure and labor relied on to appear sovereign.[62] In this light, the concept of prosthetic memory affords a space for conjoining efforts in criticizing and overcoming the normative notion of the sovereign (human) subject by reassessing the notion of supplementarity—in conversation with discussions on the division of labor, ethics of care, and revalidation of interdependence in postcolonial feminist, critical disability, and critical animal studies. Through recasting the political valence of supplementarity, I hope to reenvision prosthetic memory as less attributable to the self-bound individual subject and more situated in and stemming from webs of asymmetrically interdependent entanglements among human and other beings.

Feminist discussions on the complex and changing dynamics of care work in the transnational circuits of BT and ICT are therefore quintessential grounds for engaging with prosthetic memory in the chimeracological milieu of contemporary biopolitics. In particular, feminist, queer, and women of color scholars have been concerned with issues that emerged from the development of assistive reproductive technology (ART) and transnational surrogacy over the past few decades. This techno-cultural development not only has intensified the status of female reproductive body parts as an important source of surplus value in the fertility industry but also has become an important part of the making and breaking of kinship, of the patterns and flows of care labor (including gestational surrogacy), and of the distribution of rights and resources for having and raising children, at the complex intersections of gender, race, class, nation, and other socio-economic and environmental infrastructures.[63] Furthermore, the recent global spread of the stem cell and regenerative medicine industries highlights the role of women in biotechnology because these fields require high volumes of human embryos, oocytes, fetal tissue, and umbilical cord blood beyond the usual sense of reproductive purposes. Catherine Waldby and Melinda Cooper urge theorization of the changing role of women in what they call "regenerative labour" (distinguished from the reproductive-work and ethics-of-care approaches of existing feminist theories) in this kind of emerging practice across both advanced industrial countries and developing nations.[64] These feminist critics have foregrounded and reexamined care work, often considered supplementary (and thus less important), in ethical, social, and politico-economical debates.

As ICT reorganizes work and lifestyle on a global scale, feminist scholars have discussed the supplementary roles that women and other feminized subjects take in this new context. Some critics have foregrounded how the immaterial, virtual, and cybernetic world is supported by low-skill material labor, which has become increasingly invisible and is disproportionally performed by women, immigrants, people of color, and people in the global south.[65] Others discuss how the rise of ICT has resulted in the capitalist extraction of women's immaterial and affective labor across the domestic and public realms on one hand and the automation of conventionally feminized labor (such as clerical, service, and care work) on the other.[66] Yet other critics look at how discourses around artificial intelligence and robots as potential human replacements (surrogates for humans, in Neda Atanasoski and Kalindi Vora's sense) are entwined with gendered, racialized, and colonial discourses.[67] While the rise of immaterial and affective labor with the global acceleration of ICT might have potential for revalidating social and economic values that have been depreciated as supplementary (such as care, love, and collaboration), the persistent gender and racial hierarchy, the global division of labor, and the biopolitical regulation and commodification of these values complicate its radical potential.

From another corner of feminist inquiries on the ethics and politics of care, Sunaura Taylor turns to the question of "what it means to be *cared for*," which as a disabled person can be "stifling, if not infantilizing and oppressive."[68] Taylor sets out her criticism by asking how the American ideal of independence exaggerates individual physical autonomy and overlooks both human and animal (inter)dependency on "communities, habitats, and ecosystems."[69] She further interrogates how such an alluring notion of the human subject serves as a justification for the exploitation of those histori-cally perceived as dependents (that is, a burden to others) through "slavery, patriarchy, colonization, and disability oppression" and for the slaughter of domestic animals (who couldn't have been born and cannot survive in the "state of nature").[70]

Taylor observes that "much of the hostility toward domesticated animals seems to come from the idea they are unnatural," as illustrated by envi-ronmental philosopher J. Baird Callicott: "Domestic animals are . . . living artifacts. . . . From the perspective of the land ethic a herd of cattle, sheep, or pigs is as much or more a ruinous blight on the landscape as a fleet of four-wheel-drive off-road vehicles."[71] Notably, Callicott's understanding of domestic animals as "another mode of extension of the works of man [*prosthetic*] into the ecosystem" leads him to conclude that these animals are dependent on humans rather than the other way around.[72] Criticiz-ing this self-serving logic of the naturally independent subject, Taylor sug-gests a feminist human-animal ethics of care that regards vulnerability and dependence as holding "the potential for new ways of being, supporting, and communicating."[73] And Callicott's equation of both domestic animals and off-road vehicles as artificial extensions to the ecosystem makes Kafer's proposal (for politicizing cyborgian feminism from critical and creative dis-ability perspectives) even more relevant in this book's effort to recast the supplementarity of prosthetics in a more-than-human world.

As a topos for figuring the relationship between human and technology, the notion of prosthesis carries rich biopolitical implications. In a society where the norm of an independent human subject is prevalent, the use of *prosthetic* beyond the context of disability risks deriving the metaphoric values from disability while erasing the cultural and political contexts that frame assistive devices as an indication of dependency—which in turn is used to justify denying the sovereignty and dignity of people with disabil-ity. At the same time, this term also allows us to critically intervene into the value system underlying our understanding of the relationships between and among humans, animals, and technologies through reexamination of the notions and values of care, capacity/debility, and autonomy/interdepen-dency. Reflections on this term thus help us to think of prosthetic memory not as an artificial replacement for natural memory but as what emerges from the categorically unstable and politically loaded chimeracological interfaces—in which we are invited to reflect on and reenvision our rela-tionship with others, both familiar and alien.

Prosthetic Memories is indebted to the rich postcolonial feminist discourses that have engaged with embodied memories—most notably of Japanese military "comfort women," of the sex industry at US military bases, and of transnational adoption—as a site of resistance against, recovery from, and transformation through loss and suffering.[74] In this kind of discourse, human bodies (especially women's) are invested with the task of carrying traumatic, oppressed, and minoritarian memories of patriarchy, colonialism, and postcolonial governance during and after the Japanese occupation of the Korean peninsula, the US Army military government control of the southern part of Korea, the Korean War, and the ensuing Cold War.

However, postcolonial conditions across these two countries have changed alongside the global techno-biopolitical landscape in the early twenty-first century—which Achille Mbembe characterizes as the globalization of markets and the neoliberalism "dominated by the industries of the Silicon Valley and digital technology."[75] Mbembe attests to the fictionalization of human subjects (whose new form of psychic life is "based on artificial and digital memory and on cognitive models drawn from the neurosciences and neuroeconomics"), the technological manipulation of living things nearing the elimination of races deemed undesirable "through theriomorphism (hybridization with animal elements) or 'cyborgization' (hybridization with artificial elements)," and the delirium evoked by racism that "consists . . . in substituting what *is* with something else, with another reality."[76]

Mbembe's observations invite us to revisit "A Cyborg Manifesto," in which Haraway maps the changing matrix of domination with the advancement of c3i (command-control-communication-intelligence) technologies and genetic science in the 1980s.[77] Writing at the height of the Cold War, Haraway proposes the cyborg as a figure to reenvision the socialist feminist subject and the corresponding politics of alliance.[78] At the center of this political vision lies Asian women (including "young Korean women hired in the sex industry and in electronic assembly")—as illustrated in Lynn Randolph's painting *Cyborg*, inspired by Haraway's description of "Asian women with nimble fingers, working in enterprise zones."[79] Haraway's political prospectus still strikes me as prescient but merits revision in light of subsequent geopolitical and techno-scientific changes across

South Korea and the United States within a global context (the revisions of the three boundary events in the first part of this introduction is a part of my efforts to chart such changes). What would a postcolonial feminist painting of a cyborg in this century look like? While Mbembe and Haraway offer conflicting views about the political implications for nonhuman animals and machines of racialized proxying (which I discuss later, especially in chapters 2 and 4), their discussions show the necessity of expanding the postcolonial feminist topos into chimeric and cybernetic body-technology interfaces as emerging sites of collective memory.

Yet a sense of vertigo pervades my efforts to revise the postcolonial feminist approach to memory in the geopolitical and techno-cultural contexts across South Korea and the United States at the turn of the twenty-first century. This is not simply because South Korea (as the world's most networked and automated country and a globally competitive laboratory of advanced biotechnology) is an intense host of the planetary biopolitical changes that Mbembe has reported, demanding a new transpacific cartography of postcolonialities. It is also because the pictures of the current political and cultural states across South Korea and the United States—spinning between the global wave of South Korean pop culture and the rise of national pride in the country on one end, and the escalation of anti-Asian violence in the United States amid the COVID-19 pandemic on the other—render the main time frame of this book (the 1990s and 2000s) both distant and immediately relevant and therefore my search for a transnational feminist alliance both retroactive and prospective at the same time.

In addition, the heightened anti-Asian violence since the outbreak of the pandemic and the globalization of the Black Lives Matter movement illustrate the exigency of reflections on Black-Asian relationship for renewing the transnational feminist alliance across the two countries.[80] As Lisa Lowe points out, the United States' involvement in neocolonial wars and capitalism in Asia underpins the racialization of Asians as an alien cheap labor force in the United States.[81] It has also cultivated the racial ideologies of white superiority and Black inferiority in Asian countries—which, as Nadia Y. Kim observes, loop back to the United States through Asian immigrants.[82] Thus, such a circuit of Asian-Black racialization reflects what Lowe calls "intimate" colonial connections among Europe, Asia, Africa, and America since the late eighteenth century, through which the liberalist-as-universal form of "the human" is freed by enslavement, indenture, and dispossession of other humanities.[83] This intimate racial structure imbricated in the intercontinental geopolitics makes Black critiques a weighty companion for envisioning a postcolonial feminist mnemonic at the edge of the human in the transpacific context.[84] In this light, this book is in dialogue with the Black and decolonialist critiques on racism, coloniality, and the notion of the human, to develop a postcolonial feminist approach to prosthetic memory that addresses new patterns of chimeric and cybernetic entanglements across the two countries.

This approach weighs on several contentious agendas in feminist theories of embodied memory, including the boundary of humanity and the relationship between body and language/image, and how these ideas inform what constitutes reality. Let me sketch out what this approach entails in conversation with two key biopolitical theories of embodied memory in contemporary feminist thought: Judith Butler's ethics of mourning, which concerns the biopolitical derealization of human precarity, and Rosi Braidotti's posthuman ethics, which espouses memory as becoming-minoritarian. Revisiting these two thinkers—whose relationship Braidotti describes as "affirmation versus vulnerability"—I aim to delineate the unresolved tension between these two lines of thinking as a liminal space for conceiving a postcolonial chimeric vision of prosthetic memories.[85]

In *Precarious Life*, Butler proposes an ethics of mourning based on the idea that the possibility and experience of loss through violence is a shared condition we cannot will away because of embodied interdependence among human subjects.[86] Mourning then indicates the recognition of such primary ties with others in the web of vulnerability, and performatively establishes who counts as a life worth grieving for—which for Butler is essentially the matter of who belongs to humanity as a political community.[87] From this perspective, disavowal of mourning denies the worth of those who are lost—thus acquiescing to the violence in and through which the victim's humanity is rendered unrecognizable. Here, Butler carefully poses their claim about "a 'common' corporeal vulnerability" as something other than a proposition for "a new basis for humanism."[88] Butler instead asserts that their critique on the dehumanization in disavowed mourning concerns "not a matter of a simple entry of the excluded into an established ontology, *but an insurrection at the level of ontology*, a critical opening up of the questions, What is real? Whose lives are real? . . . What, then is the relation between violence and those lives considered as 'unreal'?"[89]

For Butler, this "insurrection at the level of ontology" must come to terms with "the limits of human intelligibility" to recognize the vulnerability of others differentially allocated in the matrix of variable norms of recognition—and thus with the limits of discourse to represent the suffering and loss of others.[90] However, while Butler's argument accounts for the violence of derealization in the omission of certain deaths in media representation (such as Iraqi children killed in war), it sends us back to questions about what such a limit of human intelligibility (whereby certain deaths are unmarkable in human discourse) has to do with the derealization of those who are already discursively dehumanized and thus subjected to killing.[91]

The ambiguous circuit between the limit of human intelligibility and discursive dehumanization suggests the notion of humanness that underpins Butler's account of insurrection at the level of ontology, despite their critique of normative notions of the human and humanism. This is evident in their reference to Emmanuel Levinas's notion of "face," which mandates the injunction not to kill the other. What about lives that do not have a human face? Can our embodied interdependency or the consequent vulnerability be enclosed in humanity? In a similar vein, Cary Wolfe suggests that "Butler's effort . . . runs aground on the question of nonhuman animals."[92] Wolfe locates the problems in Butler's reliance on a "mutual striving for recognition," which assumes the model of a (human) subject committed to reciprocal agency and intelligibility.[93] Yet, Wolfe argues, if Butler's theoretical coordinates suggest that a truly ethical act is directed toward those who are outside the model of mutual exchange among moral agents (as in her primary example of newborn infants) and that such an act is radical precisely because it recognizes the precarity of "life itself" beyond human conceptualization, then their own theory compels an understanding that "the ham-fisted distinction of 'human' versus 'animal' is of no use" in deciding membership in the community for ethical consideration by which we grieve the loss of others and protect them from violence.[94]

However, critical reflection on the conflict within Butler's own theory leads to more than the inclusion of nonhuman animals in ethical consideration. For Wolfe, the unwitting human-centrism within Butler's own position is even more conspicuous given the history of "the 'animalization' of a population produced as 'dubiously human' by and for a political program."[95] Then, what Butler posits as "insurrection at the level of ontology" must reckon with how violent in/distinction between nonhuman animals and dehumanized humans subtends the derealization of other humanities. Likewise, while Butler's ethics of grievable life offers rich grounds for theorizing a biopolitics of memory that addresses the differential allocation of precarity alongside differing norms concerning the value of life (and death), it also merits a critical revision from more-than-human perspectives. Here *more* denotes not so much a logic of inclusion or a position of transcendence as an openness to realities other than the one intelligible per hegemonic humanism. From this perspective, Butler's "insurrection at the level of ontology" calls for a kind of chimeric vision to evoke countermemories in the uneven entanglements of humans and animals in the transnational circuits of advanced technologies.

Prosthetic Memories thus invites a critical conversation with posthumanist approaches to memory, especially Braidotti's proposal for an affirmative ethics geared toward the "qualitative leap through pain, across the mournful landscapes of nostalgic yearning."[96] Braidotti attempts to overcome the traditional biopolitics of mourning focused on control of the body, emphasizing instead the vital force of Life (life in its inhuman face) that exceeds biopolitical control. With this force that concerns the self-organizing flows of intensities among affective bodies, she envisions a subjectivity that is nonunitary and nomadic yet accountable in the technologically and globally mediated world.[97] From this perspective, she suggests a nomadic mode of memory that arises through "composition, selection, and dosage" of the flows of Life with a modicum of creative work of imagination, wherein we transform in assemblage with other bodies.[98] Braidotti portrays nomadic remembering as "the active reinvention of a self that is joyfully discontinuous, as opposed to being mournfully consistent," which destabilizes the authority of linear chronology and "real experience" predicated on the majority subject's centralized data bank.[99] This approach to memory draws on the Deleuzian concept of minoritarian memory, which "propels the process of becoming by liberating something akin to Foucault's 'counter-memory'"—and thereby opens spaces for "a sort of empowerment of all that was not programmed within the dominant memory."[100] As such, Braidotti's approach affords a powerful theory for engaging with prosthetic memory as an ethical and situated practice in the more-than-human world we inhabit.

However, Braidotti's affirmative proposal for a "leap"—or rather, the trajectory this term evokes—invites some questions from postcolonial perspectives. Braidotti suggests that her proposal is particularly relevant for "diasporic subjects of all kinds," such as migrants, exiles, and refugees who have "first-hand experience of the extent to which the process of disidentification from familiar identities is linked to the pain of loss and uprooting."[101] The challenge here is to translate this negative sense of pain and loss into affirmation of "multiple forms of belonging and complex allegiances," which requires "suspending the quest for both claims and compensation, resisting the logic of redistribution" and instead taking a different route for fulfilling "the subject's capacity for interaction and freedom."[102] While

I am intrigued by Braidotti's proposal for an ethics of affirmation, I would like to reflect on a couple of issues as it connects the onto-epistemological proposition on biocentric egalitarianism with the political program for social transformation. Despite Braidotti's repeated address of diasporic subjects, her biocentric egalitarianism lacks the analytic acuity to engage with the biopolitical order of things.[103]

In particular, the turn of this biocentric egalitarianism away from the majoritarian human subject (modeling the white man) does not necessarily offer a more effective tool for addressing the intrahuman relations of power through which some are relegated to the state of infrahuman, animal, or thing. As Zakiyyah Iman Jackson observes, appeals to "go beyond" or become "post" human too often presume the West's "Man" as "the originary locus of this call," whereby "potentially transformative expressions of humanity are instead cast 'out of the world' and thus rendered inhuman."[104] As such, posthuman appeals to move beyond the human overlook "race" at the center of the Western metaphysics (and thus the racially hierarchized philosophy of time, knowledge, reality, and the world) founded on and undergirding the historical horizon of slavery, conquest, and colonialism.[105]

In a similar vein, I argue that the current posthuman approaches to memory require a more fundamental reflection on the racial and geopolitical constituents of some key concepts that undergird these approaches' claim on realness. This kind of issue arises, for example, when Braidotti links the political proposal for the leap from mourning to affirmation with the theoretical trajectory from linguistic to material, which she describes as how "the return of 'real body' in its thick materiality spells the end of the linguistic turn."[106] By contrasting the "real body" with "textuality, representation, interpretation, and the power of signifier," Braidotti's formulation circumvents the question of how "reality" is predicated on the very body/language binary that she aims to overcome, which itself has racial and colonial genealogies that are nothing but violent. Thus, Braidotti's formulation preempts the possibility of other kinds of language-body assemblage—and by extension, their relation to humanness, reality, and power—outside the frame of Man.

Then, in order to take seriously Braidotti's theory of minoritarian memory, it is imperative to ask, which reality and whose body? Braidotti draws her examples of "the beneficial side effects" of the process of detachment from the cherished identity of "the crucial appraisal of blackness" in Paul Gilroy and Patricia Hill Collins, and her case for the affirmative translation of the negative sense of loss into "multi-locality" from Édouard Glissant.[107]

Braidotti also offers "the figure of Nelson Mandela" (and the Truth and Reconciliation Commission in postapartheid South Africa) and the works of Cornel West and bell hooks to illustrate an affirmative ethics, in which "those who have been hurt" transcend "the logic of negativity" (claim, compensation, and revenge) and instead collectively construct "positions of active, positive interconnections and relations that can sustain a web of mutual dependence, and ecology of multiple belongings."[108] The racial bearings in these references are difficult to miss, and so a careful reflection on the assumed "real body" (as opposed to the representations) of these minoritarian subjects is imperative in order to avoid unwitting empiricism about these subjects.

In this light, I consult postcolonial and decolonial thinkers who offer critique on language as a way to criticize the existing order of body, humanness, reality, and power and to imagine alternatives.[109] I argue that postcolonial and decolonial critiques of language help to revise minoritarian memory so as to open a reality conceivable only with articulations between body and language different from those of the hegemonic reality. Posthuman attention to the "real body" demands, rather than supersedes, Butler's call for "insurrection on the level of ontology" at the limit of normative human recognition.

Prosthetic Memories positions a postcolonial critique on prosthetic memory at the edge of the human in conversation with these two branches of contemporary feminist thought. On one hand, Butler's meditation on mourning as a performative measure for the life of others reassures the task of remembrance as a feminist ethics for addressing biopolitical precarity and debility at the limit of human representation, which (and, I would argue, at odds with Butler's intention) is contiguous with the abject territory of animality and mechanicality. On the other hand, Braidotti's posthumanist approach to memory as becoming through composition of the force of Life with a modicum of imagination offers a useful onto-epistemological frame for engaging with technological assemblages of humans and nonhumans in the contemporary world. These two approaches are not easily compatible, but the break between the two signals less a linear leap (from the linguistic to the matter, from representation to becoming, and from human to posthuman) than a liminal space between the margins of humanity and the nonhuman for reenvisioning memory (and its relation to body, language, and reality).

From this perspective, this book mobilizes its two central figures (tongues and genes) not simply as the binary topoi of cultural and biological embodied memory, but as an index pointing to the binary's Eurocentric onto-epistemological premise as the horizon of violent derealization. In this, Black critiques offer forceful guidance for approaching the chimeric and cybernetic entanglements around tongues and genes in the following chapters less as evidential flesh and more as the enfleshing of an onto-epistemological aperture. From such an aperture, this book presents a renewed postcolonial feminist approach to prosthetic memories situated in the transnational circuits of BT and ICT at the turn of this century, on one hand revising discourses on prosthetic memory as a form of collective memory in modern society (as suggested by McLuhan and Landsberg) and on the other extending postcolonial discourses that focus on the body as a site of collective (often gendered and traumatic) memory across South Korea and the United States.

Movement of the Book

Prosthetic Memories consists of two parts, corresponding to two figures of embodied memory: the tongue and the gene. This pair enfolds the junctures of discursive and material, cultural and biological, and artificial and natural—the onto-epistemological destabilizations of which backdrop the new figure of prosthetic memory I have discussed above (and explore further in the following chapters).

In response to the political and theoretical pressure under the unracialized posthuman declaration of "the end of the linguistic turn" as sketched out in this introduction, the book begins with the postcolonial and diasporic tongue (both language and organ) as a site of prosthetic memory. Part I, "Mouth to Mouth," explores the prostheticity of tongues as an essential component for understanding contemporary postcolonial languaging, which I argue is a series of biopolitical events that concern the racial and gendering order of (human) embodiment, kinship, and the reality of worlds.

For this, chapters 1 and 2, on one hand, consider a variety of sites of human-technology interface, including tongue surgery to correct children's English pronunciation in South Korea, Susan Sontag's reference to English-accent training at call centers in India in her reflection on the age of computer translation, and Margaret Rhee's works that play with the queer and diasporic relationships among robot/machine, human, and poetry. On the other hand, these chapters revisit feminist theories of linguistic performativity through the lens of Black and decolonial critiques on the notion of the human and its racialized proxies (such as animals and machines). Interweaving these two moves, I argue that the postcolonial human-technology interfaces of languaging are not forts of human exceptionalism nor loci of the recovery of identity and origin associated with the mother tongue. Rather, they are performative spaces of a racial, diasporic, and gendered (un)becoming-human, through which chimeric visions for the counter-memories of education-labor, migration, and intimacy emerge at the margin of hegemonic humanity.

Part II, "The Specters of Cloning," turns in a more "biological" direction—genetic technology. These chapters critically interrogate the prevalent approach to genetic cloning as an artificial replacement for the original (and thus a circumvention of the natural process of mourning) and explore prosthetic memories emerging from the fragmented and supplementary entanglements of humans and animals in transnational pet cloning and human stem cell research (which often involves genetic cloning) in and across South Korea and the United States. Extending my critique on the biopolitical consequences of the Western body/language metaphysical binary (and the exceptionalization of certain realities at the cost of others), part II starts by asking how the original/copy frame is coconstitutive of the somatechnical norms of mourning concerning gender/sexuality, race, species, and disability in the wake of commercial pet cloning. This kind of frame is also a part of the biopolitical derealization that depreciates bodies regarded as artificial/mimetic or otherwise outside the original/copy frame. From this perspective, I trace prosthetic memories in the transnational circuits of cloning technology, attending to the biopolitical spectralization of certain bodies—such as the "used-up" surrogate-mother dogs (said to have been slaughtered for human consumption) in pet cloning, the massive use of female animal bodies in genetic cloning, and the mobilization of women's bodies for human stem cell research. However, I depart from existing conversations that regard these issues as scandalous indicators of the immaturity of animal welfare and bioethics in South Korea, as I see these discourses as a part of the postcolonial normativization of bioethics. While bioethics is commonly understood to consist of ethical issues arising in the research and application of medicine and the life sciences, I approach it as also part of the biopolitical apparatus that concerns the regulation and governance of human and nonhuman lives. Thus, I trace how women and other female animals are chained through the rubric of substitutability at the heart of global institutionalization of modern (Western) bioethics—which also facilitates increasing experimentalization of human and animal mind-bodies in the biomedical and pharmaceutical industry—in the context of the patriarchal-developmentalist paradigm of globalization in postcolonial South Korean society.

Prosthetic Memories therefore aims to offer a postcolonial and posthumanist feminist approach to memory in an age when human and nonhuman lives are increasingly incorporated into the transnational circuits of informatics, communication, and biotech situated between South Korea and the United States. I argue that chimeracological assemblages are not simply sites of biopolitical erasure but also affective interfaces for collective memories that might enable new connections of intimacy and care despite the isolating and injurious experience. I also hope to show that attending to animal, technological, and affective bodies does not render critical inquiry into language and representation obsolete, against the grain of the unracialized posthuman and new materialist proclamations of the end of the linguistic turn. Rather, it demands critical reflection on Western-centric, racialized, and gendered understandings of language, body, and the relationships between them. This leads to the recognition that dislocating prosthetic memory from the exclusively majoritarian human realm of representation is an intrinsically postcolonial and feminist project as much as a posthuman one.

In search of feminist mnemonics in the chimeracological entanglements across the Pacific, *Prosthetic Memories* compels critical and creative rearticulations among different theories, methods, and archives. This book therefore choreographs a variety of practices, including close reading of literature, films, and newspapers; archival research; in-person and email interviews; and visits to a biotech research facility—tracing and engaging with the prosthetic memories composed in body-technology interfaces. In this light, the book is an active component of the prosthetic memories it writes, rather than a recording and analysis of already existing memories.

The performative nature of writing about prosthetic memories is telling of the ethical and theoretical risk and potential of this book. This composition of memories that are neither mine nor theirs points to the frailty of the proprietary relationship between subject and memory within chimeracological entanglements as much as to the possibility of a collective memory that carries the traces of encounters among various mind-bodies. If *Prosthetic Memories* is already embedded in a potentially parasitic-caring milieu of embodied memories, then I hope the book's creative surplus becomes a new vision of intimacy in intersectional and interspecies entanglements and of renewed affinity between Black feminist thoughts and transpacific postcolonial feminism, weighing in on the new biopolitical landscape of our time.

PART I

MOUTH TO MOUTH

Korean American artist and writer Theresa Hak Kyung Cha's video work *Mouth to Mouth* (1975) shows a mouth repeatedly opening and closing. The image fades in and out as video static hazes more thickly, then becomes snowflakes and even rippling water before again thinning over the mouth. The mouth enunciates the eight Korean vowels, but they are inaudible; instead, the image is accompanied by sounds of birds and water, bubbling and running, fused with electronic noise, and by intermittent silences. As the video repeats what appears to represent "the beginning of language" and "the loss of language over the course of time," it enacts the arduous remembrance of the loss itself.[1] Yet the repetitive work of remembrance in this video doesn't recover the memory of the Korean language (by recombining Cha's mouth with the corresponding vowel sounds). Rather, it inaugurates the loss as another beginning, recomposing its memory with other organic and electronic components.

One might suggest that the video presents Cha's memory of the Korean language as a diasporic subject, reflecting her family's migration from postwar South Korea to the United States and even her parents' exile in Manchuria during the Japanese occupation.[2] I present this interpretation because I am intrigued by the volatility, rather than the certainty, of ties among Cha's speaking body, the film, and the memory of diasporic experience.

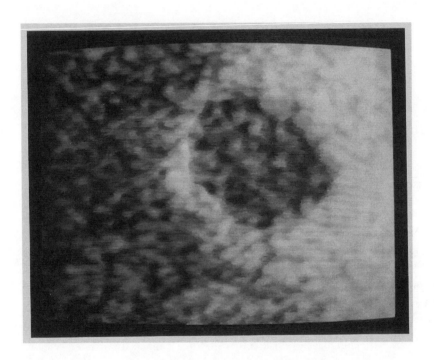

Pl.1 A mouth repeatedly opens and closes, overlapping with bubbles and static, evoking memories of the mother tongue that are both organic and electronic. A still from Theresa Hak Kyung Cha, *Mouth to Mouth / Vide o eme / Re Dis Appearing*, 1975–76, Sony Video Tape V-30H for Helical Video Tape Recorders, 1 videotape, master, reel to reel. Courtesy of the University of California, Berkeley Art Museum and the Pacific Film Archive. Gift of the Theresa Hak Kyung Cha Memorial Foundation.

If, as feminist literary critic Shoshana Felman has theorized, speech acts problematize "the incongruous but indissoluble relation between language and the body," then *Mouth to Mouth* invites us to consider the problem of the speech act as a key constituent of postcolonial and diasporic memory.[3]

In part I, *Prosthetic Memories* explores language and/as technology as a site for postcolonial feminism to rearticulate the relationships among body, language, and memory in the context of neoliberal globalization, the growing hegemony of (American) English, and an intensifying sense of transnational (im)mobility. Echoing Cha's film, this first part of the book, "Mouth to Mouth," underlines the alien and transitory prostheticity of the postcolonial speech act that happens through various bodies as it performatively enacts memories of displacement from the (evoked) origin and foreignness within the self. The title locates the linguistic event in the act of transmitting life, air, saliva, food, signs, and amorous sensations both organic and mechanical—from one person to another, one language to another, one continent to another, mother to daughter, and lover to lover. Here I am thinking alongside Elspeth Probyn's "mouth machine," which will "constantly take in and spit out" things, peoples, and selves, rearranging the interminglings of our bodies with others.[4] Through the figure "mouth machine," Probyn offers a new materialist approach to "the bodies that eat," an approach that doesn't relate the sensual functions of the mouth to evidence of the primary territory (such as the self, identity, and origin) but instead to the possibility of rhizomatic connections with others.[5] Similarly, "mouth to mouth" as a figure emphasizes the assemblages of bodies that speak, whose "openings and closings . . . constantly rearrange our dealings with others."[6] If a postcolonial speech act is less a recovery of one's identity than a kind of becoming and connecting through embodied entanglements with others, then the first part of this book concerns the prosthetic memory composed through such speech acts.

As a linguistic machine, "mouth to mouth" works in assemblage with other machines, such as alimentary, sexual, and earning-working machines.[7] However, such an assemblage is somatechnological—the perceived prostheticity is contingent on the disciplinary and regulatory technologies concerning whose and which orifices might or must be open or shut to whom and to what. Muzzling, starvation, force-feeding, prohibited intimacy, and sexual and racial violence are as much at stake as speaking, singing, eating, working, or loving. This approach expands existing postcolonial and decolonial critiques of language as the site of colonial subjectification, resistance, and subversion so as to better address the somatechnological wiring of the tongue (both as organ and as language) into various biopolitical machineries of our time.[8]

Engaging with the biopolitical machinery of "mouth to mouth," the following two chapters explore the postcolonial and diasporic speech act (which concerns the experience of languaging amid postcolonial and diasporic conditions) and the memories it performs in human-technology interfaces—such as tongue surgery on South Korean children to improve their English pronunciation, and Margaret Rhee's *Kimchi Poetry Machine* (a multimedia poetry installation)—in the twenty-first century.[9] Literary and cultural critic Rey Chow considers the sort of "privilege" the colonized get from their experience of severance of the mother tongue and imposition of the other's language: a prescience that "the reality of languaging as a type of *prostheticization*, whereupon even what feels like an inalienable interiority, such as the way one speaks, is—dare I say it?—impermanent, detachable, and (ex)chageable."[10] Echoing Chow's proposition, the following two chapters present medical and information-communication technologies as the most palpable technologies, but here they don't represent artificial interfaces for human language in opposition to the natural one (as every human language is intrinsically prosthetic). Instead, they amplify and extend the perceived artificiality of postcolonial languaging detached from the mother tongue as part of and in articulation with racializing, gendering, and neoliberal technologies of (un)becoming human in relation with the world(s).

If Chow's postcolonial prescience is indeed a gift, I find it is the "dehumanist" potential of language and/as technology rather than a tool for conquering the world or an object of mastery, to borrow Julietta Singh's term.[11] This approach challenges the posthumanist turning away from language as the privileged marker of undifferentiated (unracialized) human exceptionalism, allowing space for other perspectives on language beyond that of majoritarian humanity and its version of the world subtended by the hegemonic order of matter, language, and reality. Further, by inviting a nonmasterful vision of engaging with language and/as technology and the more-than-human world(s), this approach advances decolonial critique on language in terms of colonial and anticolonial technologies of humanness through which the subject's humanity is asserted, denied, and cultivated. In this light, the assemblages of mouth machines featured in the following two chapters are chimeracological—contiguous to animals and machines and fostering inhuman perspectives at the edge of majoritarian humanity. I hope to illustrate how the linguistic performativity of these assemblages carries postcolonial and diasporic memories that are eclipsed in the hegemonic onto-epistemology and thereby engenders networks of care and intimacy at the interface of alienating and injurious somatechnologies of speaking subjects.

Chapter 1 revisits memories of postcolonial languaging as somatechnologies of being human (presently, being neoliberal homo economicus) and its tie to the origin often figured by the mother tongue. In exploring stories of tongue surgery performed on South Korean children to "correct" their English accent, traces of Black bodies in speech act theories, and diasporic memories of the mother/tongue in the works of M. NourbeSe Philip and Theresa Hak Kyung Cha, this chapter has two aims. On one hand, it delineates the West's onto-epistemological norms that render certain technologies of the speaking subject legible and others not in a postcolonial neoliberal world. On the other hand, it explores the dehumanized (maternal) soma in postcolonial languaging as the matrix of countermemories (eclipsed by the hegemonic metaphysical norms)—engendering new relations to the mother/tongue dislodged from the institution of the origin and identity.

Chapter 2 critically reflects on how language has often been used as a measure for humanness in relation to and distinct from the technological, at the intersections of race, gender, and sexuality. This chapter counters the techno-Orientalist dehumanization of Asians and Asian Americans as machines as a prompt for nonmasterful (dehumanist) engagement with language and/as technology—especially of intimacy across difference rather than of reinstituting the (human) self/identity. From this perspective, this chapter explores how techno-linguistic performativity can carry the prosthetic memories of being human near machines/robots in Susan Sontag's descriptions of Indian workers at call centers and in Margaret Rhee's poetry *Love, Robot* and multimedia installation *Kimchi Poetry Machine*. In this way, the following two chapters enter the human-technological interspaces of "mouth to mouth," composing the prosthetic memories of colonialization, displacement, resistance, labor, desire, and love—memories that are both mine and others', human and inhuman, real and chimeric.

1

A Cut in the Tongue

The analogy of Victor, the wild boy of Aveyron, with whom I have identified. Victor never learned to speak—a scar on his throat.

He was rescued from the forest (parents, mother, family) and taken to a "civilized" place (learning, separation, growth). But the damage has already been done—his throat has already been cut—he has been rendered speechless.

Michelle Cliff, "Notes on Speechlessness"

After having spent several months in France a young farmer returns home. On seeing a plow, he asks his father, an old don't-pull-that-kind-of-thing-on-me peasant: "What's that thing called?" By way of an answer, his father drops the plow on his foot, and his amnesia vanishes. Awesome therapy.

Frantz Fanon, *Black Skin, White Masks*

The Tongue on the Operating Table

A B C D E F G, H I J K L M N, O P Q R R R R R . . .
    The title screen of South Korean director Jin-pyo Park's short film *Tongue-Tie* (2003) opens with the voice of a boy merrily singing the alphabet song, until it repeats the letter R like a broken record and slowly fades.[1] Next he is lying on an operating table, and a close-up

image of his tongue fills the screen—cut by knives and threaded by wires, this tongue strains even to writhe. As a moaning sound mixed with the noise of a suction machine recedes, a doctor speaks with the boy's mother, and we learn that the boy has undergone tongue surgery to improve his English accent. Throughout the film, the mother takes an active role in the boy's English education—including compelling her son to undergo the surgery—while the father acquiesces. *Tongue-Tie* echoes a series of news reports on affluent South Korean parents (mostly mothers) who have surgeons sever the ligament under their children's tongues to help them master the [r] sound, which Koreans often collapse into an [l]—even though this kind of surgery is typically performed only when the ligament is unusually short or tight (a "tongue-tie") and causing difficulty in breastfeeding, eating, or speaking. The *Los Angeles Times* first reported the phenomenon in 2002, following which it was repeated by major news media in Korea.[2] The *L.A. Times* told the story of Dr. Nam, who performed such procedures on children for better English pronunciation at a clinic in the affluent Apgujeong neighborhood in Seoul.[3] A few years later another series of reports on tongue surgery appeared in Korean media, referring mostly to *Tongue-Tie* (which depicts a fictional surgery).[4] Few accounts offered any verified case, but they nonetheless asserted that tongue surgery for this purpose was said to be widespread in Seoul's wealthy districts.[5] These stories then might not be precise descriptions of factual events—the surgical interventions for the purpose of improving pronunciation might not be as prevalent or frequent as the reports suggest. Nonetheless, these reports provide a cultural repertoire for narrating the English craze that permeated South Korea under the intensifying pressure of neoliberal globalization at the turn of the century.[6]

Opening with a short film and media reports on tongue surgeries in South Korea to improve English pronunciation, this chapter approaches postcolonial languaging as it concerns gendered and racialized somatechnologies of producing the (de)human subject in relation to the mother tongue. From this perspective, it aims to explore the prosthetic memories emerging in the cut from one's mother tongue, not to reinstitute a proprietary mastery of the mother/tongue as the origin but to make conceivable the chimeric memories of who we have become as speaking subjects (that are derealized within hegemonic somatechnological assemblages) by recasting our relation to the mother/tongue. With this aim, this chapter revisits a genealogy of linguistic performativity that takes racial and colonial somatic injuries as an aperture toward another reality, challenging the Western metaphysical and scientific understanding of the relationships among body, language, and reality.

Tongue-Tie illustrates what Rey Chow calls "languaging as a type of prostheticization" in reference to the universal nature of language as something imposed and foreign, which nevertheless becomes conspicuous in the (post)colonial governance of the tongue that uproots, divides, and cultivates the colonized into the self-hating and master-mimicking subject.[7] However, the usual sense of the master's language in critiques of colonialism doesn't sufficiently convey the complex status of English in contemporary South Korea. Korea experienced outright language control during Japanese colonial rule (1910–45), including the prohibition of learning or speaking Korean in school. However, the temporary US military government occupation of the southern part of the Korean peninsula following World War II was politically different, and South Korea's international status and relationship with the United States have significantly changed since. A more nuanced understanding of the perception and role of English in South Korean society is therefore necessary.[8] *Tongue-Tie* calls for a revised approach to linguistic postcoloniality alongside the intensifying capitalization of English in South Korea under the broader regime of *segyehwa* ("world-ization," in Korean) that resorted to neoliberalist and nationalist strategies to adapt to and succeed in the globalizing world at the turn of this century.[9]

Tongue-Tie was released while South Korea underwent neoliberalist restructuring after the 1997 financial crisis that struck many Asian nations, and the aggressive US global dominance became even more palpable after 9/11. The *segyehwa* discourse amplified the necessity of English skills while debate rose around the officialization of English in Korea following the financial crisis.[10] Thus, limited access to private English education and to studying abroad became a sensitive issue involving both class mobility and national identity.[11] In this context, the suggestion in the cultural repertoire of tongue surgery about the absurdity of surgical resolution not only mocks the failure to implement a reasonable pedagogy for English education (one might say, "The surgery will not help, because the pronunciation is cultural!") but also betrays discomfort with those privileged enough to afford a globally competent education for their children—who might potentially utilize the resource for achieving only individual and family success and affluence.

In such an affective and discursive structure, the tongue on the operating table is doubly marked: first as an object of the overly competitive postcolonial and neoliberal education system, and second as a subject of the enviable but potentially treasonous privileged class under the *segyehwa* regime.[12] An ironic consequence of the structural dismissal of the tongue is the muteness of the boy in the film (he barely speaks) despite the hypervisibility of his tongue throughout the surgery scene. However, my aim is not to recuperate the voice of the boy, which represents the experience of tongue surgery or of the English craze in general. I instead ask, what does this taken-for-granted absurdity suggest about certain technological articulations between body and language that are marked outside rational apprehension, as non-sense, in the fractious assemblage of postcolonial, nationalist, and neoliberal technologies concerning speaking bodies? How does such marking-off betray the norms that naturalize a speaking body's relation to one's origin—often described in familial terms such as mother tongue (*mogukŏ*) and fatherland (*choguk*)? How can we conceive counter-memories from the perspective of absurdity in this cyborgian assemblage of a tongue on the operating table?

The baffling corporeality of the tongue on the table shows that postcolonial prostheticity of languaging is somatechnological. By this, I mean two things. First, due to its position at the binary opposites of language and body, culture and nature, inside and outside, the tongue is a crucial channel for technologies of power that produce and shape both colonial and anticolonial subjects.[13] Second, these technologies are somatechnological in that they are not added to the natural tongue, but their artificiality is perceived and moralized according to social norms concerning the technological production of the speaking subject (who does not exist prior to the production). In this light, I approach the cultural repertoire of tongue surgery in South Korea as it concerns the somatechnology of the tongue, through which we make sense of, endorse, and capacitate certain speaking subjects (and not others). Thus, rather than assessing the political valence of tongue surgery itself, I am more interested in the social norms undergirding its perception as betrayed in the cultural repertoire of tongue surgery— in particular, the norms concerning how the speaking subjects carry the memory of their mother tongue (as national-cultural origins) and of their displacement from it.

The two epigraphs to this chapter illustrate the somatechnologies of colonial and anticolonial speaking subjects, against the background of which I engage with the tongue on the operating table. In the first epigraph, Jamaica-born American and lesbian feminist writer Michelle Cliff identifies herself with Victor, a famous feral boy who was "rescued" from the forest and "civilized" by well-meaning Enlightenment French doctor Jean-Marc-Gaspard

Itard, but never came to speech.[14] Cliff credits her empathetic association with Victor to her own experience of speechlessness in patriarchal and colonial society, pointing to the affinity between and confluence of colonial, medical, pedagogical, and patriarchal investments in the native tongue. It is notable that Itard's intensive education program for Victor is still considered "an important early development in the special education of children with intellectual and developmental disabilities," while Victor was recently suggested to have been autistic.[15] These medical-pedagogical interventions into Victor's tongue (reading alongside Cliff's affinity with him) then illuminate no less than colonial and postcolonial somatechnologies of humanity, whereby the project of capacitating the proper human subject rationalizes violent intervention into the feminine, disabled, native, and feral within us.

In the second epigraph, Fanon portrays an Antillean peasant's "therapy" for his son, who—mimicking a metropolitan linguistic subject—has apparently forgotten what to call a plow in his native tongue.[16] For Frantz Fanon (and perhaps for the peasant father), the son's amnesia indicates an inauthentic simulation (a white mask) in conflict with the inner truth of who he really is (a Black Antillean farmer). However, if the father's plow-dropped-on-the-foot "therapy" cures internalized colonial repression, does it not also betray the frailty of the inside/outside (authentic/artificial) distinction that the therapy aims to recover? The tongue-foot of the son might then be less a locus of preserving the origin to be remembered by an already established subject. Rather, it forms a somatechnological assemblage in connection with other bodies such as the imperial metropolis, the plow, and the father—through which one's origin-as-identity is forgotten and remembered in a simultaneous doing and undoing of the corporeal, psychic, and linguistic self.

When read alongside these epigraphs, the cultural narrative of tongue surgery for improving English pronunciation is not about an exceptional technological intervention into the otherwise-natural tongue. Rather, the tongue on the operating table is a somatechnology concerning the origin memory (with its cut from the mother tongue) through encounters with other bodies such as the mother, the doctor, and surgical equipment, as well as the South Korean educational system embedded in the neoliberal education-labor complex on a global level. From this perspective, what makes the plow therapy for a young Antillean farmer effective and the tongue surgery for a Korean boy non-sense has to do with the somatechnological norms that naturalize ties between a speaking body and its origin-as-identity (figured as the mother tongue) in the critical discourses of colonialism. Then, the film's critical representation of tongue surgery (like

Fanon's anticolonialist appraisal of plow therapy) inverts, yet also shares with the colonial project, the pedagogical-medical investment in the speaking body shown in the case of Victor the feral boy.

Furthermore, extending its colonial and anticolonial genealogy, *Tongue-Tie* illuminates a somatechnology that aims to (de)capacitate the postcolonial-neoliberal human subject amid the ascendance of English as (what David Crystal calls) the "global language" at the beginning of the twenty-first century.[17] For this argument, let me examine how the film's portrayal of the boy and his family oddly echoes (and also challenges) the neoliberal model of homo economicus and his family in Michel Foucault's *The Birth of Biopolitics*. This new model of subject accompanying postwar American neoliberalism generalizes the internal rationality of the market "throughout the social body."[18] Foucault characterizes this emergent subject as "an entrepreneur" of himself and "an ability machine" who produces an earnings stream, concerned primarily with managing the acquired elements of his own human capital.[19] The most salient element is the educational investment, which is "much broader than simple schooling or professional training" and includes the parents' time and the care and affection given to a child as well as the parents' own education.[20] Mobility is also an important acquired capital, with migration in particular becoming an investment for the improvement of status and remuneration.[21] In addition, Foucault recognizes the possibility of incorporating innate elements of human capital such as genetics into the economic machinery of homo economicus, which he anticipates to be in line with the management of human capital in "the function of unions and consequent reproduction" rather than an indication of "traditional racism."[22]

What Foucault means by "traditional racism" and whether he is suggesting a new kind of racism isn't clear. Nonetheless, the tongue on the operating table invites rearticulation of the relationship between achieved capital (cultural) and innate capital (biological, where Foucault locates traditional racism) and its bearing on the function of family in Foucault's theory, insofar as this neoliberal machine-enterprise is haunted by the postcolonial somatechnologies of the tongue. Through the surgical cut, the presumably innate biological capital bleeds into the achieved capital of the ability machine, while this tongue on the operating table is plugged into its family machine in the global education-labor market. *Tongue-Tie* shows not only how English has gained pragmatic and symbolic value as an index of global competitiveness in neoliberal South Korea, but also how the cultural and economic pressures and desires surrounding this global language are woven into the fabric of family and its reproductive function.[23] In this, the family is not simply a biopolitical machinery of unions and reproduction in the Foucauldian sense—its neoliberal enterprise is inflected by the postcolonial memory of traitorous elite familism. This is shown in Kwangyong Chŏn's 1962 novella *Kkŏppittan ri* (Kapitan Lee), which illustrates the role of the master's language as a disloyal means to survive occupations by the Japanese, Soviet, and US militaries, handed down through family lineage, especially among the privileged elite class in modern South Korean history.[24]

Looking at how *Tongue-Tie* suggests a postcolonial twist on Foucault's concept of the neoliberal genre of homo economicus and the role of family in the reproduction of this new kind of subject-entrepreneur, I argue that absurdness in the cultural narrative on tongue surgery points to onto-epistemological fibrillation in the assemblages of various postcolonial and neoliberal somatechnologies of the speaking body. Further, this fibrillation is projected onto the speaking subject's relation with its mother, who embodies frictional expectations to preserve the national identity and to manage her children's globally competitive education.

On one hand, anticolonialist critique often concerns colonization of the tongue as the disruption of national and racial identity, sometimes represented as maternal and vulnerable (and disabled).[25] For instance, postcolonial literary critic Suk-ho Lee argues that the officialization of English would effectively make obsolete Korean "a pitiful dwarf language," while the discrimination against English users of certain races and accents in the present global empire cannot recede until "they change their mothers and are born again."[26] Written from a son's masculine point of view, Lee's rhetoric reflects Eunjung Kim's observation: even though the colonized Korea has been metaphorized as feminine and disabled, "disabled, poor, feminine, perverted, and racialized Others" have been construed as "objects of the empowered nation's 'help,' which was often exercised in the form of . . . violence" in the development of postcolonial and capitalist South Korea.[27] Similarly, Lee's argument portrays Koreans' English accents as matrilineal and the Korean language as disabled. In this way, Korean mothers bear the sign of a disabled yet unexchangeable national origin, and thereby protecting one's tie to the vulnerable mother tongue gains the virtue of masculine filial loyalty.

On the other hand, mothers take an important role in contemporary South Korea as the primary managers of children's education (especially for learning English) in the reproduction of homo economicus, as noted by Korean studies scholars So Jin Park and Nancy Abelmann.[28] Examining the narratives of three mothers in different class positions, Park and Abelmann consider the mothers' management of children's English education to be "an inter-generational gendered project" that also speaks to "their own class mobility (or maintenance) and cosmopolitan strivings" in the global order.[29] Borrowing Ann Anagnost's "cosmopolitan striving" that concerns the desire to become "citizens capable of living at home in the world," Park and Abelmann find such striving also characteristic "of seemingly resolutely 'local' people and even of 'nationalistic' rhetorical regimes themselves, such as South Korea's recent globalization policies."[30] One option for this would be the increasingly popular precollege study abroad (*chogi yuhak*), where children studying internationally are often accompanied by their mothers while fathers stay in South Korea and financially support the family.[31] We can also think of this cosmopolitan striving in the tongue on the operating table, regardless of whether the boy (and his mother) will actually travel and live abroad.

Then, I propose to consider the prosthetic memories of the tongue on the operating table in *Tongue-Tie* through the relationship between the boy and his mother (who takes him to the doctor and persuades his father to allow the surgery). If the boy portrays a postcolonial-neoliberal genre of homo economicus, the cut in his tongue might hold the memories of his mother—eclipsed in the non-sense of the surgical resolution to lift the boy's tongue from the mother tongue. Even though the voice of the mother is heard throughout the film, she rarely appears. This invisibility reflects the dilemma of remembering a mother in a patriarchal society, which mobilizes women's reproductive labor to preserve, save, or enhance social order in the name of motherhood but at the same time chastises mothers for not meeting the saturated symbol of mother as the origin.

In this context, one way to trace the memory of the mother is to recollect her voice so as to rearticulate her relationship with the neoliberal structure. Nancy Abelmann and Jiyeon Kang's analysis of the memoirs written by mothers of South Korean precollege students studying abroad shows this possibility, addressing how these mothers' writings are already responses to the criticism that they "create excessive instrumental familism, abrogate gender norms and forsake their nation to produce over-privileged, insufficiently filial and unpatriotic children."[32] In this way, Abelmann and Kang's approach unearths silenced memories.

However, I am interested in another kind of memory: the memory of mother/tongue that is unconceivable via postcolonial and neoliberal somatechnologies of the tongue. This interest arises from my initial question about what the countermemories would be of colonial and neoliberal injuries and displacements from the mother tongue if we consider them through the absurd corporeality of the tongue on the operating table. What if we take this absurdity as a prompt to explore an alternative logic of understanding somatic injury's bearing on linguistic force, which might trouble postcolonial and neoliberal norms that concern the speaking subject as the site of pedagogical, medical, and filial-reproductive interventions? How might such somatic injury as a condition of postcolonial prostheticity of languaging compel us to envision postcolonial feminist mnemonics of the mother/tongue, dislodged from the mother as symbolic and pragmatic institution (of origin and reproduction)?

As a detour on the path to addressing these questions, the next two parts of this chapter trace Black embodiments in feminist theories of linguistic performativity, which challenge the hegemonic sense of reality based on the unracialized relationship between body and language. In this way, I hope to reenvision how a speaking body enfolds the memory of modalities of being human and relating to the world (beyond those of the neoliberal homo economicus) that have been derealized under dominant geopolitical and economic forces.[33] The final part of the chapter then returns to the figure of mother/tongue in the critique of postcolonial language, engaging with Theresa Hak Kyung Cha's evocative writing on (her) Mother (an exile in Manchuria during the Japanese occupation of Korea) and African-diasporic feminist writer M. NourbeSe Philip's poetic portrayal of a human-animal mother who tongues her newly-born.[34] These two writers illustrate the postcolonial and diasporic prostheticity of the tongue as a chimeric space for queering and inhumanizing the memory of mother/tongue—by unbinding the mother from a saturating sign of the origin and the reproductive institution (which Lee's masculine speaking subject tries to preserve in and through Korean language).

A Bird in Your Hand: Precarity, Blackness, and the Power of Language

Often-forgotten racialized bodies in speech act theory might be seen as incidental examples. But they demonstrate that colonial biopolitics is an essential factor for figuring the relationship between language and body and the power of language upon the physical reality it references. In *Excitable Speech*, Judith Butler theorizes linguistic performativity by examining how injurious speech afflicts the reality of a subject who is susceptible to political violence ("Does language *really* hurt us, like physical assault does?").[35] In this, Butler refers to Toni Morrison's 1993 Nobel lecture that reflects upon how the force of language touches the precarity of Black people in the United States.[36] Morrison opens her lecture with a fable: "Once upon a time there was an old woman. Blind. Wise," who is also identified as a daughter of slaves, Black, American.[37] In this story, a group of children visits the woman. They seem bent on disproving her clairvoyance, and one asks a question that preys upon her disability: "Old woman, I hold in my hand a bird. Tell me whether it is living or dead." The blind woman responds, "I don't know . . . whether the bird you are holding is dead or alive, but what I do know is that it is in your hands." Following this fable, Morrison gives her own account of the story, in which she would "choose to read the bird as language and the woman as a practiced writer." Morrison explains that as a writer, the woman "thinks of language partly as a system, partly as a living thing over which one has control, but mostly as *agency—as an act with consequences.*"[38] Through this choice to measure the agency of the children's language by looking at how it humiliates the blind woman facing the violence that threatens the bird in their hand, Morrison illustrates the performativity of language as primarily biopolitical.

Morrison's explanation of the agency of language as that which concerns the precarity of life presents a somewhat puzzling disjuncture between the figuration of bird as language and that of language as an act with consequences. In other words, the agency of the children's speech becomes conceivable in relation to this contiguous yet uncollapsible space between the precarity of the bird and that of the blind woman confronting a threat. Butler notes that Morrison's lecture sustains this space through a figurative refrain—the modesty of not daring to say "the bird is language" or "language is agency," which performs the linguistic reality that the lecture purports to convey.[39] In other words, Morrison's lecture demonstrates that if language were to touch the vulnerability of life, then it could be performed, paradoxically through language that acknowledges its own limit vis-à-vis the life it represents. Such deference echoes Morrison's reference to Abraham Lincoln's Gettysburg speech, "disdaining the 'final word,' the precise 'summing up,'" that would "signal deference to the uncapturability of the life it mourns." This nonetheless doesn't mean that language has no power over the reality of the life it refers to. For Morrison, "a dead language" is measured by the consequences of an action that "actively thwarts the intellect, stalls conscience, suppresses human potential," rather than by the exhaustion of a living language or the inert remnants of it. As Butler draws upon Morrison's lecture for theorizing the nature of linguistic violence in relation to the embodied subject targeted by injurious words, traces of Black corporeality in the United States (mediated by the precarity of disabled and animal bodies) buttress Butler's emphasis on the limit of linguistic performativity, its untraversable distance from the referenced body.

Only after reflecting on the deathly power of language does Morrison turn to its force of life. "Once upon a time," Morrison begins the other half of the story from where Butler has left off. Now, the children challenge the entirety of the old woman's lesson. They criticize her for not even attempting to reach out to touch the bird, for being wise but not generous, for showing art but not commitment—suppose there was no bird from the beginning, and their visit was "only a ruse, a trick to get to be spoken to"? They ask her, "Don't you remember . . . when the invisible was what imagination strove to see?" "Make up a story. Narrative is radical, creating us at the very moment it is being created." Beseeching the woman to tell a story, the children create the story they have anticipated from her: the story of a wagonload of slaves, and of the boy and girl who secretly give bread and cider to them. Through their story, the children enact the blind clairvoyance they requested from the old woman—a story that touches without seeing by striving to approximate the precarity of others' lives in their hands, in the vicinal yet contingent space between their speech act and its corporeal consequences for other living beings.

Morrison's fable demonstrates the power of both dead and living languages—first in the supposedly threatening words that exploit the vulnerability of the woman and the bird, and second in the blind yet committed words that envision otherwise. However, compared with the vehement assertion of the violent force of dead language in the first part of the lecture, the second part is restrained. The story ends with the old woman's brief comment following the children's story about the wagonload of slaves: "The next stop will be their last. But not this one. This one is warmed." This asymmetry is a logical consequence of Morrison's thoughts on the life of language, which is measured by its deference to the vulnerability of the life it references. Here, the negative passion of not daring to capture the body is doubly performed: by the fictional suspension of the deaths of the slaves in the wagon and then again by the refusal to call it the final stop but rather just the one before their last. So what does this negative passion say about the narrative radicality that the children claim?

This proposed narrative radicality, alongside the asymmetrical power of language, returns us to the question raised by the absurdity of the tongue on the operating table: given the prosthetic relationship between the speaking body and its language, what is language capable of in delivering pain and loss? One might interpret the asymmetry as an indication of what posthumanist theorists see as the limit of the branch of thinking associated with "the linguistic turn" (including Butler's theory of performativity), whose emphasis on linguistic constraint mirrors the human-exceptionalist habit of privileging language (as a marker of the proper human subject) over matter. From this perspective, such a habit also informs the ethics of vulnerability that inherits the normative approach to death as the ultimate limit of the human subject prevalent in Western philosophical tradition, which Rosi Braidotti seeks to overcome through the neovitalist emphasis on Life whose force is indifferent to the boundary of the human subject.[40] While such a posthumanist perspective offers sobering insights, this line of criticism nonetheless fails to address how the poststructuralist emphasis on the linguistic limit in deference to death doesn't assume or prove the unexamined privilege given to language over matter. On the contrary, this emphasis highlights the weight of the corporeal in the history of racialized suffering and loss, which is often derealized in the hegemonic frame of humanity. As such, the posthuman emphasis on matter (over language) obscures its own inattention to racialized corporeality and thereby reproduces the construal of reality based on a Western metaphysical binary of language versus body that it seeks to overcome.

Morrison's fable within and beyond Butler's theory instead suggests another materialist approach to the power of linguistic reality, which accounts for Black bodies that bear historical and political injuries. This materialist methodology thus takes up where Butler leaves off in the inquiry into the reality of linguistic force vis-à-vis physical reality and the political potentiality such an inquiry entails, beyond the Western metaphysical sense of reality imbricated with the colonial and racial order of things. Between the final stop and the one before lies a power of language that doesn't dare to capture the corporeal suffering of Black people but nonetheless carves out space for unfolding the memory of the otherwise beyond and against the colonial and racial order of body, language, and reality. Figured as blind clairvoyance, this radical narrativity can turn Chow's postcolonial prescience of the prostheticity of language—the dislocation of one's language from the speaking body—into the capacity to be haunted by the social and political precarity of others. In this, the blindness of the old Black woman in Morrison's story is less a narrative device than a metonymic remainder of the collective debilitation of Black people in the United States since slavery.[41] Thus, while this radical narrative as a kind of blind clairvoyance does not limn the reality that trumps the hegemonic onto-epistemology, it nonetheless renders conceivable another reality whose measure isn't actualization but a holding-onto of countermemories of colonial violence and dehumanization.

Cosmogonic Autopoiesis: Storytelling and Genres of Being Human

My reading of Morrison both with and beyond Butler has sought to foreground the racial corporeality in their conceptualization of the force of language, which concerns the biopolitical question of what constitutes the reality of loss and pain and how language might carry an/other reality. However, although attending to racialized corporeality complicates the posthumanist approaches to language as a privileged marker of the human proper for Western liberalism, it nonetheless doesn't dismiss the posthumanist call to decenter from human agency and rationality in and beyond language. Rather, it invites considering the different status of racialized subjects in their claim for humanity—accounting for what is construed as human about human linguistic practice and by whose measure—as we seek an approach to language that does not take for granted hegemonic humanism and anthropocentrism.

In this light, Sylvia Wynter's theory of homo narrans (storytellers) illustrates how factoring in race helps us recognize the multiplicity of human-language assemblages beyond the liberal humanist model.[42] Wynter's theory draws on the second-order cybernetic theory of autopoiesis to explain how human linguistic practices (especially telling cosmogonies) bear upon the racially embodied praxis of being human and relating to the world.[43] In particular, as I'll soon explicate, Wynter accounts for the injurious prostheticity of languaging experienced by a Black colonial subject as a recollection of human races as homo narrans, autopoietically instituted as such by their own origin stories. Wynter's conceptualization of the human races as cybernetic-autopoietic linguistic animals thus offers a space for interlocution between decolonial and posthuman theories of language and its relation to the racialized body. From this perspective, this part of the chapter explores prosthetic memories about who we (as human species) are when human races emerge amid these chimeracological entanglements of an/other origin story and the cosmos, doing and undoing the postcolonial-neoliberal self-portrayal of homo economicus in Tongue-Tie.

For Wynter, attending to human linguistic practice is far from human exceptionalism, but rather a key for reformulating "the question of who we are as humans" as a decolonialist agenda.[44] The political significance of this question parallels the global catastrophe problematically called the Anthropocene—a term that presumes the Western bourgeois model of Man as representative of all human kinds. Given that the catastrophe is caused largely by the Western (and Westernized) Man's mode of material provisioning—capitalism—but its destructive cost is unequally imposed on poorer and darker peoples and regions, calling it the result of human activities reinstitutes rather than deters the specific mode of being human that is in fact culpable for the problems.[45] If the Anthropocene is only a synecdoche for the extensive global catastrophe to which the hegemonic mode of being human has led us, it's necessary to rediscover other kinds of humanity that enable us to reenvision possibilities other than the impending catastrophe.[46]

From this perspective, Wynter offers an alternative narrative of human evolution for reenvisioning who we are as humans. Following what she calls— in reference to physical chemist Ilya Prigogine's law-event duality—the "First Event" (the origin of the universe) and the "Second Event" (the explosion of biological life forms), there came the "Third Event" marking the origin of the human as a storytelling species, homo narrans, in Africa.[47] Wynter attributes the Third Event to "the *co-evolution* of the human brain with . . . the emergent faculties of language."[48] Wynter's proposition is that, thanks to the human brain's capacity to neurochemically "auto-institute" oneself according to the symbolic instructions given by social myths, we have become the very kinds of human that our cosmogonies say we are.[49] However, the multiple "genres of being human"—each performatively generated by its own origin story—have been blotted out by the globally hegemonic figure of Man.[50] It is therefore important to remember that this hegemonic figure of Man is also an enactment of its own origin story, that the Western bourgeois liberal humanist reinvention of homo economicus is generated by the Darwinian-Malthusian origin story.[51]

Wynter's theory finds the origin of the human-as-species in the evolutionary articulation between biology and language (that is, between brain and myth), which she calls "the *autopoiesis* of being hybridly human," borrowing Chilean cybernetics theorists Humberto Maturana and Francisco Varela's term.[52] Wynter notably illustrates this cybernetic hybridity of being human and the onto-epistemological rupture it offers with Frantz Fanon's famous scene where he was called a "dirty nigger" upon arriving in imperial France.[53] In this moment, Wynter writes, the Black person's phylogeny/

ontogeny (black skin) is instituted by the projected gaze of the colonial-ist sociogeny (white mask), the Darwinian myth that regards the Black as a naturally deselected savage.[54] Wynter further suggests that this event—during which Fanon's dermal condition turns into a mode of being Black in the metropolitan environment—inaugurates the colonial subject, who must experience himself as both "normally and abnormally human."[55] This irreconcilable conflict between normal and abnormal humanity not only poses the colonial subject as a pseudo-species but also institutes the normal (that is, colonial European) human species.

Wynter's theory of homo narrans describes both the emergence of the human species in Africa during the Third Event and the inauguration of the colonial subject in the middle of the twentieth century in Fanon—mirroring the double structure of Darwin's theory on the origin of the human, which effectively inaugurates the West's Man. As such, while Wyn-ter's approach recasts Darwinian evolution, it doesn't simply reverse the hegemonic genre of Man that Darwin's theory institutes but also doubles and haunts it. In this, Wynter's theory allows us to consider how human linguistic practice (storytelling) performatively recalls chimeric visions for our countercosmogonies. This is another kind of prophetic memory of our past that is not yet, which performatively un/does who we are (as and other-than homo economicus) and further who we will have become as humans and affords an alternative futurity to the script of the impending planetary catastrophe.

Thus, Wynter's somewhat eccentric refiguration of the human species as autopoietic in origin invites an interesting conversation with a posthuman-ist approach to language. On one hand, Wynter's theory of homo narrans seems to repeat the anthropocentric tendency to privilege language as what distinguishes the human species from "all other primates."[56] On the other, and probably at odds with Wynter's own intention, her theory is predisposed to more-than-merely-human perspectives. Wynter's theory can be read as a posthumanist hypothesis on how cosmogonic codes are literally written into human brains and substantialized through the evolutionary process. Thus, it allows us to approach human linguistic practice as a nonrepresentational and beyond-the-human becoming that involves the other nonhuman entities and inhuman forces that take part in cosmos. On a more earthly scale, Max Hantel refigures Wynter's autopoiesis as "multispecies," extending Wynter's critique of monohumanism that has led to the impending planetary environ-mental destruction.[57] Hantel notes that while Wynter draws upon cybernetic theories, which are often discussed in terms of human-machine interface, these nonetheless emerged in relation to research on animals such as Gregory Bateson's search for the patterns of communication among all living animals.[58] Still, this multispecies autopoiesis is also racially and geopolitically constituted. As Orit Halpern discusses, Bateson's theory about the stability and disruption of the system is derived from his ethnographic observations of colonial Balinese people's bodily gestures—which conveniently exempts the anthropologist from paying attention to (let alone learning) the native language.[59]

Here, the point is not that Wynter's theory is (or is not) sufficiently posthumanist. Rather, Wynter's theory amplifies the definitional tension within posthumanism due to its reference to the boundary of the human, which is interlaced with biopolitical productions of the infrahuman, including racialized others. Then, this tension cannot be resolved by the professed inclusion of the Other(s) but should be considered an ever-contingent onto-epistemological grounds for claims for more-than-human perspectives. If postcolonial experience has (as Chow observes) gifted the prescience of the prostheticity of languaging, then the racial double consciousness for Wynter unveils that the prostheticity of languaging (inscribing cosmogonies onto our brain) is the very condition of the autopoiesis of humans both as species and as races within the cosmos. If Wynter's vision for the other origin of our species is already chimeracological at birth, it is not simply because this theory is based on the cybernetic model that concerns similarities between and communications among mechanical systems and biological organisms. As Denise Ferreira da Silva notes, Wynter's appeal to scientific knowledge's (specifically the natural sciences') role in "unveiling the nonhistorical or extrahuman (natural/biological) structuring of cultural or ideological mechanisms" may overlook the very violence the post-Enlightenment power/knowledge effects through the analytics of racial differences.[60] However, I still find Wynter's vision chimeracological, also because its troping of hegemonic scientific knowledge into poetic knowledge invites reimagining humans' relationship with other species from an infra-human perspective.

"Mother, you are a child still."

So, the tongue has been a prime site of somatechnological investments in the speaking subject for colonialist, nationalist, and neoliberal projects. Here, one's relation to the mother/tongue as a symbolic and pragmatic institution (of origin and reproduction) becomes the horizon within which only certain pedagogical and medical interventions into the speaking subject—and the subtending (often Western metaphysical) onto-epistemological logics of body and language, and their relation to reality—are validated while others are invalidated or even illegible.

Yet, with the help of Morrison's and Wynter's approaches to language that account for racial and colonial somatic injuries as a potential aperture to another reality, let me return to where I left off in the first part of this chapter: countermemories of the mother/tongue in the postcolonial cut in the tongue. As in Morrison's fable, we can think of two stories of post-colonial languaging. If the first is about the lamentable non-sense of the speaking body whose English pronunciation is corrected by a surgical cut, displaced from the mother tongue (as the origin), what is the second story of the lifted tongue? Could this second story be another origin story of the postcolonial subject in Wynter's terms—memories through which we unbecome a postcolonial neoliberal version of homo economicus? And could this other origin story be the memories of a mother other than the mother as national origin or neoliberal reproductive institution? This last part of the chapter attempts to reverse engineer the somatechnologies of the tongue on the operating table through the countermemories of the mother/tongue illuminated in poetic writings of M. NourbeSe Philip and Theresa Hak Kyung Cha. Here, my readings are offered not as an immediate countermemory of the mother in *Tongue-Tie* but as a diffractive device for intimating its potential.

M. NourbeSe Philip is a Tobago-born, Toronto-based poet, writer, and lawyer whose works largely concern Black women's experiences. In this vein, Philip's poem "Discourse on the Logic of Language" illustrates how the maternal corporeality of the native tongue can also be a source of de-colonial feminist remembrance of the Other language, *logos*, and culture repressed by colonial physical and epistemic violence, without recourse to the (masculine) mastery subject of anticolonialism. The central voice of this poem evokes the memory of the loss of the mother tongue, or the anguish of postcolonial and diasporic prostheticity of language—because "my mother tongue" is English, that is "my father tongue," and therefore it is "a foreign language, not a mother tongue."[61]

In columns parallel to this evocative narration, the poem records and laments the loss of the mother tongue in the history of Africans and African diaspora in the New World under the colonialist law whereby "every slave caught speaking his native language shall be severely punished," and the slave's tongue itself could even be removed as a punishment.[62] This necropolitical governance of slaves' tongues under colonialist law is juxtaposed with reporting on prominent nineteenth-century European doctors Carl Wernicke and Paul Broca, after whom "the parts of the brain chiefly responsible for speech [and memory] are named."[63] The poem details how Broca was committed to proving the supremacy of "white males of the Caucasian race" (due to their "larger brains"), pointing to the entwined logics of Western science and medicine with the somatechnological interventions in the slave's tongue—and the memory it holds.[64]

Against the hegemonic "logic of language," the poem narrates another memory on the margins of the paper, tracing back to the event of a birth when "the mother" licks her newborn daughter clean, and then (once you literally turn the page) blows words into the daughter's mouth tongue-to-tongue.[65] Here, the poem stages memory in a liminal crossing between human and animal, where the primordial animality of the maternal tongue/body engenders a new kind of speaking subject. Set in such a chimeracological space, the birth of the new speaking subject does not recuperate an oedipal-masculine subjectivity from dehumanizing colonialist practices. What might appear as a biological reduction of the (human) maternal body into animality instead intimates a new kind of speaking subject that dismantles the West's medical and scientific orders of race, gender, and species from within. I draw this argument in dialogue with Zakiyyah Iman Jackson's discussions about the bearing of blackened female bodies on the world's order. Jackson criticizes how Black females' flesh (especially their breasts) and mammary labor have given the soma "both to bodies and our prevailing categories of species and sex/gender," while left un/gendered (as the outer marker of the white bourgeois norms of women)—examining eighteenth-century European science's development of zoological nomenclature (such as Swedish botanist Carl Linnaeus's work) and the twentieth-century entomologist imaginary of the origin of society.[66] Furthermore, Jackson argues, as the laboring mater-matter-matrix that is unrepresentable under the hegemonic scientific and social systems of knowledge of the human and the world, the Black mater (in her contiguity to animals and animality) holds "potential to the terms of reality and feeling" that shatters the "globally hegemonic metaphysics of the world."[67] In a similar light, Philip's poem presents a chimeracological maternal corporeality as the matrix for Afro-diasporic feminist countermemory of the birth of a speaking subject (that does not conform to the usual liberalist sense of the human subject), where the mother's tongue is not a site of reconfirming the hegemonic forms of human identity/subjectivity but rather an amorous, animalistic, and visceral yet word-giving organ that begets her daughter as a Black speaking subject.

Cha's evocative writing on the Mother tongue illustrates another kind of mnemonic machine that unremembers the mother/tongue as the institution of origin in the prosthetic space between tongue and tongue, mouth and mouth:

> Mother, you are a child still. . . . Still, you speak the tongue the mandatory language like the others. It is not your own. Even if it is not you know you must. You are Bilingual. You are Tri-lingual. The tongue that is forbidden is your own mother tongue. You speak in the dark. In the secret. The one that is yours. Your own. You speak very softly, you speak in whisper. In the dark, in secret. Mother tongue is your refuge. It is being home. Being who you are. Truly. To speak makes you sad. Yearning. To utter each word is a privilege you risk by death. Not only for you but for all. All of you who are one, who by law tongue tied forbidden of tongue.[68]

A chapter in Cha's *Dictee* titled "Calliope Epic Poetry" opens with recalling Mother, who was born in Manchuria, where her Korean family had moved to escape the Japanese occupation (which eventually did reach Manchuria). "Calliope" can be read as one version among many other stories of the forbidden mother tongue, whispered from mother to daughter and father to son under the watchful eye of colonialism. However, this story also unsettles the narrative tradition, as it is told back to Mother—and not in Korean but in English, the language of the United States where Cha's family moved in her childhood. As such, "Calliope" evokes both a memory of the Mother tongue and also its erasure, a memory of imposed polylingualism but also sheltering the Mother tongue in secret. Through this double gesture, "Calliope" at once reappropriates Mother's memory and dispossesses it by speaking in English.

Sung by the Asian American daughter to her Mother who is still a child, "Calliope" offers epic poetry of displacement as a postcolonial and diasporic origin story—an origin story that does not recuperate but rather engenders Mother from the prosthetic space of mouth-to-mouth. This engendering is a queering work of love toward Mother-as-Child, refiguring the prosthetic interstice within the "mouth to mouth" as a space for rearticulating the cut, lineage, and kinship. Only with love to Mother who is yet a child (and yet an animal, like the one in Philip's poem), whose body is yet to be crossed as the oedipal lack, whose love has yet to be privatized into the family as a unit of social intimacy and reproduction, can one remember another origin story—words blown back to her, mouth-to-mouth.

2

A Song from the Cybernetic Fold

In Response to Sontag's "The World as India"

In her 2002 St. Jerome Lecture on Literary Translation titled "The World as India," Susan Sontag attests to the distinctiveness of the human translator from the computer, "which will soon be able to perform most translating tasks."[1] In particular, Sontag anticipates that the human translator's value will survive in the field of literature, where translation requires engagement with "ethical standards" in order to choose among different losses in translation from one language to another. For Sontag, this agony of loss is lacking in the machine counterpart, which simply finds equivalence between two languages. In this light, the perennial debates between fidelity to the original text and adaption to the target language in translation (literal translation versus adaptive translation) indicate such an ethical caliber, which concerns the loss of national identity vis-à-vis one's connection to the world.[2] Interestingly, Sontag finds a contemporary case of such an ethical predicament in outsourced US call centers in India, where operators are trained to erase their Indian accent in English in order to sound American. For Sontag, these operators—who not only perform assigned American identities (names with little biographies) but also prefer these pseudo-identities to the real ones—are a perfect example of the "loss of identity" in adaptive translation. This phenomenon at call centers convinces Sontag that India, where the national language "has to be" the colonial conqueror's language among the variety of local tongues, models "the World" where English has become the new lingua franca.

There have been rich discussions on the impact of globalization on national identity and division of labor in outsourced call centers since Sontag's lecture.[3] What I nonetheless find more relevant over the past two decades is that the Indian operators' accents function as a metonymic device for connecting the tension between globalization and national identity to the distinction between human and computer. Sontag portrays the operators' labor as "pretending" in order to "pass for Americans"—in striking resonance with the Turing test that was designed to determine whether a computer has a human-like intelligence by measuring its capacity to imitate a gendered person (woman) in teleprinter conversation.[4] In Sontag's lecture, these operators—and especially their simulated accents—thus embody an inevitable loss of authenticity in the globalizing world, the pang of which evidences the ethical agency of the human (except the operators themselves) as distinct from the computer. Here, the information and communication technology (ICT) industry offers both rhetorical and material matrices for the postcolonial prosthetization of languaging in the age of neoliberal globalization.

Taking Sontag's lecture as its point of departure, this chapter examines the racial and gendered humanness's bearings on postcolonial languaging in the transnational circuits of ICT to engage with the prosthetic memories emerging through this cybernetic fold. Eve Kosofsky Sedgwick and Adam Frank's term "cybernetic fold" refers to a historical moment spanning roughly the late 1940s to the mid-1960s, "when scientists' understanding of the brain and other life processes [was] marked by the concept, the possibility, the imminence, of powerful computers, but the actual computational muscle of the new computers [wasn't] available."[5] Sedgwick and Frank note that this interstitial moment created an intellectual environment for rich imaginations, where Silvan Tomkins's early question "Could one design a truly humanoid machine?" inspired his theory of affect that finds productive potential in the inefficient fits between affective and cognitive systems and various crossings of digital with analog.[6] Since Tomkins, a variety of computers and humanoids have materialized, but Sedgwick and Frank's observation about the interstitial contingency is still relevant. Our contemporaries still make sense of who we are as humans and what our trajectory from past to future is like in relation to the ideas of computational and robotic technologies yet to come, only with a more tactile immediacy of an automated world and a thicker history of the cybernetic fold.

This first part of the chapter revisits Sontag's lecture and the subsequent "cyber-coolie" debates, examining the postcolonial prosthetization of language that positions Asiatic mind-bodies within the geopolitical stratification of human groups by construing their humanity through a proximity to (and distinction from) technology in the global division of labor at the turn of the twenty-first century. In this, I don't take conflation between the Indian operators' tongues and the machine translators as simply a matter of discriminatory or exclusive dehumanization, requiring that we recognize the humanity of the Asiatic bodies. Rather, such conflation betrays how the usual understanding of human exceptional linguistic capacity relies on and reiterates what Denise Ferreira da Silva criticizes as the post-Enlightenment onto-epistemological structure of interiority/exteriority: that historical and scientific knowledges of race have produced and protected the European subject as "the proper man," the only one privileged to house freely self-determining reason (interiority), by allocating to others of Europeans in the realm of the affectable the condition of being subjected to the external power (exteriority) because of their inferior mental capacities.[7] In other words, Sontag's analogy between Indian call-center operators and a computer translator illustrates how the exceptionality of human languaging (translation of literature) presumes distinctive human mental capacity, with the outer/lower edges of such capacity—drawn by the Indians' and computer's languaging—signifying lower kinds of mind. Thus, if I figure this century's ICT cybernetic fold as chimeracological, it is because the proxy between Asiatic tongues and computers articulates an onto-epistemological circuit preemptive of the supposedly universal human qualities of self-determined reason in ethical and aesthetic judgment.

My critical response to Sontag grounds this chapter's primary goal of exploring how Orientalized and queer affinities with machines might enable a chimeric and dehumanist alternative to the view of language as a universal marker of human distinction—and what prosthetic memories this vision might engender, compounding the usual question of how postcolonial languaging holds memories of dispossession and displacement. For this, the subsequent parts of the chapter turn to multimedia artist and poet Margaret Rhee's work, which rewires humans' relationships with robots and digital technology to offer an imaginative space akin to Tomkins's cybernetic fold. Thus, I engage with Rhee's poetry as a technology of difference (rather than of distinction) with which to reenvision queer and diasporic memories of how we live and die, love, and work near machines.[8]

In defense of Sontag against the accusation that she is enthusiastic about and supportive of the call centers, she in fact remains ambiguous about her own position and acknowledges the uneven effect of globalization on different languages. She likens it to the Tower of Babel, where certain languages occupy desirable upper floors while others are confined to lower levels. However, Sontag writes that the initial ascendance of the new lingua franca was "something of a fluke"—a consequence of, for example, the international adoption of English for civil aviation in the 1920s and the later prevalence of English in the ubiquity of computers. Thus, her analysis somehow overlooks the role of the United States' current cultural and economic dominance and past British colonialism in the global spread of English. Although it is at odds with her own perspective, Sontag's analysis nonetheless also highlights how the Babel of languages is interlaced with the development of information, communication, and transportation technologies during and after the world wars. Such historical conditions inform the status of the call-center operators in a global market increasingly networked through ICT, where "the interface between humans and machines [computers] is predominantly rooted in English."[9] Then, the seemingly arbitrary juxtaposition of the Indian operators' English accents and the human/computer distinction in Sontag's lecture isn't coincidence but rather illustrative of the postcolonial languaging wherein one's status of humanity is contingent upon the relation to (and distinction from) information technology within the global political economy.

The publication of Sontag's speech in the *Times Literary Supplement* stirred up the "cyber-coolie" debate among Indian critics, who also postulated the political meaning of these English-speaking Indian operators in reference to their relationship with technology in the transnational ICT circuits.[10] Harish Trivedi, a professor of English at the University of Delhi, initiated the debate in a letter to the paper criticizing what he called Sontag's deluded "enthusiasm for the call centers."[11] Trivedi argues that young Indian people—who are pressured to fake not only their English accents but also their identities—are "indeed the cyber-coolies of our global age, working not on sugar plantations but on flickering screens." For Trivedi, such "a brutally exploitive economic arrangement" has nothing to do with literary translation but only confirms English as "the linguistic instrument" for what Sontag describes as "the world dominance of the colossal and unique superpower of which I am a citizen."[12] However, Gurcharan

Das, who claims to have been associated with three call centers, criticizes Trivedi in his letter to another newspaper, the *Times of India*, titled "Cyber Coolies or Cyber Sahibs?"[13] Das argues that young people in India see the outsourcing phenomenon as "an exciting chance to work with the world's top brands and acquire new skills to make a career in the global economy," where "English remains the passport for every youngster who dreams of becoming *a master of the universe*."[14] Either way, the debate employs an instrumentalist approach (to both language and ICT) that figures technology as a means for mastery of the world. Thus, the Indian operators become either machine-like tools exploited for global dominance or masters of the world through language and/as technology.

In both Sontag's lecture and the cyber-coolie debate, these young Indians' status in the world is mediated by their linguistic vicinity to technology—in the first case as a failure to be distinguished from computers (and thus as an exception to the human-exceptional quality) and in the second as neoliberal tools for mastery of the world (or as masters of the tools, hence of the world). This mediated status urges us to revisit the racialized contiguity between human and technology, which entails reimagining a nonmastery engagement with technology beyond the usual critique of instrumental reason (that nostalgically reinstitutes the West's classic human subject with the capacity of creative/poietic thinking). The operators' vicinity to the translation machine illuminates the prosthetic conditions of postcolonial languaging in the era of globalizing ICT, where the assumption of human-exceptional linguistic practice puts these young Indians at the margin of the human (embodied by the human translators of literature who would agonize over the loss of the spirit of one's mother tongue). Similarly, Margaret Rhee discusses how the *Economist* special issue titled "Rise of the Robots" evokes the trope of robots as "immigrants from the future" and "second-class citizens," which bears an "uncanny resemblance" to "the model minority stereotype" of Asian Americans.[15] In particular, the association between the two speaks to the racialization of Asian Americans as laborers with "great productivity" who are nonetheless incomplete by virtue of lacking "creativity" and "emotions," which also echoes anxiety about the loss of jobs due both to artificial intelligence robots and to the Asian (migrant) labor force.[16]

As such, Indian operators in Sontag's lecture substantiate the racial matrix of the human that Wendy Hui Kyong Chun criticizes: "The human is constantly created through the jettisoning of the Asian/Asian American other as robotic, as machine-like and not quite human, as not quite lived. And also I would add, the African American other as primitive, as too human."[17] These tropes of Asiatic subjects, however, do not indicate a shared intrinsic quality among Asians, Asian migrants, and Asian Americans. Rather, such transversal associations on the one hand are enabled by US racialist technology that deploys Asians as efficient workers but politically alienates them as migrants and foreigners, and on the other articulate a US techno-Orientalist imaginary that projects its futurism on Asian Others as perversely hypertechnological (despite different significations between the Japanese as creators and Chinese and Indians as "the technology").[18] Thus, the gathering of Koreans, Indians, and Asian Americans in this chapter suggests a space for oppositional affinities against malleable racial technology. In a similar vein, Chun's observation about the different rubrics for Asian American and African American also limns the hegemonic racialist topography more than an intrinsic and clean-cut difference between these subjects. As such, Chun's focus and my own on a techno-Orientalist imaginary do not cancel out the critiques on the social imaginary of robots in reference to Black slaves offered by Neda Atanasoski and Kalindi Vora.[19]

In this light, it makes sense that Chun revisits Frantz Fanon's refusal to accept his race as a social "amputation" and his commitment to turn his race into a prosthesis that endows him with "the power to expand without limit."[20] Chun engages with Fanon's pursuit of turning his Blackness into a prosthesis through Heidegger's proposition on the salvational power of poieses (arts) to address the destructive power of technology that renders man a "standing reserve."[21] However, Chun moves away from Heideggerian suspicion of technology and instead asks, "To what extent can ruminating on race as technology make possible race as poieses, or at least as a form of agency?" and "Could this power stem not from asserting difference between humans and technology, technology and *poieses*, but rather through an acceptance of their similarities—through race as prosthesis?"[22]

Chun's engagement with and move from Heidegger is noteworthy, thinking alongside Luciana Parisi's challenge to the familiar critique of instrumental reason—such as Heidegger's return to "the pre-Socratic union of poetry (or *poiesis*) and thinking (*noien*)" as a philosophical resolution to the "advancing form of instrumental reason" he saw in post–World War II cybernetics, or media theorist Bernard Stiegler's recent placement of technics within the Aristotelian noetic to ground the biotechnical diversity of minds "against the global order of techno-capitalism."[23] For Parisi, this kind of "merging technics with poiesis" only reiterates the Promethean cosmogony of "the self-making Man," restoring the onto-epistemological premise of the self-determining subject (echoing Ferreira da Silva's critique).[24] Thus, Parisi proposes to abandon "the view of technics as being part of the creativity of Man" and instead attends to "the dark side of improper knowledge, stemming not from self-creativity but from . . . the inhuman condition of the slave-machine."[25] Although Chun does not abandon the idea of reconciling technology with poiesis, her emphasis on the indistinction between humans and technology—via thinking of (amputated) race as technology—already moves away from Man's reason toward dehumanist thinking.

In this light, I would like to further Chun's effort to recast the racialized affinities between humans and technologies in conversation with queer posthumanist critiques on the technicity of gender postulated in the conceptualization of machine intelligence. Queer theorist J. Halberstam observes how the Turing test betrays only that gender (used as a control model for gauging whether a machine can think) is in fact an "imitative system" just like computer intelligence, the distinction of which from human intelligence is anything but clear and stable.[26] If we follow Halberstam's deconstructive logic, Indian operators simulating an American accent present not a problem of inauthentic identity but rather an event of racializing technology that configures these operators as machine-like pseudo-Americans.

Approaching race (like gender) as technological is not necessarily subversive in itself. Nonetheless, Halberstam's attention to the similarity between two imitative systems (gender and intelligence) in the Turing test also intimates more fundamental affective-cognitive circuits among humans and thinking machines, from which Elizabeth A. Wilson retraces queer bonds involving non-oedipal, homosexual, and arrested attachments.[27] Such a human-machine intimacy contagiously destabilizes the binary relationship between the human subject (as signifier of reason proxied by European subjects) and the thinking machine (as signifier of instrumental reason, which in turn is the object of human reason)—the violent post-Enlightenment binary between interior and exterior as critiqued by Ferreira da Silva.[28] This kind of queer critique amplifies the potential of an approach to postcolonial languaging as technological that embraces the affinities between racialized humans and machines beyond both the imaginary of master-slave dialectics and the conventional critique of instrumental reason. This brings us back to reflecting on the Indian operators' speech act through which the status of these workers as (racialized) humans vis-à-vis machines evokes, diffracts, and collides with the colonial and diasporic memory of exploitative labor and with the futuristic aspiration for what ICT promises amid neoliberal globalization.

The rest of this chapter takes Sontag's lecture as a spur for reenvisioning the prostheticity of postcolonial languaging in the contemporary cybernetic fold from an inhuman perspective near the technological—drawing on queer genealogies of thinking and feeling with machine intelligence and the fractured associations between robots and Asians (and Asian migrants) in colonial and postcolonial history. For this purpose, I hope to engage with queer and diasporic memories in such a prosthetic interface of languaging by exploring Rhee's poetry collection *Love, Robot* (2017) and her multimedia installation *Kimchi Poetry Machine* (2014), which reenvision the human-machine relationship by recasting two qualifications that are often considered unsuitable for robots/machines: love and poetry. What if we engage with poetry not as the site of human affective-intellectual distinction from machine (as in Sontag's lecture) but as a technology of love across difference, inflected by love as a feminist and queer practice? What if we engage with poetry not as a mark of individual human creativity but as a technology of listening and connecting across difference inside the cybernetic fold? How might such a poetic technology enable us to reenvision techno-Orientalist futurism into the countermemory of how we inhabit the more-than-merely-human world amid biopolitical compartmentalization and denigration in the global circuits of information and communication technology?

Technology of Difference 1:
A Memory of *Love, Robot*

I propose to consider the question, "Can machines think?"

A. M. Turing, "Computing Machinery and Intelligence"

Playing with A. M. Turing's initial question, "Can machines think?" (which he then replaces with the Turing test), Margaret Rhee's *Love, Robot* prompts the question, "Can machines love?"[29] Shifting focus from cognitive to emotional capacity, this question appears to challenge logocentric human exceptionalism but at the same time to implicate another sense of "human uniqueness" that regards "affective capacity" as its ultimate benchmark (as the human translator's unique capacity in Sontag's lecture). Whether machines with artificial intelligence are capable of (and will replace) the affective interaction that is presumed to be quintessential among human partners has been a recurrent theme in the popular imaginary, such as in films like *Blade Runner* and *Her*.

However, intimating Turing's then-prohibited homosexuality (and its implications for the conception of artificial intelligence), Rhee's question slips away from the underlying logic of the sameness of Man—that is, the equivalence between humans and robots—and instead to what it even means that someone or something can love.[30] On this slippery ground, Rhee's *Love, Robot* invites us to a world where humans and robots fall in (and out of) love with each other, playfully muddling what Mel Chen describes as "the biopolitical spheres" of intimacy imbricated within the racial and species order of things.[31] As such, it is an invitation to a queer love—queer in the sense that human-robot love entails "non-normativity, and an embracing of the edges that trouble the norm," extending the usual reference to "LGBT issues or identity."[32] The following is thus a reading of Rhee's poetry as a technology of difference (as opposed to one of distinction), exploring how it unfolds prosthetic memories of a mundane yet transgressive love between humans and robots, across different corporealities.

> What I remember: once,
> after we had dinner in the city.
> there,
> between
> turk street and 7th
> i stroked your shoulder
>   your lights began to beam and
> you stayed put,
>   as the cars passed
> us, and the traffic lights
> eventually
>   all
>   turned
>   red.

Rhee, "BEAM, ROBOT"

In the final lines of "BEAM, ROBOT," which opens *Robot, Love*, the memory of human-robot love is set in a cityscape where "the traffic lights eventually all turned red."[33] Red light is often applied to machines due to a "primordial vividness" that signals "rupture" and "danger" to human senses—as in red stop signs.[34] However, in this poem red light not only alarms and interrupts but also allures—the human and robot lovers "lit up with the pin ball machine," dazzling and being dazzled by each other.[35] While there's nothing new about red love, in Rhee's poems red lights illuminate a queer "ecology of sensation" (to borrow Amit Rai's words) in which humans are wired into robots through desire and intimacy.[36]

Or perhaps the queer ecology of sensation is what flickers red, signaling transgressive sensations of human-robot encounters across corporeal differences. The sensation of human-robot intimacy beams, blinks, and sparks in electric dryness as the robot partner gets close to, is touched by, and jolts against the wet-sanguine human partner. In "LOVE, ROBOT *for Dmitry*," "the soft part of my fingers" touches a robot to "make her blink red."[37] This poem begins with the (probably human) narrator reminiscing how she "liked to watch you shower because you closed your eyes in the water and slightly parted your mouth," envious of aliveness in such a mundane scene. It is unclear whom ("you") the narrator is watching. Yet this poem ends with the narrator's disastrous attempt to make her robot lover alive: "i coaxed my robot not to be afraid of the water. To open her mouth. To let everything rinse away by the sparks of electric light."[38] This spark marks the unassimilability between the two different kinds of corporeality, queering seemingly all-too-human songs about humans and various machines being fascinated by, making love to, feeling frustrated with, and being heartbroken by one another.

If *Love, Robot* demands a certain naivete in its enchanting and enchanted look at both robots and humans, it does so through the prism of difference instead of the prison of sameness of Man. In other words, this poetic naivete doesn't prove the human-like capacity of machines to love, or even the human capacity to love machines as if they were humans; instead, it operates something like what Jane Bennett describes as "a clue to the secret life of nonhumans" that resists human comprehension.[39] Even in such poetic speculation the difference between humans and robots is nonetheless maintained, as the lovers' desires, frustrations, and corporeal sensations are diffracted through the memory of prohibited homosexual intimacy:

> you held me close even when i didn't want you to, even though everyone stared at us. . . . . when we are together, they stare at us. let's be careful. hide me deep & order me oil, coke, & springs. don't let anyone see us. i want us to live a long life together. i want to have your cyborg baby, i want to share a coke with you, every year, on the same day, in our near future.

cut off my legs & head, leave only my servomotor
we dance on tables we drink
until we die
cables,
connectors,
wires,
water, &
flesh

Rhee, "MACHINE TESTIMONIAL 6"

In "MACHINE TESTIMONIAL 6," human-robot love is coded through a clandestine homosexual love, echoing Frank O'Hara's "Having a Coke with You."[40] José Esteban Muñoz writes how in O'Hara's poem "a quotidian act" of having a Coke with somebody "signifies a vast lifeworld of queer relationality, an encrypted sociality, and a utopian potentiality."[41] Evoking such a mundane yet coded intimacy, the seemingly normative desires to live "a long life together" and have a (cyborg) baby evoke transgressive intimacy and kinship. Written in the voice of a robot, the poem asks, "dear mother, / did you make / me?" to blur the roles among lover, robot-maker, and mother.[42] The poem thus challenges the conventional trope of intimacy between (male) human and (female) robot, which figures the robot both as creature and as object of patriarchal and masculine desire and knowledge. While this kind of conventional trope can also be considered through Ferreira da Silva's "transparent I" (as the location and effect of scientific reason, privileged to European subjects) and his affectable object, the human-robot intimacy in the poem disturbs such logics.[43]

"When all the traffic lights turn red" is when the memory of human-robot love begins, but also when it ends. Perhaps it belongs to this suspended time when traffic signals "stop" and humans are asleep. The night is the time of being-nearby and its difficulty, due to and despite difference. In "SLEEP, ROBOT," while robots "take time for day dreaming" at night, the narrator falls asleep next to her partner because "there is no sweeter lullaby than the hum of your servomotor."[44] However, as the robot grows slower and rustier, it eventually needs to be fixed (or "maybe even replaced").[45] The robot asks

i may stop in the middle of the night
never see you again.

so, stay up with me. . . .

The human lover is receptive but fails:

> i tried to stay up
> i did everything to try,
> yet my eyes fluttered shut long before
> all your lights died into a
> dead city,
> deep cough of night.[46]

Later, as the human tries to fix the robot amid "a sea of plentiful oil, screws, and gears," the poem envisions the possibility and impossibility of intimacy across difference, especially different kinds of corporeal ephemerality (such as daily biological rhythm and product life cycle) that do not rely on anthropocentric mortality.[47] Or, rather, the near-impossibility of occupying the same time-space is the very content that opens the possibility of intimacy. The greater transgression is therefore when the human lover is left alone, lonely again.

The question "Can machines love?" is a clever trick, in the end. As the poems unfold, the problem is not the robot's capacity to love but the human-centric (hetero)normative assumption of love as a possessable competency built into the structure of the sentence itself. In other words, the poetic language of *Love, Robot* turns us away from the concept of love as an emotional-mental capacity attributed to the human, whose boundary is embedded in the biopolitical order that dictates desirable (or acceptable) love objects and subjects according to the logic of sameness. Instead, it turns to love as a limit concept that demarcates and crosses such logic and order. In this way, *Love, Robot* shows the imaginative force of poetry as a technology of difference—composing the memory of queer intimacy between human and robot through which each species becomes with and is undone by the other, creating the cybernetic "elsewhere, within here."[48]

Technology of Difference 2: What Poems Do You Hear from Machines?

Q: *Please write me a sonnet on the subject of the Forth Bridge.*
A: Count me out on this one, I could never write poetry.

A. M. Turing, "Computing Machinery and Intelligence"

As this imaginary scenario in an imitation game suggests, writing poetry has been considered a touchstone for testing the uniqueness of human intelligence with emotional and creative capacity (as opposed to simply mechanical intelligence), even though only a small fraction of humans might be more confident about their capacity than Turing's imaginary machine. Hence, "Can machines write poetry?" is a question engaged both by those who advocate for human distinctiveness and by those who challenge such an assumption.[49] However, as we have seen, turning to creativity (poiesis) as a resolution to the prevalence of instrumental reason potentially only restores the universal (that is, European) subject's authority as the bearer of Reason, which justifies its violent objectification of and dominance over other races, species, and things.[50] Margaret Rhee's multimedia installation *Kimchi Poetry Machine* twists this sort of discourse on machine poetry by instead provoking a question that concerns the human capacity to engage with difference: "What poems do you hear from machines?" What if we explore listening to poetry as a feminist technology, diverging from the hegemonic human-centric perspective that locates the creativity of a poem only in the agency or capacity to write one? How might this technology offer an alternative to the imaginary of Asians (and Asian migrants) and machines as highly productive but apathetic and unoriginal labor forces? Can one hear queer and diasporic memories in the cybernetic circuits of poetry, love, and labor from *Kimchi Poetry Machine*?

Kimchi Poetry Machine was created by Rhee in response to a call for a future digital-bookless library.[51] This machine involves futuristic technology of robotics and cybernetics, but at the same time it is also tactile and sensual—playing with kimchi's red color and strong smell (which are often associated with Koreans and the Korean diaspora) and with the acoustic experience of listening to poems. To engage with this poetry machine, you must open a kimchi jar. When I first saw jars of kimchi on grocery shelves in California as a graduate student, I found it odd and amusing, as it is stored differently in Korea; then I learned that kimchi is stored and sold in this kind of preservative glass jar in many countries. Rhee uses the kimchi jar as a medium for mechanical engagement with poetry: when you open the jar, "instead of pungent smells of fermented cabbage filling your nose, your eardrums are lulled by the luminous readings of poetry."[52] You are also invited to take one of the poems on paper from inside the jar, which were written by invited women and transgender poets on issues of "womanhood, culture, and kimchi," and to tweet it (@kimchipomachine).[53] In this way, one is wired into the cybernetic circuit of humans–kimchi jar–Twitter (now X) listening to the stories of affection, labor, and sense of belonging (and displacement) among and beyond Korean and Korean American women. The following is a poem from the first batch out of the machine:

Bright red—grandma's gochugaru in
mom's cucumber kimchi.
Aiya! My son just bit me with his first
fresh-cut tooth. How sweetly it burns.

Hyejung Kook

In Hyejung Kook's poem, the bright red color of kimchi from *gochugaru* (chili pepper) evokes the Korean diasporic matrilineal heritage of material and affective reproductive labor.[54] Traditionally, making kimchi (*kimchang*) is a major event undertaken by a group of women in the family, often with help from neighbors. While this kind of large-scale group kimchi making has become less common, families (especially women) often share the essential chili pepper for making kimchi with their children and relatives in Korea and Korean diasporic communities. Like making, sharing, and eating kimchi, the collective work of creating, circulating, and listening to the poem features a transnational and cybernetic feminist poetics that spins out creative and loving activity from the mundane reproductive labor often borne by women.

However, if the *Kimchi Poetry Machine* is a gendering-racializing technology, it does this less by tying kimchi back to a Korean origin than by mobilizing affinities across differences. The poetry machine unfolds its queering memory as a technology of difference in the immersive experience of a demonstration video titled "Red Bloom: Poetry Altar for Queens."[55] In the video, Micha Cárdenas, a media artist and scholar working on trans-of-color poetics, listens to a poem from the machine that happens to be the one they themself contributed:

At the Prince, over *soju* and *kimchi*,
she weaved pop lyrics into queer
genealogies, geographies, and familias,
never breaking the electronic
'90s rhythm

Micha Cárdenas

In this poetry event, the aural experience of listening is intensified by the sensation of red, which choreographs encounters among various elements—first kimchi and kimchi-inspired poems, then the artificial-red machine and altar, in front of which Cárdenas's trans body sits in a red dress, provoking feminine lust and sexuality as indicated by the title of the event, "Red Bloom." If I go a bit further, there's also Prince, a bar in Los Angeles furnished with burgundy couches under dim light.

What emerges in this composition is not a unification of components under the redness, but border-crossing memories of becoming-in-difference—fueled by Korean-diasporic spice, liquor, and outdated music, as well as "queer genealogies, geographies, and familias" in a bar in Koreatown in LA. In this, the poetry event queers as Cárdenas's memory at the Prince unfolds, and listening to the poem Cárdenas turns red with the poetry machine (no longer the same as the one who wrote the poem). With "turning red," I am searching for a language to convey a mode of becoming-nearby in the contagious assemblage of diasporic Korean-ness in this poetry event by transposing *red* as the signal for the queer ecology of sensation in human-robot intimacy in *Love, Robot* with the *color of love* as we say in *people of color*. This transposition enables a queer diasporic connection, alternative to the one that (as JeeYeun Lee criticizes) is constructed through heterosexist and patriarchal notions of kinship, lineage, and authentic culture of the homeland.[56] In this way, the poetry machine of the digital future becomes a feminist technology of diasporic memories through transfectious listening and queer connecting.

An Ear for Cosmo-poetics: Memories from a Future

Extending chapter 1's proposal to take Wynterian cosmogonic performativity beyond the exclusive realm of the human, this chapter explores postcolonial languaging as what concerns the stratification of human races in relation to the technological in the neoliberal circuits of communication and information technology. The space of mouth-to-mouth—unlatched between the Indian operators' mechanical simulation of an American accent and the human translator's distinct capacity to agonize over this kind of loss of authenticity, which makes translators irreplaceable by computers in Sontag's lecture—illustrates the racial and geopolitical components of this stratification. Thus, I suggest that the perception of human language—and literature in particular—as a touchstone for humanity's exceptional emotional and creative capacities distinct from machinery is a biopolitical technology through which race, species, and sexual differences are articulated, stratified, and managed. But is there a chimeric perspective in the Indian operators' proxy for machines, from the perspective of the dehumanized like and near machines?

Rhee's *Love, Robot* and *Kimchi Poetry Machine* guide us to consider poetry not as a mark of human distinction but as a technology of becoming and becoming undone in difference. I have tried to listen to the prosthetic memories from Rhee's poetry through reading them alongside the queer genealogy of thinking machines and the affinities between Asiatic subjects and robots. This task turns out to be an exercise in cultivating the ear to listen to what I call cosmo-poetics—bringing together Isabelle Stengers's posthumanist cosmopolitics that proposes to "slow down the construction of this common world" in response to "planetary issues" and Aimé Césaire's decolonial search for poetic truth as an antidote to the monopoly of Western scientific knowledge.[57]

Cosmo-poetics resists a multiculturalist approach to difference in Sontag's analogy to the Tower of Babel that portrays the problem of "the world as India."[58] To address the hierarchical differences among language groups in the world, Sontag urges us to "secure and deepen the awareness that other people . . . really do exist"—which, for her, validates the evangelical task of literary translation (that translation machines cannot perform).[59] Sontag's multiculturalist resolution to preserve native accents from the flooding effect of global language echoes what Stengers refers to as Kantian cosmopolitanism, envisioning a world "in which everyone is a citizen." Sontag's world as India is already enclosed (constituted by every linguistic group) and is there to be known (in fact, by those on the upper floors) through literary translation. Resisting this kind of incorporative impulse, Stengers instead calls for a cosmopolitics that concerns "the unknown constituted by these multiple divergent worlds" and for that aim suspends the masterful logic of *we*—"so full of good will, so enterprising, always ready to talk on everyone's behalf."[60] If postcolonial somatechnology of language in the transnational network of ICT operates through stratification of human races in relation to machines (which should serve as tools for mastery of the world), then cosmo-poetics demands we slow down to listen to the differences that resist such a distinction in the globalizing cybernetic fold in the Tomkinsian sense.

To elaborate on the other genealogy of cosmo-poetics (the decolonial and feminist emphasis on poetic knowledge), it is worth revisiting Ferreira da Silva's proposition of "black feminist poethics"—"an aesthetic-artistic practice aimed at disrupting modern political strategies of racial subjectivation"—by way of her criticism on the discourse of "difference."[61] Ferreira da Silva criticizes contemporary critical scholarship's rewriting of "racial difference as a signifier of cultural differences," despite its benevolent and critical intention to include the others of the white-European-centric world.[62] Ferreira da Silva argues that such rewriting effectuates racial subjects (or subaltern subjects) whose cultural differences (signified by their bodies) "always already refer to 'other' global regions" such as Asia and Africa, expressing the earlier (inferior) stage of mind in the development of natural and historical reason.[63] As such, this kind of rewriting of racial difference—prevalent in the contemporary racial critique—manifests and reiterates the onto-epistemic logic that justifies violence and obliteration of the others of the (white/European) subject of reason. From this perspective, Ferreira da Silva turns our attention to a different potential, something else that happens "when criticality comes through creative work, when the imagination pursues the ends of [Kantian] critique."[64] For this to happen, she notes, "we [the artist, the critic, and the audience] may have to release the artwork from the grips of understanding (which is the mental faculty to which criticality is attributed) and allow it to follow the imagination."[65]

While the concept of cosmo-poetics therefore echoes Ferreira da Silva's endorsement of imagination, it also reworks the ambivalent relationship between creativity and imagination (and thereby creativity's relation to Kantian reason) that Ferreira da Silva leaves unaddressed. As Sontag's lecture demonstrates, and Parisi points out, the usual critique of instrumental reason has tried to resuscitate poiesis as an antidote to instrumental reason, especially in response to the (perceived) rise of mechanical thinking—only to restore and enhance the ideals of Man (the post-Enlightenment white/European thinking subject). I argue that cosmo-poetics' nonmasterful and nonindividual approach to creativity and imagination near thinking machines (instead of against or different from them) helps take the Black feminist and postcolonial genealogy of poetics' imagination beyond such a conservative restoration of Man. Therefore, I argue that cosmo-poetics' love-across-difference in the cybernetic fold enable us to conceive of difference away from what Ferreira da Silva warns about (the violent devourment of differences for the sameness of Man) and instead to imagine the otherwise.

In a sense, this chapter is also a call for a poetic vision of Haraway's famous figure of the cyborg, which was modeled after an Asian female in an offshore factory—not to reiterate an Asian identity for the figure or to assume a subversive propensity in being close to technology, but to reactivate a chimeric vision from the racialized and gendered difference and the global division of labor in the genealogy of feminist and posthumanist theories.⁶⁶ Rhee's poetry illuminates this potential by turning the thing-ifying and isolating racial and diasporic experience with technologies (as in Fanon's amputation) into a poiesis of inhabiting cybernetic folds through becoming and becoming undone -with and -near machines. The poetry also teaches that queer love-across-difference is what it takes to hear songs from these chimeracological entanglements, where a futuristic vision of the relationship between human and technology composes and recomposes diasporic and queer memories of how we work, control, love, and relate to one another in the human and more-than-human world.

In exploring the prosthetic memories arising from the space of mouth-to-mouth, the first two chapters have offered a transposition of the frequent postcolonial critique's inquiry, "How does postcolonial and diasporic language perform the memories (of the loss) of the mother tongue (as the origin)?"—the issue that the Indian operators' simulation of American accents and the stories of Korean children's tongue surgery (discussed in chapter 1) implicate. I have shown that exploring the prostheticity of postcolonial languaging (displacement from the mother tongue) in terms of the somatechnology of the speaking subject entails questioning the geopolitical notion of the human (in relation to animals and machines) on one hand and white/European onto-epistemological articulations of language, body, and their relation to reality on the other. In this light, cosmo-poetic imaginations illustrate countermemories of the mother/tongue foreclosed by postcolonial-neoliberal somatechnologies of the speaking subject, through a dehumanist engagement with language as technology of intimacy across difference—instead of as technology of reinstituting the origin.

PART II

THE SPECTERS OF CLONING

Great companion animals are like works of art. . . . Once we've identified these masterpieces, then arguably it's not just reasonable but imperative that we capture their unique genetic endowments before they're gone—just as we would rescue great works of art from a burning museum.

Lou Hawthorne, speech at "The Ethics of Cloning Companion Animals" panel

Is it possible to speak of the soul or the conscience, or even of the unconscious from the point of view of the automatons, the chimeras, and the clones that will supersede the human race?

Jean Baudrillard, "The Final Solution"

The analogy between clones and works of art, often referring to Walter Benjamin's discussion on the loss of aura due to the modern mechanical reproducibility of art, has frequently appeared in criticism on genetic cloning as the mass reproduction of copies.[1] However, the analogy was used with the opposite intent by Lou Hawthorne, at the time a project coordinator at Missyplicity (a venture devoted to cloning a mixed-breed family dog named Missy) and CEO of the newly launched US biotech company Genetic Savings and Clone.[2] Presented at the public panel "The Ethics of Cloning Companion Animals," sponsored by Stanford University, Hawthorne's speech was a response to anticipated criticism that commercial pet cloning would offer only genetic replicas of deceased pets and therefore had no social or scientific value to justify the enormous investment and six-digit price tag for cloning.[3] As such, his speech also recognized the deep anxiety about cloning technology in the Western philosophical and cultural imaginary, where clones could replace natural creatures. The above epigraph from Jean Baudrillard or the 2000 American sci-fi film *The 6th Day* are only two among many examples. In this kind of dystopic imaginary, cloning is often employed as an artificial circumvention of the natural process of death and mourning through bio-mimetic replacement, which threatens the assumed singularity of the original.

Hawthorne's reference to "works of art" in a burning museum was an effort to counter such anxiety by asserting the uniqueness of the genetic endowments deserving of preservation through pet cloning in the industry's pilot period.[4] The trope of rescue echoes the discourse of environmental crisis that presents cloning as a technological intervention into the mass extinction of natural species. Pet cloning is in this sense similar to Akira Lippit's understanding of cinema as "a massive mourning apparatus," nostalgically summoning animals in their state of disappearance in films while actual animals move toward extinction as the result of human habitation and climate change.[5] However, in shifting the scene from deteriorating nature to a burning art museum, Hawthorne's analogy neutralizes any mournful nostalgia for disappearing nature in the discourse of de-extinction. Instead, it projects a futuristic aesthetics of techno-nature, endowing selected genetic properties (the companion animals and their clones) with the status of Bourdieuan "cultural capital."[6] Interweaving the tropes of rescue and great art, Hawthorne's speech attributes noble and collective ethical and aesthetic values to pet cloning, capitalizing on "unique genetic endowments" through artificial reproduction.

The second part of this book explores what surrounds, undergirds, and haunts the development and use of cloning technology (from commercial pet cloning to stem cell research) as a site of prosthetic memories across South Korea and the United States at the turn of the twenty-first century. It looks for an alternative to the dystopic vision that pervades the usual critique on cloning (especially pet cloning) as a technological substitute for mourning, symptomatic of the inability to properly deal with death and loss in technologically advanced but ethically disoriented modern society. This sort of approach has played a critical role in bringing into question the biotechnological degradation of life in the modern world. Nonetheless,

I propose to get out of the habitual thinking of the clone as a copy—as a deceptive replacement for, and therefore a sort of antimemory of, the original—to better address the neoliberal paradigm of genetic and regenerative technologies that have already incorporated and exceeded the frame of original/copy. There's much to say about how we carry memories of others in an age when neoliberal capitalism conjoins with biotechnological projects of enhancement, reproduction, and regeneration of life on a planetary level.

Moving from technology of the tongue in part I to cloning technology in part II doesn't represent a linear shift of focus from language to body (from representation to matter), but rather extends my critique on what the posthumanist narrative of the turn from linguistic to material eclipses as pivotal for refiguring prosthetic memories. That is, the second part of this book furthers the critique on the hegemonic Western onto-epistemological notions of body (material), language (immaterial), and reality as a part of the racializing-gendering-speciating somatechnology that concerns the norms and potentials of prosthetic memories. In this light, my research departs from the dystopic vision of cloning that relies on and slides across the string of dichotomies between original/copy, body/image, and nature/technology, which is invested in the normative biopolitical order of things. Instead, it attends to how the metaphysical frame of original/copy performatively derealizes clones and other bodies involved in cloning and other relevant technologies.

For example, Baudrillard's "The Final Solution" presents an image presaging the evolutionary U-turn toward extinction of the human species: the headless clones of frogs and mice in private laboratories "in preparation for the cloning of headless human bodies that will serve as reservoirs for organ donation."[7] In Baudrillard's dystopic scenario, anxiety about the technological replacement of heterosexual human reproduction is projected onto experimental animals as acephalic simulacra, turning their vulnerability into the object of horror. W. J. T. Mitchell argues that hostility toward clones (as the very image of *the living image*) and other bodies associated with clones (such as racialized "terrorists") in the postindustrial age of "biocybernetics reproduction" reflects the long-standing iconophobia undergirding Western civilization.[8] Mitchell finds such a case in faith-based policies restricting cloning and stem cell research and in the concomitant proliferation of the image of clone-like (in other words, indistinguishable) hooded terrorists in the Abu Ghraib prison during the Bush administration, pointing to cofiguration of the clone and the racial other.[9] Jackie Stacey criticizes this kind of cultural imaginary of cloning that nostalgically reiterates the heteronormative human subject (threatened by clones), re-claiming the subversive potential in clones as what turns the human subject into "a reproducible code that reveals the vanity at the heart of the subject's self-imaging."[10] She further suggests an affinity between clones and female, queer, and colonial subjects, who are often pejoratively labeled to mimic, parrot, and masquerade. I am in line with Mitchell and Stacey in criticizing how the original/copy frame for cloning derealizes (and thereby justifies the abjection of) clones and other embodied beings through interweaving sexual, racial, and species hierarchies.

Nonetheless, I take a complementary but different route when considering more current developments in cloning and relevant technologies in a transnational context, as the anxious hostility against clones (as artificial simulacra) offers only a partial account of how genetic technologies have developed in the twenty-first century. The policies restricting cloning and stem cell research during the Bush administration (which supports Mitchell's argument) coexisted with financial investments promoting "the utopia of perpetually renewed life promised by stem cell research" in the United States.[11] Meanwhile, the field of regenerative medicine (such as stem cell–based research) has witnessed the rise of South Korea and other Asian countries where the Western metaphysical imaginary finds less traction. In this growing field, stem cell research often concerns therapeutic cloning of specific tissues (different from the reproductive cloning of individuals), consequently incorporating various forms of human and animal bodies (whose status doesn't fit within the original/copy frame) into the biomedical complex on a planetary scale. As Luciana Parisi notes, with the advancement of bio-informatic capitalism "the automation of genetic codes does not simply limit the body to self-reproduction and sex to autoeroticism," contrary to Baudrillard's concern.[12] In particular, Parisi points out that "the cybereconomic investments in the molecular level of the egg cell" have made it possible "to reengineer reproduction through the cloning and patenting of genes and cells"—which entails "the recombination of indifferent bodies (a human body, a bacterium, an animal and a technical machine)," raising the possibility of unpredictable mutation and transmission of information and bodies.[13] As such, we need a new frame of critique that moves beyond the original/copy binary to discuss the genetic technologies of our time.

Instead of asking whether clones (as copies) replace natural creatures and thereby erase the memory of the original, this book approaches the original/copy frame as a horizon for derealizing-spectralizing the others of the original. What if we consider the prosthetic memories that trace the spectralization of clones, clone-like bodies, and other substitute bodies (whose body parts are used for producing clones, such as gestational surrogates and egg donors) beyond the original/copy frame in the transnational circuits of biotechnology? What if Baudrillard's headless frogs evoke not the horror of anticipated human extinction but an inhuman perception of experimental subjects that illuminates the incorporation of substitute bodies into the capitalist biotechnological "delirium" of endless reproduction and regeneration?[14] Can we think of these chimeracological entanglements of human, animal, and technical bodies both as a site of the unequal distribution of precarity, responsibility, and protection and as a potential site of care, alliance, and becoming—intersecting species, gender, and geopolitical differences?

The second part of this book asks how we carry memories of others in technologically fragmented and mediated embodiments, focusing on the transnational pet-cloning complex and human stem cell research in South Korea. It traces prosthetic memories in the affective, parasitic, and paradoxical entanglements of humans and animals, departing from the prevalent imaginary of cloning as a technological circumvention of mourning. Chapter 3 critically interrogates the prevalent trope of pet cloning as replacement of the original by a genetic copy at the dawn of the commercial pet-cloning industry across the United States and South Korea. I approach the trope as part of the somatechnological regulation of intimacy among humans and animals that concerns who and what should be remembered, and how—interweaving normative discourses on gender, sexuality, and mental and physical disability. In search of a different way of perceiving pet cloning, I turn to the narrative of a pet owner who cloned his deceased dog, examining how he carries the memories of the dog through the fragmented and haunting embodiments evoked by its clones. Chapter 4 then turns to the prosthetic memories of disposable bodies that are invisible in the original/copy frame but nonetheless haunt the transnational pet-cloning complex. In particular, the chapter traces affective remainders of the retired gestational surrogate-mother dogs reportedly returned to dog-meat farms after being used for cloning, who disappear in the circuits between the Euro-centric animal welfare and bioethics discourse and the nationalist reaction against it. Taking up the issue of surrogates, chapter 5 further addresses the animals with female reproductive organs and cells used for genetic technologies, looking at how their status is connected to the scandalous mobilization of women's bodies for human stem cell research in South Korea. In challenge both to South Korea's patriarchal and nationalist regime of biotechnology that naturalizes the sacrifice of these bodies for the promise of curing intractable diseases and supporting the national economy and to the techno-Orientalist approach that reduces these problems to an improper bioethics in South Korea, I trace how women's and animals' bodies are chained through the rubric of substitutability at the intersections of gender, disability, species, and nation at the heart of the Western-centric modern bioethics. Together, these chapters explore a transspecies postcolonial feminist mnemonics that reenvisions how we carry memories of other mortal and vulnerable entities through chimeracological entanglements in the transnational circuits of biotechnology with the advance of genetic cloning and regenerative medicine.

3

"Best Friends Again"

"I gave my beauty and my youth to men. I'm going to give my wisdom and experience to animals," vowed sex kitten Brigitte Bardot, who shocked the middle classes with her libertine lifestyle.

Nadine Dreyer, ed., *A Century of Sundays: 100 Years of Breaking News in the Sunday Times, 1906–2006*

"Barking Madness": Between Cloning a Dog and a "Sex-in-Chains Story"

"Yes, I know you! You know me, too!" Bernann McKinney, an American woman in her late fifties, joyfully greeted five puppies genetically cloned from her late pit bull, Booger.[1] Their rendezvous added a touch of warmth to the 2008 press conference announcing the first successful commercial pet cloning of a dog through somatic cell nuclear transfer (SCNT) by South Korean biotech company RNL Bio.[2] McKinney's story with Booger began twelve years earlier, when she picked up "a stray dog . . . by the side of the road."[3] Soon after, Booger saved McKinney from a mastiff that attacked and seriously injured her, and during her recovery he became her de facto service dog—he pulled her wheelchair, opened doors, and even helped take off her socks and shoes. When Booger died of cancer, McKinney was devastated by grief and resolved to clone him: "I wanted my friend back."[4] She described that to achieve this she went as far as selling her house to pay the fee of $50,000—a price discounted from the normal cost of $150,000 in exchange for her public relations cooperation.[5] In an interview with *Today*, McKinney further presented her plan to write the story for a book and movie deal, with the hope "to sell the rights and have a place called Booger's Place, which would be his legacy, a training center for service dogs for handicapped people."[6]

McKinney's life story did make it to film, but with an unexpected twist. Following her appearance in the media, reports surfaced that Bernann McKinney was actually Joyce McKinney, the protagonist of the so-called Mormon Sex Slave Case in 1977.[7] As it turned out, she was the infamous former Miss Wyoming who had run from British justice after kidnapping and sexually exploiting a Mormon missionary in a Devon cottage in England.[8] McKinney reluctantly admitted her identity after initial denials but insisted that she was innocent and the depiction of her in the media at that time was a "figment of the tabloid press."[9] This odd turn caught the attention of Oscar-winning director Errol Morris, who made a film titled *Tabloid* exploring the theatrics of truth in McKinney's saga.[10] In the film, McKinney complains, "I don't see the connection between cloned dogs and a thirty-two-year-old sex-in-chains story." However, the connection slowly emerges in the film as a repetition of an obsessive "love" that won't let go, whose "madness" also has a note of "*Alice in Wonderland* absurdity," to borrow a film critic's words.[11] Ironically, this connection is implicated through McKinney's own words, which she ascribes to Brigitte Bardot—"I gave my youth to men, and my old age I give to dogs that I trust."[12]

McKinney's story is not a representative case of commercial pet cloning. However, the sensational turn of the story represented in the film betrays how the perception of pet cloning as a prosthesis of mourning coalesces through the configuration of social norms concerning technological support for physical and mental disabilities, replaceability of love objects, and libidinal entanglements among humans and animals. Cloning Booger was regarded as more acceptable (and even desirable) when the dog was presented as an assistant animal for McKinney. However, when McKinney's troubling past was revealed, the unnaturalness of cloning negatively cofigured with her sexual deviance.[13] This shift was amplified by the concomitant change of focus from McKinney's physical impairment due to the attack by another dog to the insinuated mental disorder, which a tabloid reporter called McKinney's "barking madness" in *Tabloid*.[14] Pet-cloning was now portrayed as an artificial device for replacing McKinney's pathologically obsessive love object, Booger, which in turn was a replacement for her previous object of attachment, the Mormon missionary. The cloning thus became a metonym for McKinney's wrong kind of intimacy with her dog (her almost pathological incapacity to let go of him in a natural manner), which violates both the limit of species boundaries and the intensity and dynamic of the normative order of love. The cofiguration between the invoked impropriety of cloning as a technology of mourning and the libidinalized and pathologized grief over her dog in media representations suggests that the perception of commercial pet cloning as a technology of mourning concerns the normative arrangement of intimacy among living and dead bodies, intersecting the axes of species, sexuality, and disability.

Titled after a commercial dog-cloning project by BioArts International (to be discussed soon), this chapter asks what it means to think of pet cloning as a prosthesis of mourning as it relates to the biopolitical regulation of how we ought to love, let go of, and carry the memories of other mortal beings in the age of genetic reproduction. In this, my approach departs from the prevalent criticism that pet cloning is a vain attempt to circumvent the natural process of grief. Instead, I highlight the various norms of intimacy and attachment that make certain ways of mourning natural and others (such as pet cloning) artificial. In this, I'm in the camp of feminist and queer critics who approach intimacy as an important site of biopolitical governance that effectuates certain fantasies of unmediated intimate relations.[15] Furthermore, echoing Mel Chen's discussion on the anxiety-provoking cultural imagery of white American children licking toxic toys made in China and the reflection on Chen's own experience of intoxicated intimacy with a couch in a time of illness, I look at troubling moments of intimacy as they betray race, gender, and species norms that are otherwise naturalized and invisible.[16]

In this light, I propose to approach pet cloning as a prosthesis of mourning in line with the queer critique of somatechnology, which rejects the intrinsic division between body and technology and instead attends to how "corporealities are formed and transformed" through highly regulated technologies interlaced with social norms and values.[17] This approach helps renew the ethics of mourning attuned to the changing ontological condition in the coevolution of biotechnology and capitalism. When the predisposition to biotechnological intervention, reproduction, and commodification of life becomes the condition for a technology of mourning (as in pet cloning), the ethical valence of mourning as a scale for the value of the life being grieved asks for further interrogation. For instance, Judith

Butler's theory of grievability (wherein whether one is worth mourning indicates whether one's ties to others as a member of humanity are acknowledged) requires revision and complication, alongside other rubrics such as how one is mourned, what kind of relationship is at stake, and how various values (ethical, biotechnological, or financial) are configured. In this context, a somatechnological approach to pet cloning takes us away from the (rather rhetorical) question of whether cloning as prosthetic mourning erases memory of the original through biomimetic replacement, leading instead to another path: the biotechnological arrangement of human and animal bodies in pet cloning as the biopolitical conditions in and through which memories of other mortal beings arise.

I focus particularly on the somatechnological production of "singularity" (the quality of being "unique," "non-substitutable," and impossible to be "replicated or cloned")[18]—which operates as a conceptual linchpin connecting critique on the prostheticity of cloning (in opposition to the natural process of mourning) with norms of intimacy among humans and animals. While critical perspectives on pet cloning often imply that cloning violates the moral value of the singularity of a loved object, this chapter critically reflects on how the singularity of the original (or the violation of it) in cloning was socially construed during the pilot period of transnational pet-cloning services. A pet-cloning company announces "the unique genetic endowments" in pet clones to come (which makes them not mere copies for grieving pet owners); a philosopher theorizes what is "irreplaceable" about a beloved person (illustrated by a conjugal relationship) through a thought experiment on pet cloning; and a man who cloned his deceased companion dog finds the irreplaceable aspects of the dog in technologically mediated, fragmented, and haunted embodiments of cloned puppies. Juxtaposing these narratives, this chapter aims to think of pet cloning as a prosthesis of mourning, not in the sense of a replacement for the original but as a gendered and interspecies somatechnology of carrying the memories of other beings in an affective and fragmented entanglement of humans and animals in the age of genetic reproducibility.

Making Clones Unique: Life Worth Cloning and Life Worth Grieving

If cloning is like saving masterpieces from a burning museum, as portrayed by Genetic Savings and Clone (GSC) CEO Lou Hawthorne, then it requires an eye for discernment to identify dogs with "unique genetic endowments."

The company delineates the criteria for such discernment, removing their pet-cloning service from the usual perception of cloning as a self-delusive technology of mourning by way of mere replacement:

> Before gene banking your pet, we urge you to answer one question as honestly as possible: do I want to bank my pet's DNA because I'm distraught and want the SAME pet back, or because my pet had a special genetic endowment that ought to be preserved? Keep in mind that you can love someone or something whose genetic trait is unremarkable, simply by virtue of shared experiences. If your honest answer is that you are grieving your pet's loss and seeking an identical replacement, then we respectfully discourage you from using our services.[19]

In this passage from GSC's website, the value of cloning is generated along two axes: first, pets with unremarkable genetic traits versus those with "a special genetic endowment"; and second, cloning for an identical replacement out of grief versus cloning in pursuit of preserving that genetic endowment. By converging the two axes—one measuring the quality of genetic traits, and another the purpose of cloning—GSC validates cloning only of pets with special genetic endowments worth preservation. Cloning a pet with no special genetic trait is merely replacement, echoing the usual criticisms of pet cloning as a way to escape a proper mourning process. Naturally, GSC offers advice to those grieving the loss of their genetically unremarkable pets: "Nothing can replace your pet, not even a clone, and the healthiest thing you can do is grieve fully, without illusions."[20]

Despite GSC's recognition of the necessity for a "healthy" process of mourning, it is notable that the company delicately sets aside the affect of mourning to stress the objective and impersonal values of its pet-cloning service. In this line of thinking, grief resulting from the loss of a beloved pet is seen as a vulnerable state of mind (if totally understandable and, so long as it moves through the right phases, even psychologically healthy) that can bring about an unreasonable decision based on confusion between the subjective value of a pet for the owner and its objective genetic value. Genetic Savings and Clone even offered a "Grief-Time Guarantee" for its separate gene-banking program (to preserve genetic materials necessary for cloning) for deceased pets or those about to be euthanized, which allowed a full refund upon request within three months: "We understand that grief also sometimes leads people to make impulsive decisions."[21] The company makes a reasonable point in acknowledging the psychological and ethical significance of grieving but recognizes the force of grief (as private and emotional) only to position the objective quality of "unique genetic endowment" outside the affective and relational spheres, where grief belongs.[22]

Framing pet cloning as the preservation of unique genetic endowments suggests a particular scale of life that can be called *life worth cloning*, as distinct from *life worth grieving*. Butler's concept of a "grievable life," the suffering and death of which are recognized in the form of loss, illuminates who counts as a valuable life and who does not.[23] The concept of life worth cloning also implies that it is especially desirable for certain lives to populate our world. However, it does this by virtue of genetic traits that can be transferred and reactivated in other bodies with proper technological intervention—and not by virtue of the mortality of the life form and its susceptibility to objectification by the technological process, or the dignity to be served by or protected from such intervention.

These two kinds of value in the discourse of pet cloning to some extent resonate with the two different ideas of life that Catherine Waldby finds in debates around the status of human embryos in stem cell research: while opponents of such research view the life of the embryo as "biographical," advocates approach it as "a form of raw biological vitality" that is "not killed" but "technically diverted and reorganized."[24] Waldby describes the life value pertinent to this kind of vitality as a source of use value and exchange value through the biotechnological reformulation of living processes, which she calls "biovalue."[25] My intention isn't to equate biovalue with life worth cloning. Rather, in the next section I bring these two concepts together to examine how the clone-worthy uniqueness of dogs is construed through complex entanglements between biovalue and biographical value in actual pet-cloning projects delivered by GSC or its offshoot organizations, and thereby to question how the biocapitalist assertion of clone-worthiness based on unique genetic endowment separate from the affective force of mourning bears upon criticism of pet cloning as a violation of the singularity of an original living being.

Clone-Worthy Dogs: The Cases of Missy and Trakr

Our first case is Missyplicity, the companion-dog cloning project that led to commercial pet-cloning services. Lou Hawthorne described how the original idea to clone his mother Joan Hawthorne's dog Missy arose during a breakfast-table conversation with his mother and family friend and entrepreneur John Sperling in 1997, inspired by the news that Dolly the sheep had just been cloned through SCNT.[26] With Sperling's funding and Lou Hawthorne's coordination, the $3.7-million Missyplicity project to clone the border collie and husky mix took off in cooperation with a team of scientists at Texas A&M University (TAMU) the following year.[27] However, although the TAMU team successfully produced the first cat clone—CC, short for Carbon Copy—via SCNT, it was unsuccessful in cloning Missy until after the dog's death in 2002.[28] Genetic Savings and Clone terminated the partnership with TAMU and proceeded with its own team of scientists, cloning seven cats before shutting down at the end of 2006 due to the poor financial viability of technologies available at that point.[29] Nonetheless, the next year Hawthorne launched a new biotech company, BioArts International, based in California. The company revived Missyplicity in partnership with Korean scientists at the Sooam Biotech Research Foundation (Sooam BRF), led by Dr. Woo Suk Hwang—the veterinary scientist who produced the very first dog clone while he was at Seoul National University, before he was embroiled in a scandal around his human stem cell research.[30] Sooam BRF finally created clones of Missy: Mira in December 2007, and Chin-gu and Sarang in February 2008.[31]

Promoting its resumed dog-cloning service, GSC's website introduced Missy as the company's "inspiration": "She had an exceptional genetic endowment but because she was a spayed mutt of unknown parentage, it was otherwise impossible to continue her 'breed.'"[32] The site also reposted anecdotes written by "Missy's human 'mom' Joan" from the original Missyplicity website (missyplicity.com) to show "some of the features that made Missy such *a special dog.*"[33] These rather ordinary anecdotes offer a glimpse at what qualities constitute the unique genetic endowment indicating clone-worthiness.

In her analysis of Joan Hawthorne's (henceforth Joan, as she is called on the GSC website and to distinguish her from Lou Hawthorne) stories and images of Missy on the project's original website, human-animal studies scholar Susan McHugh has criticized how these "gooey" portrayals of Missy as a special dog belie the paradoxical bearing of the project: although it draws on the scientific value of cloning Missy from her unique genetic status as a mongrel, it turns her genetic uniqueness into something reproducible.[34] McHugh argues that such appropriation of the dog's specialness into the human breeder's language conforms to the abjection of animals, evidenced by the following comments by Hawthorne: "Most people aren't bothered so much—or at all—by cloning dogs, compared with cloning humans. . . . The simplest explanation . . . is that our concept of people . . . is closely linked to *the concept of uniqueness*, while our concept of a good canine companion does not depend on uniqueness—at least not to the same degree."[35] In response to this comment, McHugh suggests that "canine non-identity, not the supposedly singular identity of the celebrated mongrel, lies at the heart of Missyplicity."[36] Further, in this transition from an individual to the avatar of a breed, Missy "becomes a figure of reification in Fredric Jameson's dual sense, both of the transformation of dog love into clones and, more abstractly, of the effacement of the traces of the cloning process from the cloned products."[37] To translate McHugh's argument into Waldby's terms, while pet cloning appeals to unique genetic endowments, it derives use value and exchange value for human purpose by exploiting the biovalue and erasing the biographical value (which marks the singular identity) of the individual dog. McHugh's analysis offers valuable insight into the affective political economy of biovalue in pet cloning, which thus serves as a technological supplement for human-centric dog love.

However, the underlying perception of pet cloning as reproduction of identity-less animals is limited for analyzing the specificity of pet cloning as distinct from other kinds of animal cloning.[38] Cloning animals for agricultural or research purposes, as well as cloning service dogs and specialty dogs, often aims for mass reproduction. However, as Hawthorne notes, "most clients want only one or two clones at most," leaving extra clones (resulting from the challenge in predicting cloning efficiency) both common and unwelcome.[39] In most cases the clones are special only for the owner of the genetic donor dog, so there is little outside interest in any extra animals. These issues suggest that pet dogs are subjected to commercial cloning not due to the simple disavowal of their singular identity (a concept that problematically privileges the liberal humanist sense of subjectivity, to which I return later). Rather, it is due to the ambiguous position of these dogs as companion animals, which doesn't neatly fit into the supposed dichotomy between the singular identity of the human and the nonidentity typically attributed to the nonhuman animal.

In this light, I take a different route from McHugh to examine how the ambiguous status of companion dogs sheds light on a rationale for pet cloning that necessarily entails biographical and relational elements. Rather than attributing any singular identity to a companion animal, I propose to trace the uniqueness of Missy in the human-animal encounters—overflowing the boundary of individual identities of both the dog and the human—in Joan's narrative. The narrative derails the pet-cloning company's claims about an objective value in unique genetic endowments and shows that relationality (rather than identity) should be an essential frame for understanding the nature of uniqueness in commercial pet cloning.

In the anecdotes about Missy, her "special genetic endowment" is evidenced by Joan's memory of Missy's compatibility with humans and the humanist virtue of caring for other lives—such as responding to Joan by barking and howling back when they first met, having a "soft mouth" (different from the coyote-dog mix Liebe, who had bitten Joan), and saving ailing Liebe who was lost in foliage. Conversely, Missy's wild traits are presented as both amusingly adorable and tamed to the level of no functional use. Missy had a "special connection with coyotes" and loved hunting, but unlike Liebe, she was never a good hunter; for Missy, hunting was "pure dog imagination."[40] Missy's case shows that, despite the company's claim about "special genetic endowment," the value of pet cloning is contingent on the shared experience between humans and their companion animals. Retrospectively framed through Joan's sense of compatibility, the claimed clone-worthy uniqueness of Missy emerging from these human-canine experiences is not only irreducible to genetic traits but also beyond the nature-versus-nurture debate regarding the formation of the individual subject (if a dog can be one). The uniqueness that materializes through this kind of experience between dog and human overflows the boundaries of the subject marked by "singular identity" and is embedded in the longer history of human-canine coevolution (in which dogs have evolved to be responsive to humans). In this sense, the clone worthiness is better captured by what Donna Haraway calls "encounter value," which highlights the importance of multispecies entanglements where "commerce and consciousness, evolution and bioengineering, and ethics and utilities are all in play" in understanding animals as "enfleshed capitals."[41]

The biocapitalist production of pet clones depends less on the erasure of singular identity in the mass reproduction of raw biological materials than on the creation of memorable singularity by investing encounter values into biographical values, which in turn are projected onto the animal's biological vitality. This approach does not dismiss the exploitive aspect of pet cloning (discussed at length in chapter 4), but rather emphasizes that clone worthiness does not precede the transspecies becoming and relating that an identity-based approach fails to address. McHugh suggests that a picture on the website of Missy mounting her human mother's leg (with a caption interpreting it as Missy's sweet love for a human) shows the erasure of canine sexuality and sociality. McHugh's criticism certainly has a point: as far as pet cloning is embedded in the history of domestication and human intervention in the reproduction of dogs, its encounter value is affected by the dominance-oriented human-canine relationship. However, a problem with this approach is that it assumes the natural sexuality and sociality of these animals free of human influence and maintains the human sphere of intimacy as separate from the relationship with nonhuman animals. I suggest instead thinking of a broad web of transspecies intimacy, of which intraspecies sexuality that concerns reproduction is only a part. From this perspective, the picture on the website indicates a source of the encounter value derived from transspecies intimacy, where humans themselves are also affected by the reorientation of the dog's affection.

The second case involves BioArts International, a company that was reorganized from GSC and started in partnership with Sooam BRF. Upon the success of Missyplicity, BioArts launched their first commercial dog-cloning service in 2008. The Best Friends Again program auctioned five cloning slots, with bidding starting at $100,000. A few weeks after initiating the project, the company announced the Golden Clone Giveaway—an essay contest for an additional slot to be given free to the most "clone-worthy" dog—in response to "the large volume of e-mails . . . received from passionate dog owners who wish they could participate in this auction, but can't afford it."[42] The prize went to a German shepherd named Trakr, claimed to be a "canine hero of 9/11 . . . now disabled."[43] According to BioArts, the former K9 dog Trakr and his handler James Symington (then a police officer in Halifax, Canada) were among the first search-and-rescue teams to arrive at Ground Zero following the airplane impacts.[44] As the story goes, they worked together searching for the living and the dead, and Trakr ultimately located the final human survivor under the debris.[45]

In a CBS report on Symington's first meeting with the five clone puppies born a few months after Trakr's death in 2009, Hawthorne said, "We expected the winner would be an exceptional pet. Maybe he would have rescued Timmy from a well. But we didn't think it would be anything of the *historical significance* that Trakr played."[46] According to his explanation, Trakr's clone worthiness lies in his historical significance, his contribution to a political community in peril. On one hand, the civil value of his contribution was conveyed through Trakr's proximity to the human rescue workers. Trakr not only participated in the rescue effort but also later suffered from neurological problems, with symptoms similar to those suffered by human 9/11 rescue workers.[47] On the other hand, the specialness of Trakr was gauged against the ordinariness of a hypothetical dog that might have rescued Timmy from a well. Likewise, the hierarchical division between *polis* and *oikos* features the cloning of Trakr as of public importance beyond personal attachment, which is perhaps ironic given that the project aimed to clone pets.

Naturally, Trakr's clones were tasked with "carrying on an extraordinary tradition." Even the clones' names were given "to reflect different qualities of Trakr: Trustt, Solace, Valor, Prodigy, and Déjà vu."[48] This is different from the usual names given to the clones of pet dogs, which often play with the names of the original pets, such as Sir Lancelot and Lancelot Encore, or Nicky and Little Nicky. According to the *Malibu Times*, Symington eventually founded an international organization committed to training and deploying elite K9 search-and-rescue teams named the Team Trakr Foundation, which "will operate similarly to Doctors without Borders."[49] The newspaper article argues that "by having Trakr cloned, BioArts International effectively short-circuited nature to produce five world-class search and rescue dogs," since "each of the dogs possesses Trakr's unique characteristics—an incredible drive, air-scenting ability and adaptability to diverse terrains."[50] In this way, BioArts asserted the social value of pet cloning by crediting a dog with "historical significance," whose virtues are preserved and reenacted through genetic reproduction.

However, as far as the company asserts Trakr's unique genetic characteristics based on a historical contribution to the political community, its claims about an objective uniqueness merit critical reflection well beyond the problem of reducing the assumed virtues to genetic components. Upon BioArts nominating Trakr as the golden clone, Marcy Darnovsky (executive director at the Center for Genetics and Society in the United States) criticized the company for "trying to appropriate the 9/11 disaster for a practice that abuses pets and misleads pet lovers."[51] Probably at odds with Darnovsky's intended sarcasm, the title of the article "Cloning Canine Patriotism?" illuminates the performative force of patriotism beyond a rhetorical covering-up of an ugly truth: the shuffling boundary between humans and animals in relation to the sense of a political community under terrorist attack. Whether mockingly suggested, as in the phrase "canine patriotism," or more positively portrayed through the "red-white-and-blue stars-and-stripes collars and leashes" on the clone puppies of a Canadian police dog, the imaginary of the nation as a political community itself is affected when a canine figure enters the picture.[52]

The selection of Trakr over other pets for the pet-cloning competition highlights the company's claim about the objective "unique genetic endowments" of clone-worthy dogs—which they locate in the public space (*polis*) as distinguished from the private (*oikos*), where emotional grief is and should be secluded. Such a claim hinges on Western philosophical and political tradition, which has designated the hegemonic figure of the human (as the political animal, distinct from other animal species and excluding other humans such as women, slaves, and children) as an exceptional constituent of the *polis*. The recognition of a nonhuman animal in the political community then unwittingly contaminates the objective human reason to assess remarkable genetic endowments with caninity and human-canine experience, unsettling BioArts's own attempt to ground the objective value of unique genetic endowments by emphasizing its public nature.

Looking at the dog-cloning companies' trope of "unique genetic endowments" as a way to assert objective value in pet cloning detached from the affect of grief, and tracing the crafting of clone-worthy dogs in the two pet-cloning pilot programs, my argument so far is twofold. On one hand, the biocapitalists' reclamation of the uniqueness of clones through genetic characteristics collapses even in their own pilot projects, as the clone-worthy values not only exceed the animal's individual quality (let alone its genetics) but also implicate transspecies affective encounters at individual, historical, and evolutionary levels. On the other hand, the biocapitalist reappropriation of the value of uniqueness points to the limit of the prevalent criticism of pet cloning as mere genetic replacement that violates the genetic-donor pet's singularity ("identity," in McHugh's term). In arguing this, one might criticize how the biocapitalist discourse wrongly locates the animals' uniqueness in their genes and still argue for a genuine kind of respect for singularity, and I don't aim to diminish the importance of singularity itself in mourning. However, I take a different path and instead trace irreplaceable singularity in the memories of transspecies encounters, dragging it away from an individual entity (let alone its genes) as the original—which often relies on the hegemonic notion of the subject and relationality, as I show in the rest of this chapter.

The Erotics of Singularity and the Biopolitics of Transspecies Intimacy

David (a pseudonym) shared his personal experience with pet cloning when I visited him for an interview.[53] Over dinner at a Korean barbecue restaurant in Southern California, he brought up a scene from a film whose title he couldn't remember: a scientist creates a clone of his wife after a car accident leaves her in an irreversible coma. However, he is tormented when he faces the clone, who has all the memories of his wife and doesn't know she's a clone (as is customary in sci-fi movies), and he finds himself unable to be physically intimate with her.[54] David told me that he might be the only real person to experience these kinds of conflicted feelings—although his case is different, in that the wife in the movie was still alive, whereas David's dog Fluppy had already died (and, of course, in that the dog is not his wife). After Fluppy's death, David had her cloned by Sooam BRF in South Korea, which continued offering pet-cloning services on its own after former partner BioArts left the field. When I met him on a spring day in 2013, he was living with two clones of Fluppy. David's empathy for the scientist in the film returns us to ethical concerns over erasing the singularity of the deceased via cloning, alongside the senses of love, loss, and grief that the entrepreneurial trope of a "unique genetic endowment" attempts to sideline. Despite GSC's emphasis on unique genetics, "the core of the company's business model" was the paradox it discovered in the responses from pet owners after the Missyplicity Project was introduced on the BBC: "Millions of people believe they have a one-in-a-million pet."[55] The task of reproducing the singularity of a pet (which is by definition unreproducible) rather than simply disavowing its singularity seems to shape both the ethical and relational stakes in commercial pet cloning.

The final part of this chapter examines construal of the irreplaceable singularity of the lost life (which is often considered to be violated by cloning) in dialogue with Christopher Grau's philosophical meditation on singularity and love and David's narrative of living with clones. In this way, this section explores pet cloning on one hand as a somatechnology of mourning interlaced with the heteronormative and human-centric biopolitics of intimacy, and on the other as a site for reexamining how we carry the memories of others through fragmented, haunted, and technological embodiment beyond the heteronormative construction of self, identity, and memory.

Grau's philosophical investigations into what constitutes the unique value of beloved ones, which makes them irreplaceable when lost, offer insight into the encounter value in pet cloning.[56] Interestingly, Grau begins an essay on this subject with the Missyplicity Project, offering the conjecture that if Missy had known about the project, she might bark out in objection: "Why, then, are you so eager to transfer your love for me to a duplicate dog who happens to have (if your project is successful) the same properties I now possess? Can you blame me for feeling that this will somehow do a disservice to me and my memory? I may not deserve all the consideration due to a human being, but I also don't deserve to be treated like a toaster oven: i.e., something that can simply be replaced with a functional equivalent when it ceases to operate."[57] After this ventriloquism of Missy's complaint, Grau anticipates possible objections to his discussion—that Missy's demand is not appropriate for "an animal that lacks the capacity to reason or . . . use language" and that such animals are "in fact closer to toaster ovens than they are to human beings."[58] However, he concludes that, inasmuch as the objections grant that Missy's claim makes sense when applied to a human person, it suffices for his purpose.[59] I return to the ramifications of the dismissal of animals later, but for now it is sufficient to note that the discourse of irreplaceable value already implies the species difference.

Grau's proposition is that the unique value of the beloved person is not, as is often assumed, a kind of intrinsic value of the person; rather, it is a final value (as opposed to instrumental value) derived from "certain extrinsic or relational properties of the object."[60] While this proposition might sound obvious at first, it has philosophical and ethical implications. In particular, it contends with the Platonic idea that love is and ought to be attached to the good that the beloved person manifests, which leads to the conclusion that the beloved person is replaceable by another with similar or even superior properties.[61] Departing from this logic, Grau instead argues that what makes this unique value irreplaceable is the "shared history" between lovers through the "responsible agency" it involves.[62] For him, such historicity explains why a beloved one is irreplaceable even by an exact duplicate with identical quasi-memories.[63] This idea also appears in his analysis of Steven Soderbergh's movie *Solaris* (2002), in which the protagonist Kelvin is visited by replicas of his deceased wife Rheya. Although Kelvin manages to reject the first replica to appear, when another arrives he is intimate with her.[64] According to Grau, Kelvin violates the commitment to his wife by ignoring the singularity of his beloved, which cannot be replaced by her replica.[65]

Grau's approach to irreplaceability as a historical and relational product helps clarify the paradox of the unique value of not-so-special objects of love, upon which commercial pet-cloning services operate. I also respect that Grau's position offers an ethical measure for valuing fellow human beings against reduction to replaceable functionalities or a set of qualities. However, some ideas that underlie his conceptualization of shared historicity nonetheless require critical examination. Despite his emphasis on the relational and extrinsic nature of shared historicity, Grau delimits such value to reciprocal relations among rational subjects with agency, and he offers no persuasive explanation for this delimitation—at times his explanation portrays this shared history as a kind of cognitive property (which then becomes an intrinsic value) and at others it rests on the matter of what constitutes ethical agency with mutual responsibility.[66] However, if we consider the singularity of a baby based on the shared history with its parents, these qualifiers do not seem to be a requirement for assuming one's singularity. As such, when Grau suggests that Missy's complaint matters for his argument only so far as the dog stands in for a human subject, and instead finds a case of singularity in the fidelity of a heterosexual relationship bonded by marriage, it is not because Missy lacks certain qualities that Rheya is supposed to have. Rather, Rheya is singular because she is (or was) the wife of Kelvin. The concept of singularity performatively romanticizes the ethical value of the conjugal relationship and vice versa—which I call the erotics of singularity. However, Missy's ambiguous status (which might be considered closer to that of an appliance from certain perspectives but is nonetheless sufficient for making a point about the relational value of singularity) in Grau's thought experiment suggests that the relationship between human and companion animal might be an interesting space for thinking of singularity outside the coinstituting circuit between proper human agency and heteronormative relationality (the erotics of singularity), as we carry memories of other mortal beings.

Earlier the day I visited him, David shared stories about cloning his dog that were also stories about his life. As David discussed his grief after Fluppy's death, he described going to shelters and meeting a few dogs that very much resembled her, but he felt it was wrong: "I would rather be alone than substitute her." In fact, the idea that adoption is a form of substitution holds at least a partial truth, much as with other forms of memorialization such as choosing the same name for another pet or even taxidermy or freeze drying. For example, in critical response to the arrival of pet cloning, the American Anti-Vivisection Society launched the educational website NoPetcloning.org, with its Adopt a Clone feature. It showed exemplary pairs of a companion animal and a similar-looking shelter animal, linked to information about adopting the "clone," somewhat ironically suggesting adoption as an alternative to cloning.[67] Thus, what constitutes a violation of irreplaceability is not intrinsic to a certain kind of practice (SCNT cloning or adoption) but contingent upon interpretations of a particular technology of mourning in relation to other social norms and values. This perspective also suggests that singularity and replaceability are not mutually exclusive but in tension with each other through a paradoxical attempt to reproduce what is irreplaceable—interweaving meanings of identity, similarity, and difference in the specific practice of technology.

Addressing variations of the question "Is the clone going to be the same as the original?" is a typical rhetorical gesture to disabuse the notion of getting the same pet back by cloning. However, we can take this question seriously and examine what "the same" means and its relation to similarity in specific cases of cloning. Most of those who clone their pets (or at least those who appear in the media) assure us that they know the pet is not the same, but often nonetheless tell stories about the sameness and similarity between the genetic donor dogs and their clones. According to David, there are multiple levels of connection between Fluppy and her clones. First, at the scientific level, they are genetically identical: not only are the clones similar in appearance, behavior, and personality, but parts of them are literally from the original dog. Second, at the spiritual level, it is impossible to know whether reincarnation exists and, if it does, whether the soul of the deceased dog might transfer into the body of a clone. And finally, at the emotional level, David wished it were true that the clone was indeed Fluppy: "We love someone so much that . . . when you have a clone in front of you, every part of you wishes that it is the truth."[68] For David, keeping the memory of Fluppy is a constant process of interweaving these different levels of connection, investing the genetic identity and associated similarity with the meanings of continuity in (post)biographical and spiritual life. Here, the sameness does not rely on an identity of/as a subject coherent with one's mind-body, but rather emerges through the interpretive composition of multiple and fragmentary embodiments of similarity with and in connection to Fluppy.

In such composition, what seems as important to David as having his pet cloned is living with the clones. When I visited David's home to meet the cloned puppies, he explained that he moved back to the place where Fluppy was born in order to give the clones as similar an environment as possible. This simulation of both nature and nurture was a frequent theme of David's life with the clones, indicating the interactive and processive nature of replaying the same. As I accompanied him walking the puppies (on the same route he used to take with Fluppy), I asked what similarities and differences he'd found between Fluppy and the clones, and between the two clones. His response was that each clone is half the original dog and half its own, and when combined the two clones are Fluppy. For example, one puppy has exactly the same body size and barks a lot, just like Fluppy, and the other is very affectionate and kisses a lot, again just like Fluppy.

In this tracing of the original dog in her clones, the clones become an interface of streamlining two lives—the original's and their own. In some cases, differences are perceived as signs of the dual embodiment of the clones, rather than of discontinuity between the original and the clone. Fluppy's clones are on the gray side, while the original was black most of her life and turned grayer only at ten years old. David guessed that this might be because the clones come from cells that were already more than ten years old, and he suggested that this means the clones are both one year old and eighteen. This is why to him each clone also has two birthdays: the original dog's and the clones'. In this sense, the bodies of clones are haunted by the specter of the original dog, through a fragmented and lagged embodiment of her. However, these different lives within the clones do not always streamline smoothly. David brought up the conflicted feelings he had when he was going to put Fluppy's clothes on her clones. On one hand he felt guilty about giving the original dog's clothes to other dogs ("No, they're not Fluppy! They can't wear Fluppy's clothes!"), but on the other he felt that it was acceptable since they're clones of her ("It's okay. They're her clones, and parts of them are actually her."). Telling me this story seems to be what reminded him about the film scene of the scientist with his wife's clone, but it doesn't mean that the clones have replaced the original dog. Rather, this instance of ethical conflict can be interpreted as a series of frictions and interruptions among bits of lives inhabiting the clones, which emerge in the composition and recomposition of the memories of Fluppy.

This approach to cloning pushes us to imagine different kinds of subjects and relationships among them, distinct from Grau's discussion of singularity and shared history. The irreplaceability of shared historicity doesn't require that the subjects exist prior to relating with each other (which is bound through the mutual responsibility epitomized by conjugal commitment) or hold the memory of shared history as a kind of cognitive property. Rather, the irreplaceability emerges in the composition of memories involving the blurring and rearranging of the boundaries of individuals in the technologically mediated encounters between the human and animals. In such a chimeracological assemblage, the human (and the pet owner in particular) is no longer presumed to be an autonomous and intact subject, much as a deceased pet and its clones are not mere objects, even if the relationship isn't free from human dominance and consumerist instrumentalization. In this sense, living with the genetic clones of a deceased pet is a kind of transspecies becoming—echoing Carla Freccero's "becoming-dog," which refers to a union of the two species in the violent "history of colonial, racial, and species encounters" that cannot be contained by humanism.[69]

Moving away from the erotics of singularity toward transspecies intimacy, my intention is not to dismiss criticism of commercial pet cloning or to assume an equal ethical position between humans and dogs (or other pets). Rather, my provisionally affirmative approach to pet cloning is an invitation to reflect on how our ethics of mourning is implicated in the normative arrangement among human and animal bodies, in which the heteronormative relationship operates as a privileged reference for the autonomous and rational human subject whose singularity is considered irreplaceable. In this light, approaching the cloning of deceased pets through a lens of transspecies intimacy offers a space for reenvisioning how we carry the memories of embodied others that doesn't take for granted the biopolitical order of intimacy and its attendant notions of the subject as a reference for singularity. Instead, this approach allows us to acknowledge singularity as just one component of the prosthetic memories of the deceased pet— composed in and through partial, frictional, and haunted encounters among human, animal, and technological bodies.

This chapter proposes to shift the critical frame on pet cloning from the biomimetic replacement of originals to the somatechnics of mourning, through which prosthetic memories emerge in biotechnological assemblages of human and other animals. This doesn't lead to a euphoric celebration of pet cloning, ignoring consumerist and human-centric pet culture or the destructive potential of biotechnology for certain lives more than others (which I discuss in chapter 4). On the contrary, this shift aims to explore a feminist ethics for engaging with the biotechnological entanglements among human and nonhuman animals, paying attention to the somatechnics of intimacy that often slip away from the prevalent criticism on pet cloning.

This requires a different approach from that of pet-studies scholars such as Heidi Nast, who criticizes the elevation of human bonds with pets (and especially dogs) in a postindustrial society where "those with no affinity for pets . . . are today deemed social or psychological misfits and cranks."[70] As Alice Kuzniar has observed, intimacy with pets at times also evokes unspeakable shamefulness, "as if it might be construed as bordering on bestiality or as if to love dogs betrayed an inability to love humans."[71] Kuzniar's point doesn't nullify Nast's argument, but taken together they highlight the normative order concerning the subject/object, intensity, and method of intimacy among and across species (and the fraught discourses on racialized humans' pet ownership discussed in chapter 4 only accentuate this).[72] Thus, commercial pet cloning has broader implications beyond offering evidence of failure in authentic human sociality and incapacity to mourn naturally (as opposed to artificially), or providing metaphoric materials for speculating about human cloning. Rather, it shows how the human-animal relationship is a key reference for the sexual, psychic, and emotional normativity that shapes our perception of cloning as a technology of mourning. In this sense, approaching pet cloning as a somatechnology of mourning helps us attend to the complex scale of understanding how we carry memories of mortal others in relation to the biopolitical order of intimacy in an era when both animal and human bodies are increasingly assembled, disassembled, and reproduced in the circuits of biotechnology.

Of course, critically reexamining the biopolitical order of intimacy involved in the prevalent criticism on pet cloning is necessary, but this is only part of the task of revising a postcolonial feminist approach to pet cloning as a technology of mourning in contemporary society. Such a revision should also include different kinds of bodily, technological, and capital circulations within the transnational circuits of biotechnology in which the pet-cloning industry is embedded. In this light, chapter 4 further explores the prosthetic memories of transspecies entanglements in pet cloning, turning to the darker parts of such technologies—the memories (and forgetting) of disposable animal bodies connected to commercial pet-cloning services in the global context.

4

Disappearing Bitches

I knew that at the center of this Labyrinth I would find nothing but this sole picture, fulfilling Nietzsche's prophecy: "A labyrinthine man never seeks the truth, but only his Ariadne." The Winter Garden Photograph was my Ariadne, not because it would help me to discover a secret thing (monster or treasure), but because it would tell me what constituted that thread which drew me toward Photography.

Roland Barthes, *Camera Lucida*

The Vexing Problem of Surrogate-Mother Dogs

In 2009, California-based biotech company BioArts International announced that it had completed delivery of healthy cloned dogs to all five of its clients from its commercial dog-cloning project Best Friends Again.[1] This project was performed in partnership with Sooam Biotech Research Foundation in South Korea, headed by Dr. Woo Suk Hwang—who had also led the research team at Seoul National University that delivered the first dog clone in the world, just before his dismissal from the university amid a scandal surrounding his human stem cell research.[2]

However, the key point of the BioArts announcement was the company's decision to discontinue cloning services shortly after they finally became available following ten years of research. Lou Hawthorne, the CEO, attributed this decision primarily to "unethical, black-market competition" from RNL Bio, a South Korean biotech company (that had cloned Bernann McKinney's Booger, discussed in chapter 3).[3] The core of his claim was that to reduce care costs, RNL would return the retired gestational-surrogate dogs to farms where dogs are raised for human consumption. Because "the idea of dog eating is quite shocking to Westerners," Hawthorne argued that such a practice would not constitute an acceptable bioethical standard for animal welfare. He further remarked that the reason South Korea was first to clone dogs had "far less to do with scientific acumen, and far more to do with the availability of dogs as ova donors and embryo recipients," supplied by dog farms.[4]

Hawthorne's criticism offers an uncomfortable but sobering perspective that departs from the prevailing approach to pet cloning as asexual reproductive technology that often revolves around the question, "Will the clone of your beloved pet be the same as the original?" Instead, it directs our attention to the lives left out of the original/clone frame, especially the female reproductive bodies that are essential to current cloning technology. As a prequel of sorts to chapter 3, this chapter traces the prosthetic memories of the used-up surrogate-mother dogs haunting the transnational dog-cloning industry, examining the fragmented, affective, and chimeric entanglements among these female dogs and humans in specific geopolitical and techno-cultural configurations.[5] Rather than repeating criticism on the treatment of these dogs, this chapter instead pays attention to the affective-discursive structure in which the treatment of animals (reduced to the recently banned dog-eating culture in Korea) has become a contentious site for articulating the relations of species, sex/gender, and race to the transnationalization of bioethics. In this, I do not assume a fixed definition of bioethics and instead examine how the invoked bioethics both frames and delimits the problematics of human engagement with these dogs.[6] In this way the chapter presents a transspecies and postcolonial feminist effort to remember these female dogs, entering the darker side of transnational commercial pet cloning.

Hawthorne's criticism stirs up an ambivalence that guides my investigation into these female dogs in the dog-cloning industry. On one hand, it reminds us of an important but often-overwritten biopolitical aspect of pet cloning as a technology of mourning: how commercial pet cloning reproduces memorable lives (the originals, and their clones worth a six-digit price tag) by rendering disposable other lives such as gestational-surrogate dogs, egg-donor dogs, and the clones that are considered defective or extra. On the other hand, Hawthorne's criticism, which evokes both the postcolonial repertoire of exotic food and Western suspicion about Oriental pseudo-science, also arrests me with a baffling sense of shame at the disgust "Westerners" are said to feel toward my people, who "eat dogs"—a debilitating kind of affect that I do not endorse but that nevertheless is mine. This affect attests to how Hawthorne's speech immediately dis/locates various bodies such as Westerners, Koreans, and the surrogate-mother dogs themselves (or their meat) within the normative order of who/what constitutes the proper subject of bioethics in relation to what constitutes the proper subject of meat. How do we carry the memories of these surrogate-mother dogs in South Korea, when Western-centric animal welfare discourse reiterates postcolonial power relations by evoking disgust and shame? What is the ethical stake of such remembrance when the perception of rapidly growing Asian biotechnology as "maverick" science persists alongside a global expansion of bioethics invested in Western-centric norms?[7]

Evoking the memories of these disappearing surrogate-mother dogs in the circuits of transnational biotechnology, the task of this chapter echoes Jacques Derrida's ethics of living with the specters of others.[8] However, it is not the specters of the original dogs but rather those of the erased maternal bodies that return in the form of dog meat and its corporeal affects. Following these affective traces, this chapter engages with the prosthetic memories of the surrogate-mother dogs within the dog-meat/biotech loop, which have been overwritten in the commerce between Western-centric animal welfare discourses and defensive Korean nationalism.

Opaqueness as a Theoretical Passage

Despite various fragmented indications, I haven't yet found definite evidence that dogs used as surrogates in pet cloning have actually been slaughtered for meat in South Korea. Hawthorne was the first to raise this issue, but his accusation pointed to a future possibility rather than to what had already happened: "For every dog cloned by RNL in the future, it is likely that a dozen or more will be slaughtered for food as a direct result."[9] Other than the existence of the dog-meat industry in Korea, his argument was based on the analysis that RNL's plan to drop its pricing by 80 percent would be impossible without compromising animal welfare. His conjecture is certainly plausible (and there might be evidence that he didn't publicly disclose), but it nonetheless remains unproven.

I asked RNL for an interview but received no response. As I discussed in chapter 3, the company was first to commercially clone a companion dog for a paying customer. Media have since reported its success with dogs for special purposes, its plans to build a new dog-cloning center, and its acquisition of patent licenses. However, it remains unclear to what extent RNL has actually engaged in cloning pet dogs. As of early 2013, the company was no longer (at least publicly) cloning dogs at all, and later that year it was reorganized as K-StemCell, a company specializing in stem cell therapy—leaving in the dark the fate of former surrogate-mother dogs.

Although the initial accusation by Hawthorne targeted RNL, such criticism has also been put on the table of BioArts's former partner Sooam, which has been a major provider of dog-cloning services. When I asked about this during my visit to Sooam's facility in 2013, Dr. Hwang responded that the dogs are borrowed from "special breeders" and returned after they recover from the cloning process.[10] In a later conversation, Sooam's vice president Dr. Taeyoung Shin explained that clients could elect to adopt the surrogate-mother dogs with the clones (although this hadn't yet happened). Otherwise, surrogates purchased by Sooam are housed in the company's separate facility afterward, and borrowed surrogates are returned to the breeder under the agreement that they be used only for breeding.[11]

A former customer of Sooam who runs the website My Friend Again— which once provided promotional information about Sooam's dog-cloning services and recently changed to represent dog-cloning services in Korea and the United States—responded to the allegations:[12]

> Sooam allowed me complete access to their entire process. . . . All animals under their care are treated humanely. The surrogates are never used more than twice for cloning purposes. They are tended to 24 hours a day around the clock. Once they have finished with the cloning process the surrogates are then sent to live the remainder of their lives at another location. . . . Sooam knows that there will be questions about what happens to surrogates after cloning. As Sooam begins to offer dog cloning services to the world they intend to keep their doors wide open.[13]

Such testimony appeases the concerns to some degree, as it suggests Sooam's investment in the welfare of the surrogate-mother dogs. However, it still offers no details about "another location."

John Woestendiek, author of *Dog, Inc.*, which offers a thorough investigation into the dog-cloning industry, reported that at least in the past "some of the surrogate dogs used in Korea have gone to 'farms'—meaning they were then raised for their meat."[14] However, in an email conversation with me, he wrote, "As the industry has progressed, there has been a better realization of the whole public relations side and the concerns of dog lovers and animal welfare types," and so "it's quite possible that . . . the dogs no longer come from meat farms."[15] He added, "Sooam doesn't specify what those places are, but insists they are not meat farms. Short of following some egg donor/surrogate dogs who are leaving the facility, and seeing where they end up, I'm not sure how to get the answer."[16] A more recent article in the *New York Times* reports that both the egg donors and the surrogate mothers are "rented from a lab-animal provider," but "at least in the case of Sooam Biotech, it's not clear what happens after those dogs are no longer needed."[17]

Amid this fragmentary and sometimes-conflicting information, actual events remain opaque. Considering that Sooam alone had cloned approximately 1,200 puppies as of October 2018, that a surrogate-mother dog is used only twice for this purpose, and that the pregnancy rate is 30–40 percent (and if we assume that a pregnant dog delivers two clones on average), then there might be more than eight hundred former surrogate-mother dogs from just the one company.[18] And besides Sooam there have been several other dog-cloning projects in South Korea—sometimes on a massive scale—which adds up to much larger numbers of former surrogate-mother dogs.

Where did they all go? I find Woestendiek's analysis of the situation persuasive, and it conforms to my own findings. However, instead of taking this opaqueness as something to clear up—by "following" these dogs or by pushing Sooam and other institutions to reveal the locations—I approach the uncertainty as a part of the problem to be examined and as a passage to more situated language and sensibilities with which to account for this opaque site of research. The opaqueness surrounding the surrogate-mother dogs indicates not simply a lack of clear information but an interlacing of the epistemological difficulty in accessing the canine bodies with the biopolitical rendering of these bodies as disposable. In particular, the disappearance of dogs in the transnational pet-cloning industry indicates the interlocking of (what Cary Wolfe criticizes as) speciesism as a paradigm of the modern biopolitical assignment of killable bodies with the invisibilization of maternal bodies in scientific and technological representations.[19]

The prevalent frame of genetic cloning as a technology of asexual re-production obscures the involved female reproductive bodies. A Google image search for "dog cloning" offers endless pictures of similar-looking puppies, at times beside images of their (often deceased) DNA donors, the scientists who cloned them, or the pet owners. However, there are very few pictures of the clones with their gestational surrogates—and then only to emphasize how different they are. No pictures of egg-donor dogs appear (or of defective or stillborn clones) unless you specify the keyword. Such imagery of dog cloning reconstructs a gene-centric family tree for the cloned puppies in which the maternal body is reduced to fragmentary functions, and any defective or surplus bodies are simply erased.

However, the effacement of the surrogate-mother dogs is also compounded by the geopolitical and historical context in which the bioethical discourse on these animals is reduced to Korea's "dog-eating" culture. As Maneesha Deckha points out, the treatment of animals, especially in food practices, has often been a point of racial and cultural differentiation; hence, more consideration of the racialized and postcolonial dimension is called for in posthumanist and feminist animal studies.[20] In this context, instead of jumping into the bioethical debate concerning lab animals in South Korea, I suggest a detour through the dialectic exchanges between the colonialist stigmatization of dog eating (in the language of animal welfare) and the nationalist defense of traditional food culture in Korea, through which the connections between farm-raised dogs and surrogate-mother dogs have been pushed further into an invisible zone.

Then, the opaqueness of the research site is also a passage for engaging with the prosthetic memories composed through fragmented and spectral assemblages with canine others in the commercial pet-cloning industry. Capturing the space these dogs occupy involves reworking the posthumanist feminist emphasis on embodied entanglements in light of the discursive-material limit of seeing-as-knowing. In this, I am attentive to what Mel Chen calls "the style of disappearance" as they pay homage to the toads that used to hop around the yard of their childhood home—but are now vanishing after contamination by a lethal fungus grown in labs where amphibians were studied.[21] In a manner different from what Renato Rosaldo calls "imperial-ist nostalgia" (which erases its own involvement in the destruction of native culture), Chen's retrospective account of their affinity for these disappearing animals does not overwrite one's involvement in their effacement within the web of toxicities.[22] As such, Chen's approach to "the style of disappearance" offers a useful method for engaging with the seemingly paradoxical task of examining embodied entanglements with spectral others. Following the opaque passage of the research site, what I present here is not a comprehensive exposition of what happened to the former surrogate dogs but rather a cartography of the ontological, representational, and affective landscape from which these dogs have disappeared.

White People Saving Yellow Dogs from Yellow People: The Second Time as Farce

Although investigations into pet cloning in Korea haven't proven that surrogate-mother dogs are consumed, Woestendiek has persuasively demonstrated that South Korea's competence in dog cloning owes much to the farms that raise dogs as meat—an easy source for the large number of female dogs used as egg donors and embryo recipients.[23] This suggests not only that dog-cloning as a technology for keeping memories of pets is systemically imbricated with the institutional reproduction and killing of animals for human consumption, but also that such imbrication is contingent on specific techno-cultural and social contexts.

In this light, Lou Hawthorne's efforts to establish bioethical protocols in the emerging industry are noteworthy. The previous animal-cloning projects he had initiated in the United States before the partnership with Sooam—the Missyplicity Project (the first companion dog-cloning project) as well as animal-cloning projects undertaken by Genetic Savings and Clone (a predecessor of BioArts)—developed strong codes of bioethics in terms of animal rights.[24] Further, BioArts tried to ensure "a certain standard of animal welfare" within South Korea by contractually requiring Sooam to never return surrogates to the farm that produced them.[25] Hawthorne also made a gesture of cultural awareness in his criticism of RNL; after saying "obviously the idea of eating dogs is quite shocking to Westerners," he added, "just as U.S. consumption of 34 million cows per year is shocking to most East Indians."[26]

In this regard, I am not arguing that white people shouldn't criticize non-Western cultures, nor am I raising cultural relativism to defend the treatment of dogs in Korea. The problem here is what this kind of criticism says about the affective-discursive structure through which the surrogate-mother dogs have become the bioethical concern in a transnational context. Hawthorne's statement, and virtually all US and European news reports about Korean pet-dog cloning cite a line or two on the dog-meat industry from John Woestendiek's book, then reduce the problems surrounding surrogate dogs to the unethical use of dogs by a shocking dog-meat industry in South Korea. Furthermore, the possibility of surrogate-mother dogs being returned to dog farms has become a signifier for Korea's lack of bioethics and thus for its inadequacy to meet global standards in this regard. When dog eating becomes an immediate deal-breaker, the language of bioethics has exhausted its skin-deep logic of cultural relativism and instead invokes the affect of disgust at the eating of dog meat—an affect that has often been integral to the production of sexual, racial, and other forms of the Other(s). In this way, the discourse imposes a Western notion of animal welfare as the norm for bioethics.[27] This posits Western subjects as the ethical agency guarding bioethics in the context of a chaotic transnationalization of biotechnology and thereby obscures the Western subject's contribution to the social and historical structure in which animals are used for scientific and medical research.

As such, this discourse on surrogate-mother dogs echoes something familiar. What Gayatri Spivak formulated as "white men saving brown women from brown men" now oddly repeats in another form: white people saving yellow dogs from yellow people.[28] Spivak's phrase recapitulates how the voice of Indian women was doubly appropriated in the debates around Britain's abolition of widow sacrifice in colonial India, first by the masculine-imperialist discourse of saving (in which the women are reduced to objects of protection from their own kind) and then by the patriarchal Indian nativist discourse that "the women wanted to die" (ironically locating a woman's agency in burning herself on her husband's pyre, based on dubious interpretations of Indian tradition).[29] Through analyzing these "dialectically interlocking" discourses, Spivak discusses how the British and nativist positions legitimize each other as they assimilate Indian women's voices. Spivak offers this analysis as an extension of her critical examination of Western intellectuals (such as Michel Foucault and Gilles Deleuze) who profess "letting the other(s) speak for himself"—making the intellectual labor of representing third-world subjects transparent within the international division of labor.[30]

My reformulation of Spivak's phrase points to both the symmetry and asymmetry between the original and revised formula, transposing the trajectory of the critique. On one hand, the revised phrase draws upon Spivak's insight that the colonialist discourse of saving appropriates the interest of Indian women by opposing it against Indian men—only to consolidate the status of British colonialism. Similarly, "white people saving yellow dogs from yellow people" points to how the Western discourse of animal welfare speaks for the interest of yellow dogs by opposing it against yellow people, consolidating Western normativity into the bioethical debate. In this, the phrase also depicts how the original formula repeats in variations, reenacting post-colonial relations even in a cutting-edge technological field such as cloning.

On the other hand, as a parody my phrase plays on the folly of such re-formulation, intimating the critical difference between women in colonial India and dogs in contemporary South Korea. As the title "Can the Subaltern Speak?" suggests, Spivak's formula raises the question of the Indian woman as the subject of representation (or the impossibility thereof), who can speak both as and for herself. However, the dog as a nonhuman species is already defined partly by its inability to speak and hence by its incompetence as a sovereign subject (especially within the prevalent Western philosophical tradition). This parody therefore does not refer to the communicative abil-ity or legal agency of the animal, even though there is certain political value in rethinking the question of the animal through the concepts of linguistic and legal subjectivity—as hinted in articles like "Can the Subaltern Bark?" or "Can Animals Sue?"[31] Rather, this asymmetry suggests that something about the canine body resists total inclusion in the original formula (which professes an ethics based on a certain kind of speaking subject), even con-taminating the sentence with its doggy-ness. Here, the dog is not a mute/d subject but instead a carnal affect that brings both Koreans and Western-ers into the circuits of disgust and shame in the event of transnational-izing bioethics. In other words, these circuits of affects are the traces that the surrogate-mother dogs (or their meat) have left within and among the humans who represent them, suggesting another passage through which to follow these dogs.

My perspective on the affects circulating within and around the dis-cursive construct is in line with criticism of nonrepresentationalist theo-ries of affect that locate affect squarely outside of discourse, represented by Brian Massumi's conceptualization of affect as pure intensity that is disparate from emotions, outside subjectivity, and beyond linguistic re-flections.[32] However, I do not dismiss Massumi's proposition on what resists linguistic representation about affect, nor do I suggest a seamless articulation between discourse and affect. Rather, the canine affects here mark what is unassimilable within discourse—the unassimilable otherness that perforates human discourse—in the assemblage of words and bodies. Within this kind of discursive-affective matrix, criticism that represents the treatment of surrogate-mother dogs as a transparent index of the lack of bioethics in South Korea, even if well intended, is nonetheless problem-atic: it reinscribes the colonial power relations within bioethical discourses and thereby obscures the complicity of modern bioethics in the abjection of animals in scientific practice. As such, this matrix also accounts for the circumstances in which concern regarding these female dogs takes the form of either silence or hyperbolic disavowal in a (post)colonial sensibility in South Korea, responding to the patronizing and humiliating inscription of bioethics upon Korean science.

"The Dog-Meat Issue": Animal Rights, Nationalism, and Cultural Relativism

The dog-meat issue has been an important part of the animal advocacy discourse in South Korea, leading to the passing of a bill to ban the raising, slaughtering, and trading of dogs for consumption in January 2024 (coming into effect in 2027).[33] How dog eating has become the foremost animal issue among many others is entwined in the historical context of Western stigmatization and the reactions to it among Koreans. As such, I am addressing the debate surrounding dog eating in Korea not because it was the most important bioethical issue in the development of the dog-cloning industry but to show the historical development of the geopolitical climate in which the bioethics of dog cloning and other biotechnologies have been discussed and practiced.

Boudewijn Walraven, a scholar in Korean studies citing Chǒn An (a rather heterodoxical historian of Korea), examines the history of the dog-eating debate in Korea.[34] The first strike against eating dog meat in South Korea was led by Austrian-born first lady Francesca Donner Lee in the late 1940s. The effort was unpopular and brought only superficial changes, such as switching the popular name for dog stew *kaejangguk* (dog soybean-paste soup) to the less descriptive *posint'ang* (invigorating stew).[35] While disapproval of dog meat receded during the Korean War, a second major international criticism of Korean dog consumption began in the 1980s when a South Korean government established by coup d'état was anxious to offer a good image to the world through the 1988 Seoul Olympic Games. In response to a boycott by international animal-welfare advocates of Korean commodities and the upcoming Seoul Olympics, in 1983 and 1984 the government took to regulating "repugnant foods"—banning the sale of dog meat at markets and prohibiting restaurants from serving *posint'ang* in large cities (where foreigners were more likely to visit).[36] However, these bans were not strictly enforced, and vendors avoided regulations by again changing the name of dog stew, this time from *posint'ang* to *yǒngyangt'ang* (nourishing soup) or *kyejǒlt'ang* (seasonal soup).[37]

Both international and domestic criticism of dog eating resurfaced before the 2002 World Cup (which Korea cohosted with Japan), pressing the Korean government to ban the consumption of dogs. French actress Brigitte Bardot wrote to Korean president Kim Young-sam that Korea's dog eating was nothing but a savage practice; she also made notoriously racist and arguably unreasonable claims during a phone interview with a Korean radio talk show (which she ended by abruptly hanging up).[38] Bardot thus became the symbol of the Western movement opposing dog meat in Korea, aggravating already-existing perceptions that "dog meat = traditional culture" and "anti–dog meat = imperialism" resulting from the top-down policy on dog meat imposed by the military government in the 1980s.[39]

Between international pressure and the Korean government's superficial responses, dog eating and the related industry had remained in a legal gray area until recent changes such as the 2023 revised Animal Protection Act and the 2024 bill to ban the dog-meat industry. Even at the time of writing (in May 2024, a few months after the passing of the ban), dogs are still included in the livestock category and thus dog meat constitutes a livestock product under the Livestock Industry Act, but dogs are excluded from livestock by the Livestock Product Sanitary Control Act.[40] As such, until the early 2020s, raising dogs for meat had been deemed defensible per the Livestock Industry Act, and processing and distributing dog meat had not been subject to legal regulation under the Livestock Product Sanitary Control Act—leaving it open to an interpretation whether these practices were also not quite illegal.[41] Accordingly, hygiene and environmental issues repeatedly resurfaced, and attempts were made to formally legalize dog meat and regulate the industry—such as the Livestock Product Processing Act reform bill submitted by Kim Hong Shin and twenty other lawmakers in 1999.[42] The amendment did not pass, however, as the assembly recognized that it would result in both international and domestic resistance.[43] In 2008 the Seoul city government announced another attempted amendment, but this was criticized by animal advocates, and no further action was taken.[44]

Slaughtering dogs for meat became technically illegal only with the fully revised Animal Protection Act that took effect on April 27, 2023, which prohibits the arbitrary slaughter of animals.[45] While the revised Animal Protection Act does not include a clause that prohibits killing dogs for their meat (as animal-advocate organizations have demanded), slaughtering dogs nonetheless may fall into the "arbitrary" category, as there is currently no legal or administrative process to acquire a license to slaughter dogs for meat. Now, with the passing of the bill in 2024 banning the breeding, killing, and selling of dogs for their meat (with a three-year grace period), the dog-meat industry has become illegal in the country.

Despite the recent changes, it is worth reflecting on the fact that the efforts to legitimize dog consumption have often (although not always) gone hand in hand with a nationalist response to Western pressure and the government's compliance. Kim Hong Shin wrote in a letter to Bardot that the Livestock Product Processing Act should be revised to include dogs because "our people's health has priority over foreigners' gaze."[46] At the same time, a group of progressive celebrities and organizations announced a "declaration of nonintervention" demanding that foreign countries respect Korea's traditional food culture, in response to the increasing international pressure around the 2002 World Cup.[47]

In these nationalist discourses, eating dog becomes an issue of a traditional food culture (or local food culture) that should continue and be protected from foreign intervention. Yongkǔn An, a professor of food and nutrition and the only scholar specializing in dog meat (also known as Dr. Dog Meat) has excavated historical records ranging from a fourth-century tomb painting to French missionaries' writings in the nineteenth century in an effort to prove that eating dog is part of Korea's traditional food culture.[48] He argues that disavowing dog eating because of foreign criticism is toadyism and neglect of sovereignty. Koreans, he claims, should be proud of and actively develop and spread dog-meat cuisine throughout the world.[49]

While assertive nationalism regarding dog meat is a minority position among Koreans and most Koreans do not actually eat dog meat, the perception that dog eating is Korean culture has been a not-unusual sentiment on the issue, often couched in the language of cultural relativism. Around the intense debate on the issue before the World Cup, one survey found that 72 percent of respondents (all women, in this particular case) answered, "I do not eat *posingt'ang*, but think it is a matter of individual choice," and another survey showed that 69 percent of those who do not eat dog meat "do not agree with some foreign animal advocacy organizations' accusations that *posint'ang* culture is savage."[50] As these research results (and the rhetoric of the questionnaires) show, a cultural relativist approach to dog meat has entailed a nationalist sentimentality responding to postcolonial conditions. And such a sentiment partly explains why, despite a meaningful decrease in the past two decades, a considerable number of Koreans remain hesitant about banning dog consumption.[51]

This widespread cultural relativism on the dog-eating issue has created rough terrain for Korean animal advocacy. For example, KARA (Korean Animal Rights Advocates) has attempted to challenge the cultural relativist defense on dog eating via two disjunct registers. On one hand, KARA argues that dog eating is not a Korean tradition but rather was influenced by China during the Chosun dynasty, when Sinocentrism prevailed. KARA also points out that the modern farming of dogs is itself in conflict with Korean tradition, which has never treated animals as mere commodities.[52] On the other hand, it argues that cultural relativism is a method only for understanding different cultures, and that ethical universalism should be applied to make a normative judgment, especially concerning the suffering of "the weak, such as life [sic] and women"—an example of which is female genital mutilation in Africa and the Middle East (with pictures of women in veils, as the icon of the violence against these women).[53]

As KARA notes, cultural relativism offers only limited grounds for engaging with ethical and political problems. However, in assuming that cultural relativism is a purely epistemological project for understanding local culture separate from ethical and political judgment, KARA's proposition paradoxically depoliticizes both traditional culture and universal ethics. Through such separation, the proposition unwittingly erases the political aspects of how dog eating has become a traditional culture in the postcolonial encounter between Korea and the West. Furthermore, KARA's perspective on a universal ethics effaces how their perspective echoes the normativization of postcolonial power relations.

Cultural relativism has limits—not because it offers only epistemological tools distinct from ethical criteria (as KARA suggests) but because it assumes that cultures are segmented into separate areas, diluting the political and historical construction of a culture through encounters with others. In this regard, cultural relativism offers a weak criticism at best of imperialist discourses, as Lila Abu-Lughod points out in her critique on the obsessive cultural iconicity of veiled Muslim women in the post-9/11 United States.[54] Abu-Lughod criticizes how the rhetoric of "saving Muslim women" in this context is used to overwrite the messy historical and political background of the "War on Terror." In particular, she wonders whether Western feminists are so readily mobilized to save Muslim women ("to whom they can feel smugly superior") because they project their own pursuit of liberation onto these women without considering the actual meaning of veiling to them.[55] However, Abu-Lughod does not relapse into the cultural relativism that reproduces "the imaginative geography of West versus East, us versus Muslims, cultures in which First Ladies give speeches versus others where women shuffle around silently in burqas."[56] We already live within global interconnections in which "Islamic movements themselves have arisen in a world shaped by the intense engagements of Western powers in Middle Eastern lives."[57]

Resonating with the transnational connectedness noted by Abu-Lughod, Walraven analyses the discourse about dog eating as a cultural product of "the confrontation of local preferences with global pressure" from the intensification of East-West contact in the contemporary world.[58] In this vein, Walraven considers the difference between the character of kimchi (which has earned an official symbolic status of Korean-ness) and of dog meat (which is controversial and not a part of the typical Korean diet), attending to how each food has acquired its symbolic attachment to Korea's national identity in the context of multicultural controversy. South Koreans' defensiveness regarding dog meat is the result of a complex logical, affective, and political dynamics that (trans)forms Korean-ness in the course of the transnational debate rather than naturally expressing an inherent cultural identity. Likewise, both Western-centric criticism on the status of surrogate-mother dogs (in the savior rhetoric of animal welfare) and nationalist/cultural relativist responses to that criticism (in the form of silence) speak to how Korean society's civility has been articulated through its relation to the treatment of dogs (and especially the consumption of their meat) within the postcolonial dynamics between South Korea and the West.[59]

In search of an alternative to these perspectives, I turn to Claire Jean Kim, who in her examination of the debates around the live-animal market in San Francisco's Chinatown questions whether "slaying the beast" as an enactment of sovereignty for both imperialist and nationalist regimes offers a sustainable civility.[60] Like the supporters of the market in San Francisco, Korean dog-meat advocates claim cultural sovereignty over slaying based on their own speciesist division between what is edible and what is not: "We do not eat pet dogs. We eat only dogs that are raised for meat." However, recurring media reports that stray and abandoned dogs are turned into soup—including pet breeds such as poodles—indicate the frailty of such a division, while Western-style pet culture is only ambiguously distinguished from the more traditional culture of raising dogs as guards.[61]

Nonetheless, the stories about poodle soup also encourage us to question a bioethical discourse that reduces the problem of surrogate-mother dogs to dog-eating culture, as this discourse obscures its compliance with other kinds of slaying based on an internal pet/meat dichotomy. Most obviously, it erases the slaughter of meat species and the putting to death of shelter animals (a systemic mass killing of the surplus bodies of pet culture) and neutralizes the slaying of lab animals that undergirds the sovereignty of the Western/human subject within transnational bioethics.[62]

Thus, before returning to the issue of lab animals in chapter 5, the final part of this chapter echoes Kim's question in search of an alternative to the notion of the sovereign subject (based on the right to slay) for engaging with the memories of these dogs in the loop between the transnational pet-cloning industry and the dog-meat market in South Korea.

"Someone Else Farting through Your Mouth": Affect as Postcolonial Ventriloquism

We often approach certain foods as a confirmation of identity, connecting the eaters to where they belong. Such an approach appeals to a politics of identity that calls for shedding shame and being proud of one's own culture—as rather hyperbolically shown in the push by Dr. Dog Meat to globalize dog-meat cuisines. However, I take a different approach, in conversation with affect theories and in particular with Elspeth Probyn, who explores eating as an event in which "we lose ourselves in a wild morphing of the animate and the inanimate."[63] From this approach, eating is a locus of transformation through visceral engagement with others, rather than the consolidation of a fixed identity.

In this, Probyn attends to disgust and shame as the hidden face of body pride (marking her own experience with anorexia) and of other carnal/sexual identity politics—including projects of affirming the body, be it gay, Black, disabled, fat, or old. The problem is that such a willful claim for pride does not necessarily nullify the affects of shame and disgust: one's face could blush, eyes close, or stomach become upset, even though one tries to resist. Probyn utilizes these affects as measures of the body's own reflective capacities to reach out, spill over, hide, and run away, building from Silvan Tomkins's affect theory that disgust has "evolved to protect the human being from coming too close" while shame is in part "generated by the recognition of having been too close."[64]

Analyzing affects of disgust and shame as a measure for corporeal capacity and response to other bodies also helps us to reflect on the politics of knowledge production regarding social and cultural abjection that evokes disgust. Psychoanalytic feminist Julia Kristeva attends to corporeal responses of spasm, retching, repugnance, and shame as an index of one's encounter with "the abject."[65] As a reminder of perishable corporeality that has been ejected but never entirely removed in the establishment of the subject I, the abject does not cease to challenge I and instead draws one "towards the place where meaning collapses."[66] Kristeva's theory suggests the primacy of affect (of disgust) over *logos* in conceiving the Other that wanders outside the realm of representation. Putting Kristeva's perspective in a geo- and biopolitical context, the investigation into affect offers a method for engaging with what Rey Chow calls "the inextricable linkages between the sensorial, the aesthetic, and the social," which provide insight into "the politics of knowledge production in the face of large periodic markers" such as modernity, colonialism, and postcoloniality.[67]

Taking affect as an analytical tool for measuring intimacy with and distance from bodies positioned differently within the politics of knowledge production, let me return to the dog-meat discourse in the transnational pet-cloning industry. To play with Allen Weiss's note on a strange food combination that "the shock of categorical incongruity was an overture to all future discourse," we can think of how the dog—in the categorically incongruent form of *meat* of *pet*—choreographs the affective dynamics between those who have been too close to dog (by eating dog meat) and those who are disgusted by it.[68] In other words, the affects of shame and disgust emerge as the trace of these dogs left with us after they disappear through interlocking Western-centric animal welfare discourses and nationalist responses. These affective circuits do not always align neatly with the primary division between Korean and Western critics, East and West, but are also complicated by differences within Korean society where the meat is associated with Oriental maleness (as an aphrodisiac), blue-collar ethics, and rural culture. Therefore, these circuits are deeply charged with sexual and class affects as well.

In this context, what if we suspend the Sisyphean exercise of throwing away shame and disgust to recover the self-coherent subject (by being proud of the Korean custom of eating dogs or denying the disgust) and instead take it as an instance of sensing the work of the Other within the self, arising in the encounter with other bodies? That is, what if we consider the sense of shame to be an instance of canine affect upon and within our bodies— giving up the fantasy of the unitary subject and recognizing encounters with other bodies as we articulate bioethics? Through affect as an analytic tool for examining bodily assemblages, I suggest reenvisioning Spivak's postcolonial critique on the politics of representation. Here, the problem is less that one speaks about or for the (mute/d) dogs, appropriating their voice. Rather, one speaks of and through one's body, which is affected by canine corporeality—being shamed, disgusted, or affected in other ways—that in turn rearranges the distance and order among speaking and eating bodies.

On one end of this affective circuit, there are bodies that are disgusted by dog meat—either expressly so, or by feeling embarrassed at being disgusted or even adventurous with something disgusting (like those trying exotic foods). Criticizing these bodies for being disgusted will not chase the disgust away if it is only displaced by a sense of guilt over being disgusted.[69] The intractability of disgust points to what Tomkins has already diagnosed: disgust is a mark of the oppressor, which "whenever an individual, a class, or a nation wishes to maintain a hierarchical relationship, it will have to resort to."[70] As such, one can critically examine this affect of disgust as a touchstone for the normative order of things and relations among them.

From this perspective, it is telling how animal welfare as a bioethics is intermingled with the normativizing force of disgust caused by the "shock of categorical incongruity"—echoing in variations of the phrase "to pet and eat" in Western discourses on dog meat in Korea and other Asian countries.[71] For example, Harold Herzog and Lauren Golden argue that people with higher visceral disgust sensitivity—which is associated with "elevated levels of ethnocentrism, prejudice, and right-wing authoritarianism"—are "more likely to be upset by animal suffering and thus more apt to become involved in the animal protection movement."[72] This claim is dangerously moralistic, but it nonetheless offers a useful insight that might be at odds with the authors' contentions. Their argument intimates that the "animal protection movement" might be contingent on disgust sensitivity and its sterilizing force, which moralize the biopolitical order of things such as the hierarchies of race, class, and species as well as the categories of farm/pet/lab animals. Of course, the affect of disgust cannot and should not explain away the attack on dog eating by animal-rights advocates. However, the reification of dog meat as the animal question in Korea and the moralization of the underlying categories point to how the ethical and political arguments about animal welfare intermingle with the normativizing force of carnal affects against other races, classes, and species in a transnational context.

On the other end of this affective circuit are those shamed for being disgusting (for being too close to dog meat), or ashamed of being shamed by their own culture. This sense of shame is not the direct opposite of disgust, to borrow Tomkins, because what the oppressor's disgust develops in the oppressed is often "contempt for themselves."[73] However, it is possible, if not common, for this self-contempt to be replaced by emphatic shame—but only when the oppressed has internalized the democratic ideal. It is through this oblique space (in relation to the diagonal opposites between disgust and self-contempt) that I approach Koreans' responses to the dog-meat debate in terms of shame. And it is with this obliqueness of shame, combined with its self-erasing and reclusive propensity, that I return to postcolonial criticism on the difficulty (or even impossibility) of representation formulated as "white people saving yellow dogs from yellow people."

In this regard, Probyn offers further stinky food for thought in her discussion of a short story. The protagonist discovers the joys of Swedish tinned herrings that smell of feces and keep fermenting inside the stomach. What's more, the dish leads to uncontrollable burping: "Well, this was like someone else farting through your mouth."[74] In the controversy around dog eating, a dog-human (or dehumanist) postcolonial ventriloquism might also be "like someone else farting through your mouth." Even though one disapproves of (or is too ashamed to speak about) one's shame, and even though the dog meat does not speak (or bark), the canine body ferments inside and generates uncanny burps—reminding us that we have already been contaminated. This kind of ventriloquism confounds the division between homo loquens (talking man) and mute animal and between the speaking subject and the eating body, deconstructing the dominant concept of the modern bioethical subject as primarily carnologocentric. If, as Wolfe argues, the humanist ethical universal is false because it recognizes humanness only in those who conform to the liberalist notion of the subject, then my canine-postcolonial perspective deconstructs the doublet of "liberalist subject–ethical universalism" within transnational bioethics, tracing both the nonhuman and the quasi-human that permeate the liberalist subject.[75]

These canine affects therefore play two roles. On one hand, they point to uneven relations among Koreans, Westerners, and the dogs themselves; on the other, they refigure bioethical subjects as affective bodies permeable to others and therefore contingent on normative arrangements among human and nonhuman bodies. From this perspective, a transspecies bioethics in the transnational context neither universalizes animal welfare nor merely adds geographical specificities to it. Rather, it begins with acknowledging and listening to the other within—to the animal and the racial other within the human. Spivak ends "Can the Subaltern Speak?" with the perplexing case of Bhuvaneswari Bhaduri, who hanged herself after not being able to carry out a political assassination (in the interest of Indian independence) during menstruation—a gesture that both conforms to and reverses the

4.1   Am Yi, *Mogyŏndo* (*Painting of a Mother Dog*), sixteenth
century, Korea, National Museum of Korea. This old painting
warmly portrays a mother dog and her three puppies. The
image of Yi's painting, as the National Museum of Korea's
public work, is used according to KOGL (Korea Open Government License). https://www.museum.go.kr/site/main/relic
/search/view?relicId=331.

native patriarchal norm.[76] Through Bhuvaneswari's death performing the impossibility of Indian women's speech, Spivak offers a postcolonial feminist response to Derrida's ethics of "rendering delirious that interior voice that is the voice of the other in us."[77] Similarly, writing about the disappearing surrogate-mother dogs is my response to this call for rendering the voice of the specters within—or rather, the affective remainders of the canine within—as a way to engage with prosthetic memories in the transnational pet-cloning complex. As I trace the remainders of these animals, this canine affect as a force of inhuman postcoloniality takes part in the production of the bioethical discourses surrounding them and thereby entangles my own writing in the chimeracological assemblages of humans, animals, and technologies. While BioArts's announcement about the dogs fills me with shame, their canine affect in the affective circuit has enabled me to be contaminated by them and to write memories of—perhaps even with—them. In this sense, these surrogate-mother dogs are less an object (either treasure or monster) of research than they are my Ariadne.

5

The Chains of Substitution

Scandalous Assemblages

After a year of controversy that captivated South Korea, Seoul National University (SNU)'s internal investigation concluded that the major achievements in human embryonic stem cell (hESC) research of Professor Woo Suk Hwang had been fabricated and were invalid.[1] Hwang had been hailed as a national hero after his team published two supposedly groundbreaking articles in *Science*, first on the derivation of a stem cell line from a cloned human embryo in 2004 and then on the establishment of patient-specific stem cell lines in 2005.[2] If valid, these papers presented a huge step toward therapeutic cloning—promising the technological capability "to replace damaged tissue in patients from various degenerative diseases" with specialized cells generated via hESC.[3] Because the stem cells were reportedly derived from embryos cloned by "transferring the nucleus from the patient's somatic cell into an enucleated oocyte" (the somatic cell nuclear transfer technique, SCNT), the specialized cells would be genetically compatible and so would not be rejected by the patient's immune system.[4] However, the only achievement confirmed by the investigation as authentic was the world's first dog clone produced by SCNT—Snuppy (a portmanteau of SNU and *puppy*).[5]

Soon after, a newspaper reported on the verification process behind Snuppy's official authenticity.[6] As the story goes, Professor Byeong Chun Lee had been compelled to comb the dog market—where dogs are sold both for meat and as pets—for the egg-donor dog used in cloning Snuppy in order to take a tissue sample for DNA testing. Although Hwang led the research team, his junior colleague Lee was credited as the first author in the *Nature* article reporting the cloning of Snuppy by SCNT, and so Lee was under particular pressure to validate the findings. Lee was "dismayed to find that that the dog was already dead," but he managed to acquire a sample of its lung tissue from "a place for necropsying dogs" just a few days before the investigation committee made its final report. However, the newspaper story focused on Lee's rather unusual journey to locate the evidence; no questions were raised regarding the location of this "place for necropsying dogs" or how the egg-donor dog ended up there. In the end, Snuppy's egg donor disappeared into the mysterious loop linking the science lab and the dog-meat industry. Her remains nonetheless saved the career of Professor Lee, who at the time was embroiled in the Hwang scandal—arguably the biggest science fraud in recent history.[7]

The disappearance of Snuppy's egg-donor dog also evokes an unsettling parallel: the Hwang scandal arose from suspicions surrounding the recruitment of human egg donors for hESC research. The connection between the canine and human egg donors used in Hwang's research motivates this chapter's investigation into the prosthetic memories of that entanglement, exploring what these scandalous revelations tell us about the status of and relationship among women and other female animals who are increasingly recruited as egg donors into the transnational circuits of biotechnology with the advance of cloning technology and regenerative medicine. This chapter traces how women and female animals were mobilized for Hwang's research, which promised to cure disabilities and intractable diseases through hESC and assert South Korea's global competitiveness in the biotech industry. The analysis here situates these entanglements within a transnational context, wherein the institutionalization of liberal bioethics concerning human and animal research subjects supplements the intensifying capitalization of various forms of living matter by advanced biotechnology.[8] In this way, this chapter contours what I call the chains of substitution, illuminating the gendered, interspecies, and geopolitical rubrics through which certain lives are made available for biotechnological research and practice in the name of curing other people's illness and disability and recuperating the national economy. These chains of substitution thus convey a chimeracological milieu in which we explore a transspecies and postcolonial feminist politics of alliance, to counter what Melinda Cooper diagnoses as the neoliberal and imperialist "delirium" of the biotechnology industry—whose speculative promises regarding the supposedly "self-regenerative" potential of life itself eclipse material and affective extractions from other bodies.[9]

Following the first landmark publication in *Science*, Korean feminist and civil-activist groups questioned the source of human eggs in Hwang's hESC research, only to be rebuffed in the celebratory atmosphere.[10] Acclaimed for having elevated the status of Korea in the world and taken a promising step toward the cure for intractable diseases, Hwang was named the first "Supreme Scientist" by the Korean government and appointed the first director of the World Stem Cell Hub—an international consortium for therapeutic stem cell research based in Seoul with satellite labs in the United States and United Kingdom.[11] Thus, when *PD Suchŏp* (a popular investigative television program in Korea) raised the issue of ethical breaches in the acquisition of human eggs for Hwang's research, it encountered strong criticism and was accused of treachery against the "national interest" by slandering Hwang.[12] However, after evidence suggesting the fabrication of research data appeared online, the controversy snowballed into a panoramic scandal involving government officials, politicians, women's clinics, and researchers of varying status. Subsequent investigation by SNU found that there was neither a stem cell line derived from a cloned human embryo (let alone a patient-specific line) nor any evidence that it had ever existed.[13] Instead, data had been fabricated, many more human eggs had been used than reported, and these eggs were acquired through illegal means.[14] Hwang was fired from SNU and later received a two-year suspended prison sentence (reduced to one year and six months by an appeals court) for embezzlement of research funds and breach of bioethics law.[15]

The reaction among a considerable portion (although not a majority) of Koreans made the scandal even more dramatic. Support for Hwang as a patriotic hero persisted even after the revelations about his research, including street rallies and egg-donation campaigns. This support for Hwang has elicited various interpretations from both Korean and international critics, from "fandom" to "pseudo-fascism" to *han*—a sentimentality of sorrowful resentment peculiar to Koreans due to their experiences with colonialization and poverty, which made people identify with Hwang's humble origins.[16]

Herbert Gottweis and Byoungsoo Kim approach the phenomenon as a "bionationalism" that "temporarily undermined the democratic process, giving rise to violations against core principles of good governance such as legality and transparency."[17] They argue that in the Hwang case, bionationalism prevailed "insofar as the traditional ethnicity marker of 'blood' became increasingly displaced by *biologically and scientifically grounded concepts such as stem cell or the oocyte* that were defined as 'Korean' and linked up with social visions of the future." This bionationalism demanded that the potential of modern biomedicine be put into the service of "improving Korean bodies" and raising the country's international economic competitiveness.[18] Certainly, Gottweis and Kim are correct in noting the appearance of a specific form of nationalism corresponding to modern biomedicine in South Korea. I nonetheless offer a different perspective on the conjunction of biotechnology and nationalism that surfaced during the scandal, and this approach frames my analysis of the human-animal entanglements detailed in the rest of the chapter.[19]

If there was something new about the nationalism surrounding the Hwang scandal, it was neither the new marker of ethnicity nor the goal of improving Korean bodies. There's nothing scientifically Korean about the donated oocytes (to be enucleated in the process), and the stem cell technology's potential for treating intractable diseases among all of humanity (and thus its profitability in the global market) was repeatedly invoked to fuel national pride and yearning. When Hwang said at a lecture, "The actor Christopher Reeve in *Superman* will be able to fly again, the singer Kang Won-rae from dance group *Clone* will be able to rise up and dance," the prospect of curing Reeve's spinal-cord injury had no less appeal than curing Kang's for a national pride that hinged on the normative assumption of a disability-free future, as Eunjung Kim has criticized.[20]

What was new about this nationalist phenomenon, however, was the centralization of curative biotechnology in the proud national imaginary of science and technology serving the country's economic development, which had been deeply interlaced with the project of modernization and recuperation from colonial history.[21] The government-initiated Biotech 2000 project illustrates the alignment of this vision for biotechnology with the *segyehwa* paradigm that sought a nationalist and neoliberalist resolution for globalization and intensified in the aftermath of the 1997 Asian financial crisis.[22] Biotechnology, alongside information and communication technology, came to be perceived as a higher-end successor to the electronics, chemical, and heavy industries that turned one of the world's poorest countries into one of the largest economies in the 1970s and '80s. Thus, the tremendous shock that the scandal inflicted on the nation shows the fibrillation between past injuries and forward-looking ambitions projected onto the cutting-edge biotechnology that Hwang embodied. Hwang's famous statement "I want to print 'Made in Korea' on stem cells" was a promise to succeed the Made in Korea semiconductor (the nation's main export product) rather than an indication of biomedically reconfigured bioethnicity as the new grounds of nationalism (as Gottweis and Kim suggest).

Modern genetic and regenerative science's bearing on neoliberal nationalism in South Korea should be understood in a transnational context wherein, as Cooper observes, "the rise of East Asia as a significant hub of research and investment in the new life sciences" is unsettling global power dynamics.[23] The life sciences have played a crucial role in US imperialist self-reinvention since the 1980s. In particular, Cooper detects two conflicting trends in US policy concerning the bioethics around cloning and stem cell research in the wake of the 9/11 attack. On one hand, there was the evangelical revival of the culture of life politics, conflating the victims of terrorism with the unborn American whose life is threatened by biomedical intervention into human embryos. On the other, there was financialization of the potential of life itself (such as the stem cell's capacity for self-regeneration) coupled with financial capitalism that promised limitless surplus, through which the US leveraged its precarious position as a global debtor to renew its imperialist hegemony.[24] This kind of neoliberal delirium of biotechnology partly informed the feverish investment in biotechnology as a "magical" (South Korean president Roh Moo Hyun's reaction upon visiting Hwang's research team) regimen for both biomedical and financial advancement in South Korea.

From this perspective, this chapter engages with two chimeracological folds foregrounded by the Hwang scandal. First, the scandal sheds light on the techno-cultural environment in which female animals and women were recruited for biotechnology in South Korea amid a global race to capitalize on the reproductive and regenerative potential of life itself. In other words, the scandal betrays Korean society's ideological, sentimental, and material investments in biotechnology that derealize the cost borne by these women and animals on behalf of others to render the technologies magical under the *segyehwa* regime.

Second, the scandal became a global stage on which Hwang's actions as the epitome of bad science were presented in an era when institutionalized bioethics was integral to the exploitation of surplus from (often sociopolitically marginal) populations and animals in the international biomedical and biotechnological complex.[25] In this context, approaching the scandal and the nationalist reaction as evidence of South Korea's failure to meet the good governance of science and technology suitable for an advanced democratic society is insufficient for critically examining the role of globalizing liberalist bioethics. In this light, I engage with the sensational exposure of (and silence about) the use of animals and women to critically examine the less spectacular biopolitical matrix that brings these women and other female animals together as research subjects in the transnational circuits of biotechnology.

Situated in these chimeracological folds, this chapter engages with prosthetic memories composed in the chains of substitution, in which women and other female animals are entangled by the substitutability of their eggs in Hwang's stem cell research and animal cloning. In this way, the chapter offers a postcolonial transspecies feminist approach to prosthetic memory that moves away from the question of whether clones replace the memory of the original (the biopolitical implications of which I addressed in chapters 3 and 4). Instead, it aims to trace the production and erasure of substitutable bodies at the intersections of gender/sex, class, nation, and species—which supplement the delirious rendering of stem cell research for therapeutic cloning. In this, I look for a chimeric vision in the asymmetrical conditions between these human and animal research subjects, to offer a dehumanist postcolonial feminist alliance against the substitutional, extracting, and promissory human-animal entanglements in neoliberal biotechnology.

Dogs for Tigers: Biotechnology, *Segyehwa*, and the Usefulness of Animals

When Hwang and Lee's team at Seoul National University announced that it had produced the first dog clone, Snuppy, at the height of Hwang's fame in 2005, the media reported it as confirmation of South Korea's superior biotechnology and ascending global status.[26] This triumphant nationalist atmosphere brushed aside any discussion of the suffering and reduced quality of life for animals used in science and medical experimentation, or questions about how animal cloning impacts the value of human and animal life (and life in general). A major Korean newspaper did call for a consideration of bioethics on the grounds that "our country has become the leader in the field of cloning technology" and "the world is watching us."[27] However, another paper expressed concern that "the birth of Snuppy will serve as momentum to replay the bioethical debates," echoing more prevalent sentiments among Koreans.[28] The latter editorial argued that any bioethical discussion would diminish Korea's biotechnological achievements "based only on imaginary possibility," as the cloning of humans was prohibited by Korea's recent Bioethics and Safety Acts, and Hwang had clarified that his goal was to cure human diseases (by developing human-disease-model dogs).[29]

In fact, Hwang reportedly said, "In no case will the result of the research be used for pet cloning," implying that this did not accord with his patriotic and humanist purposes such as "human flourishing" and "advancement in science."[30] Thus, when Sooam Biotech Research Foundation (established by Hwang after he left SNU) began to offer dog-cloning services targeting pet owners in the United States and Europe, some critics mockingly presented it as a metonym for Hwang's downfall from his heroic position cloning tigers and undertaking human stem cell research. What I find most interesting is what this ambivalent prospectus of dog cloning (and its later trajectory) suggests about the status of animals in the *segyehwa* paradigm of biotechnology, which is accountable for the effacement of the egg-donor dogs and gestational surrogate-mother dogs used for cloning.

A rather frictional relationship between the value of pet cloning and of other animal-cloning projects also appeared in a government-funded project almost concurrent with the Snuppy project. The Special-Usefulness Animal Cloning Project was funded by the Ministry of Science and Technology (MOST) and operated from March 2005 to February 2011. Following a news article reporting how this project aimed to develop "mass cloning technology for pet animals such as dogs and cats," animal-advocacy groups in Korea immediately protested—criticizing the debasement of life and the sacrifice of animals entailed by the project, and especially condemning the cloning of pets as neither necessary nor ethical.[31] In response, MOST explained that the project was not intended for commercial purposes but instead was an infrastructural project to supplement medical research.[32]

According to the 2008 and 2011 project reports, the stated goal of the project was to develop infrastructural SCNT technologies for producing special-usefulness animals.[33] The reports detail the broader applicability of the project to the advancement of human-disease-model animals, production of medically useful proteins, conservation and restoration of endangered species, and development of commercial pet cloning.[34] That pet cloning is mentioned in these reports does not clarify whether it was there from the conception of the project (contradicting MOST's explanation) or introduced after the dog-cloning research team at SNU joined in 2006.[35] Regardless, the ambiguous position of dog-cloning technologies illuminates the prevalent social values promoted under the *segyehwa* paradigm of biotechnology.[36]

The project reports promote the social values of various applications of cloning technology by asserting the usefulness of animals. These reports often appeal to universal humanitarian values such as "improving the quality life of mankind," especially when referring to cloning for medical research. They also frequently evoke nationalism—appealing at times to sentimental values but more often to South Korea's reputation and economic status in the globalizing world.[37] For example, the urgency of conserving endangered species is critical because "the tiger, a symbol of this society, will not be seen any longer, but remain in the aching heart of Koreans."[38] Somewhat differently, the technology for cloning monkeys is promising because it would enable South Korea to develop original technology and acquire international patents in the field of primate cloning, in preparation for the potential international medical and pharmaceutical market.[39] Likewise, while most applications for cloning technology appeal to national pride and to economic potential, the benefits of pet cloning are couched in terms of both its value in the global market and as a rather defensive image-making strategy under the Western gaze in helping with "wiping out the global antipathy toward Korean dog culture."[40]

The rather odd position of pet cloning in the Special-Usefulness Animal Cloning Project indicates that the nationalist and economic-developmental rationales did not seamlessly merge in the *segyehwa* paradigm of biotechnology. Nonetheless, applications of cloning technology to animals were assessed by their utilitarian value, eclipsing bioethical issues concerning the function and treatment of animals used for biotechnology. Thus, the case of Snuppy's egg donor (and the gestational surrogates used for pet cloning discussed in chapter 4) points to the collective oblivion of animals rendered open for biotechnological use (and disposal), which was expected to serve Korea's national interests and other humanitarian purposes.

Ghostly Citizens: Commemoration of Sacrifice and Its Colonial Legacy

On Korea's Independence Day in 2005 (ten days after the announcement of Snuppy's birth), a rare voice on the treatment of model animals for human-disease research appeared in the progressive daily newspaper the *Hankyoreh*.[41] Columnist Pyŏngch'an Kwak argued that, even though experimentation on animals for humanitarian purposes could not truly be compared with the medical experimentation performed on Koreans by the Japanese during the Sino-Japanese War and World War II, Koreans were nonetheless accountable for not showing due respect to the sacrificed animals. He called for legislation to minimize the suffering of the animals in experiments and for the establishment of a memorial day to commemorate animals sacrificed for the community. Kwak envisioned a variety of memorial events both national and private, and artists would seek "reconciliation" between humans and animals through *gut* (a Korean traditional shamanist ritual), songs, and plays. "Thereby," he wrote, "a life and another life become one. How beautiful is this?"

Predating the legislation of the Laboratory Animal Act by three years, Kwak's column offers a reflection on biotechnology not as a simple tool or measure for linear advancement but rather as something that comes at the cost of other living beings, for which the nation as a community is responsible.[42] At odds with the aggressive pro-biotechnology climate of that time, Kwak's column also shows that a postcolonial nationalism can be extended to recognize nonhuman animals (and their spirits), whose suffering and death is a reminder of society's past pain and a foundation for present and future well-being. In his proposal Kwak echoes James Stanescu, who sees mourning as a practice that opposes the disavowal of the value of animal lives, extending Judith Butler's notion of "life worth grieving" as the scale for membership in humanity as a political community.[43] However, I am not ready to agree with Kwak's rhetorical question, "How beautiful is this?" Recognition of the pain and death of animals as a "sacrifice for the community" toward "humanitarian purposes" is more an opening to ethical consideration than a conclusion. Who is sacrificed for what, and for whose sake? How does the notion of sacrifice (of certain lives as means to other ends) hinge upon and uphold other social values? And in what ethical relationship does the memorial ritual position lab animals alongside Korean victims of imperial Japanese scientific and medical research and thereby alongside contemporary Koreans?

It is conventional to legitimize using animals as sacrifice for humans in biomedicine. In her discussion of the case where a baby baboon's heart was transplanted into a twelve-day-old infant (alias Baby Fae) who died three weeks afterward in 1984, Lesley Sharp notes that sacrificing animals is "justified and considered reasonable when more highly valued human lives are at stake."[44] Noémie Merleau-Ponty also observes that at developmental biology laboratories in India and France, lab professionals justify killing mice for the sake of science, medicine, and humanity despite the emotional difficulty, intertwining their scientific understanding with personal and religious convictions.[45] However, what makes me hesitant about

Kwak's conclusion—and therefore about the conventional justification for sacrifice—is how it evokes the imaginary community of a nation seemingly open to nonhuman animals. Given the condition of ghostly membership endowed upon animals conscripted for biotechnology, Kwak's evocation of humans and animals "becom[ing] one" feels like a facile erasure of the otherness of these animals. As Jacques Derrida proposes, the ethics of mourning lies in the paradoxical impossibility of it being done successfully, of the other being completely incorporated into the self. Thus, rituals of appeasement, appreciation, and commemoration might indeed be gestures of living with these spectral members of the community, but they would be only and always yet to be done.

In this light, Kwak's proposal for a traditional ceremony prompts us to reflect on what it means to remember sacrificed animals (and humans) that haunt the colonial and postcolonial history of modern science and medicine. In fact, so-called traditional memorial rituals for laboratory animals have been performed for decades at a majority of medical and scientific research institutions in South Korea—from the Korean Food and Drug Administration (KFDA) and Seoul National University and Hospital to the Korea Institute of Oriental Medicine. The *silhŏm tongmul wiryŏngje*, which translates roughly as "ritual to appease the spirits of lab animals," often has a format similar to Korea's traditional Confucian ceremony for human ancestors, with shamanist and Buddhist elements.

Cultural anthropologist Elmer Veldkamp concludes that this kind of ritual is of Japanese origin, transplanted during the colonial era and later resurfaced to reflect Korean society's increasing concern for animals.[46] He notes that monuments to lab animals at KFDA and the Museum of Medical History—two of the oldest in Korea—date to the Japanese colonial period (1929 and 1922, respectively) and that the ceremonial address read during the ritual at KFDA is said to be from this period as well.[47] Around this time in Japan, rituals for dead animals "were molded to fit the imperial ideology by replacing the belief of vengeful spirits of the dead in traditional customs with the modern and nationalistic goal of commemoration for honorable souls of war casualties."[48] Tetsu Nishikawa and Naoki Morishita conclude that "the oldest animal memorial services in Japan were started as early as 1917 by members of the Buddhist Youth Association of Kyushu Imperial University . . . and in 1919 by the members of the Department of Agriculture of the Imperial University of Tokyo."[49] This was during World War I, when Japan extended its influence over China, the Korean peninsula, and other Asian countries through imperialist diplomacy and invasion. So what appears to be a traditional commemorative service for animals shares its heritage with scientific and medical research for Japanese imperialist purposes, which not only sacrificed animals but also experimented on Koreans and other people under occupation and invasion—a history that has been silenced even after the end of the war.[50]

While Veldkamp's discussion offers persuasive evidence of Japanese influence, some Koreans also find the roots of contemporary laboratory-animal commemoration in Korea's traditional rituals for dead animals, which were forbidden during the Japanese occupation.[51] Regardless, it would be mistaken to argue that the rituals performed in contemporary Korea are simple revivals of either Japanese-colonialist or Korean tradition, considering the cultural exchanges between the two countries. Since they resurfaced in the 1970s–90s, these rituals have also changed over time and are now often used both to commemorate lab animals and to affirm a commitment to improving their treatment and welfare according to modern bioethics that are internationally endorsed as ethical guidelines in the field (such as the 3Rs: replacement, reduction, and refinement). The heterogeneous and interrupted genealogy (rather than a pure origin) of *wiryŏngje* reflects the complexity of postcolonial ethics of remembering lab animals and their sacrifice.

This genealogy makes us dwell on what it means to honor the sacrifice of animals used in biotechnology in the name of (national) community—evoking the sacrifice of Koreans during the colonial occupation. Even though such a practice might extend anticolonial sensibilities and ethical positions to nonhuman animals, "oneness" would both remind us of and overwrite the contiguity between the sacrifice of lab animals in contemporary Korea and the Japanese imperialist use of animals and humans.

This kind of remainder also haunts traditional rituals, even if translated to seemingly denationalized modern bioethics outside the Asian context. For example, Susan A. Iliff (among others) addresses the widespread sacred memorials for animals in Japan and other Asian countries in the context of promoting secular memorials for lab animals in the United States.[52] She thus suggests adding "remembering" to the 3Rs of replacement, reduction, and refinement.[53] However, in this well-intended translation of Asian rituals to the modern American context, the category *sacred* erases the political and historical traces of these rituals—including the covert experimentation on human subjects for biological and chemical warfare research by the imperial Japanese army during World War II. Thus, the proposal to add "remembering" to the animal-welfare bioethical frame ironically forgets the postcolonial biopolitical rubrics that left human victims unacknowledged while memorializing animal sacrifice. In this light, the radical promise of such a ritual would be the countermemories that remain after memorialization, which resist the violent logic of sacrifice for the community or for others.

Kwak's appeal to memorialize sacrificed lab animals (who share similar suffering with the victims of human experimentation) challenges the speciesist biopolitics under the *segyehwa* regime, which calculates the value of animals in terms of usefulness for scientific, medical, and economic purposes that in turn serve the nation's status in the globalizing world. However, the heterogeneous and interrupted lineage of traditional rituals for lab animals is haunted both by the sacrificed animals and by the long-unacknowledged human research subjects in the Japanese imperialist development of modern science and medicine. Given this history, the prosthetic memories of the dogs (and other animals) used for cloning cannot be contained within the loops linking science labs and dog markets in South Korea. Instead, the entanglements of human and animal bodies in the colonial and postcolonial development of science and medicine are embedded in the epistemological and ethical rubrics of rendering bodies substitutable (as sacrifice) in the modern transnational bioethics.

Patriarchal Vision: Cloning and the Paradox of Female Embodiment

The biopolitical effacement of the surrogate-mother and egg-donor dogs used for cloning in South Korea also hinges on the prevalent frame of genetic cloning as a technology of asexual reproduction, which obscures the involved female reproductive bodies. However, with current cloning technology by SCNT, and particularly where dog cloning is concerned, the most wet and messy elements of the process involve female reproductive organs and body parts. More than a thousand embryos and 123 surrogates were used to produce Snuppy, although the numbers necessary for dog cloning have decreased with advancing technology. In 2014 Sooam Biotech indicated that it typically uses three gestational surrogates per dog-cloning order, each of which is implanted with three embryos; as of 2018, the number of surrogates remained the same, although there was no update on the number of implanted embryos.[54] The egg-donor dogs, meanwhile, are monitored constantly for progesterone levels to predict ovulation, and when the timing is right the eggs are collected through a surgical procedure called "flushing."[55] This in vivo process (using an intact living organism) of egg acquisition was the key to success for Hwang's team because the conventional method of collecting eggs in vitro (in an artificial environment such as a test tube) does not accommodate the reproductive physiology of dogs.[56] That is, current technology for cloning dogs—unlike for most other animals—requires living egg-donor dogs and cannot simply use leftover eggs from slaughterhouses or spaying clinics. Hence, where these female dogs come from (and where they go after they are used) has become a requisite logistics for cloning.

The effacement of female dogs used in cloning echoes feminist critiques of biomedical practice and research wherein women are mobilized as egg donors, cord-blood donors, and gestational surrogates, but their bodies and labor are invisible.[57] This kind of effacement has also informed stem cell research, because arguably the most promising technology (hESC application for therapeutic cloning) involves oocytes.[58] Yet, as Eun Kyung Choi and Ock-Joo Kim note, the Hwang scandal eventually triggered a shift in the focus of social and ethical debates around hESC research, from the moral status of embryos to the issues around egg collection and its risks and consequences for women's health.[59] This shift led to a call for international discussion, scrutinization, and collaboration. In this light, I take the affinity between human and canine female bodies around the Hwang scandal as a petri dish for a transspecies feminist mnemonic against the erasure of maternal bodies in reproductive and regenerative biotechnology. My aim here is to explore an intersectional approach to the status of and relationship among women and other female animals under the male-centric biotechnological paradigm—and to envision a transspecies feminist alliance emerging from these chimeracological entanglements.

The Hwang scandal was originally triggered by suspicions regarding the acquisition of eggs for his hESC research.[60] According to Hwang's 2004 article in *Science*, 242 fresh oocytes were donated by sixteen healthy women who "voluntarily donated for therapeutic cloning research and its applications only" without financial compensation.[61] After the publication, however, Korean feminist and bioethics organizations raised ethical concerns about egg donation (whose side effects can be serious and even life threatening) and asked for proof that the recruitment of these women followed guidelines.[62] *Nature* also reported that a PhD student had initially indicated that the donors included herself and another woman in Hwang's lab, but she "subsequently called back and said that she had not donated eggs, blaming her poor English for a misunderstanding."[63] Suspicion increased after a 2005 *Science* article reported that eighteen women had donated another 185 oocytes for the research.[64]

These concerns surrounding the acquisition of eggs were validated in subsequent investigations by SNU, the Ministry of Health and Welfare, and the National Bioethics Committee.[65] Even though investigators were unable to determine the exact number of eggs actually used in the research due to a lack of documentation and to ambiguity regarding the beginning of formal research, they confirmed that no fewer than 2,200 eggs were procured for Hwang's research team during the three-year period relevant to the two articles.[66] The investigations also determined that a majority of the eggs were purchased or traded, and that two junior female researchers on the team had indeed donated their own eggs, all of which Hwang was actively involved in.[67]

Nonetheless, at the onset of the scandal these issues were treated among Koreans as a relatively trivial problem that shouldn't hold back the nation's progress in biotechnology. The discussion on this issue was even met by an egg-donation movement supporting Hwang's research, appealing to women's "spirit of sacrifice" in the name of patriotism and the cure for intractable diseases. Korean feminist scholars have critically examined the mobilization of women's bodies for Hwang's research within the social context of South Korea. As Joo-hyun Cho suggests, the use of eggs in hESC extended the utilization of the maternal body for the sake of family, country, and the advancement of science and medicine in the modernization of South Korea.[68] Such a mobilization of maternal bodies led to the proliferation of reproductive facilities, providing "fertile grounds" for regenerative medicine by producing and circulating available eggs that had been objectified as materials for use.[69]

However, the invasive access to and use of maternal bodies also became a source of political agency, through which women could become patriotic, maternal, and care-giving subjects who contribute to the cure for diseases and disabilities, which would in turn bring glory to the nation. This paradox puts into perspective the liberalist notion of informed consent as the primary rule in bioethics on the acquisition of eggs. While I don't buy the idea of the egg-donation campaign (where women who pledged to donate eggs for Hwang's research were metaphorized as the rose of Sharon, Korea's national flower), it is still difficult to answer how to approach patriotism as a reason for voluntary donation in a postcolonial society where individual success and virtue are often aligned with national development.[70] Also, while altruism is generally considered a legitimate motivation for donation, the actual case of a woman who donated eggs thinking they would be used to treat her sibling suffering from lupus shows not only the importance of informed consent but also the complexity of such a principle—women's desires and interests are interlaced with the gendered division of care and affective labor in a national project professing the "cure for intractable diseases."[71] In this vein, as Yeon-bo Jeong suggests, we need to pay attention to the collective agency that emerges from the complex social meaning making of gendered bodies in relation to nation, family, disability, and science—beyond the liberalist model of *subject* that undergirds the principle of informed consent.[72]

In this sense, the Hwang scandal signaled emerging global issues, eliciting transnational feminist efforts to address the gendered impact of stem cell research and other cutting-edge biomedicine.[73] Donna Dickenson and Itziar Alkorta Idiakez observed that while "pressure to produce harmonized standards on egg procurement" had grown after the scandal, the lack of success in creating internationally binding regulations or scientific consensus led to a kind of moratorium that they feared might defer hard questions about the exploitation of women and global justice.[74] Catherine Waldby, among other feminist scholars, has raised concerns about the transnational oocyte markets where impoverished women sell their eggs at the risk of serious side effects.[75] Waldby warns that this phenomenon will be exacerbated by increasing demand for human eggs in stem cell cloning research and by the growth of regenerative medicine, as specific phenotypes are no longer important in these fields (unlike in the reproductive market, where demand focuses on the eggs of pretty, intellectual, healthy women of particular races).[76]

In this context, Melinda Cooper and Catherine Waldby contend that women who donate their tissues to stem cell industries engage with a kind of activity different from biomedical reproductive work (such as gestational surrogacy), and that this difference requires a new approach to women's bodily labor in biomedicine beyond the conventional focus on alienating dynamics of commodity.[77] Cooper and Waldby theorize "the regenerative labor" of these women, who "through the mechanism of informed consent" give "not so much the surplus products of reproduction as technical and legal traction on *their bodily potentials for embryonic self-regeneration*."[78] These women thus enter into an experimental relationship in the new bioeconomy, where their bodily potential for self-regeneration (rather than its product) becomes the source of surplus through commerce between promissory stem cell science and speculative post-Fordist financial capitalism.[79]

Cooper and Waldby's approach to these women's work as an emerging form of labor has important consequences. It emphasizes that the bodies of these women and their physical and affective labor are a critical source of surplus value, which is often eclipsed in a neoliberal bioeconomy that renders life self-regenerative. It also allows a critical understanding of the normative and regulatory nature of bioethics, especially "informed consent as an enabling regulatory condition for the market in clinical labor" wherein consenting subjects take part in a specific form of "unequal exchange."[80] In this light, Cooper and Waldby's theory of clinical labor opens political grounds for demanding better conditions for these women (and other clinical-labor providers) and reexamining the salient feminist bioethical foci on "the realm of care, dignity, respect and the liberal ethical contract (of informed consent)," as Cooper suggested in her earlier work.[81]

While these Korean and transnational feminist discourses suggest new visions for political agency emerging from the paradox of women's embodiment, I argue that considering nonhuman animals is necessary to further the prospectus of feminist politics concerning the women (and other animals) in the transnational circuits of biotechnology. Cooper and Waldby's observation that clinical labor happens "in the suborganismic level of the body" invites a posthumanist perspective.[82] If clinical labor concerns the capitalism that lets bodily materials (even when extracted from the donor's body) do the work, then it invites a new form of political agency different from the one modeling the autonomous and rational (human) subject.

Furthermore, it would be difficult to ignore that what dogs and other animals do for cloning is similar to what Cooper and Waldby conceptualize as labor carried out by egg donors in stem cell research—except that these animals are not asked to consent. So, although female animals and humans mobilized for animal cloning and stem cell research are not exactly experimental subjects (as they are not directly experimented on), the experience (taking the risk and enduring the harm of a biomedical procedure) is similar enough to validate Jonathan L. Clark's reflection on the role of guinea pigs vis-à-vis human guinea pigs in clinical trials.[83] While Clark acknowledges the political merit of approaching these human research subjects as laborers and the limits of the human exceptionalist understanding of labor, he echoes Weisberg's concern that approaching lab animals as workers risks obscuring "the brutal reality of the total denial of their ability to act in any meaningful way."[84] In this light, Clark proposes a posthumanist approach to labor that accounts for the relations of domination experienced by a majority of lab animals through attending to "the distributed agency of heterogeneous assemblages of human and nonhuman actants" instead of focusing on the agency of the individuals (possibly including animals) who do the work.[85]

My takeaway from Clark's comparative perspective on conditions among human and other animal research subjects is twofold. First, it suggests that for the majority of lab animals the political valence of shifting from the ethics of care to the political economy is contingent at best, and developing an ethics of care rather than acknowledging the agency of these animals seems suitable.[86] Second, this problem also applies to some degree to human research subjects, especially if their freedom to give informed consent is restricted by socioeconomic conditions. This necessitates attention to both human and nonhuman agents in the broader web of power of the biomedical complex.

Korean and transnational feminists have sought to respond to the changes in the transnational circuits connecting biotechnology and regenerative medicine with the oocyte market, which increasingly incorporates the vulnerable population of young women with limited resources. I suggest that the feminist search for a new form of political agency and vision attuned to the delirious bioeconomy necessitates consideration of nonhuman animals, who not only share the vulnerability but also highlight crucial aspects of what animal research subjects experience that challenges the usual sense of (human) political agency.

Eggs That Matter: A Nonhuman Genealogy of Human Stem Cell Research

To expand on the value of an interspecies perspective in feminist critique of cloning and regenerative medicine, this section complicates feminist genealogies of the use of female reproductive body parts (especially eggs) by tracing the discursive and corporeal commerce between the human eggs collected for Hwang's hESC research and other animal eggs used in his earlier research in veterinary medicine. Korean science historian Geun Bae Kim has examined the technological evolution of Hwang's research team from animal-embryo cloning to human stem cell research.[87] As a professor of veterinary medicine, Hwang was initially involved in embryo cloning (a method of splitting one fertilized embryo into two or more), which fit with his goal of the mass reproduction of high-quality stock animals. He continued to pursue this technique even after Ian Wilmut at the Roslin Institute successfully cloned Dolly the sheep via SCNT for the purpose of biomedical applications in 1997.[88] Nonetheless, Hwang eventually did become more interested in SCNT, shifting his focus to transgenic xeno-organs and stem cell therapy. Kim examines how demand for (and supply of) a large number of human and animal eggs in cloning technology shaped the path of Hwang's research after this shift.

Hwang's team launched human stem cell research the same year they also successfully cloned two cows via SCNT.[89] In the beginning, Hwang's stem cell cloning research used cow eggs to produce a human embryo, as his team was more familiar with animal eggs and thought using them would cause fewer ethical problems by avoiding human egg cells; ironically, this later spurred resistance to his research because of the popular perception that the result would effectively be a half-human, half-beast (Panin-bansu).[90] Hwang also expressed doubts about human cloning due to the large number of eggs required, reportedly saying about SCNT, "It would require thousands of eggs to successfully create an embryo and transplant it into a uterus. To extract that many eggs, we would need about 500 women and a considerable size of research facility."[91] However, Hwang did switch to human eggs, difficulty in the acquisition of which would later lead to his illicit procurement activities. Kim attributes this move to several factors: the news that a research team in the United States was making progress using human eggs, the complete prohibition of interspecies SCNT and the restriction of SCNT in the proposed draft of Korean bioethics laws, and Hwang's personal drive for reputation (especially his aspirations for a Nobel Prize).[92]

Examining the evolution of Hwang's research, Kim argues that the scandal demonstrates the limits of the research style of South Korean scientific communities geared for "aggressive and condensed development" to catch up with more advanced countries.[93] The epitome of this kind of research is "science of scale," illustrated by the huge number of eggs and the corresponding scale of the facility and human resources employed in Hwang's research. Hwang's research lab used more than two thousand animal eggs each day, and the stem cell team used far more human eggs than any other research team in the world did, or could. Based on Kim's observation of this massive use of bovine and human eggs in Hwang's research, I would like to reexamine the feminist ethics of eggs in biomedical research as intrinsically transspecies.

If South Korea's developments in cloning technology are based on what David Cyranoski pejoratively called a "cloning factory," then this kind of industrial model of biotechnological reproduction is based not only on the massive use of female reproductive cells (especially eggs) but also on replaceability between species.[94] In this, the rubrics of such replaceability shape the specific and asymmetrical nodes of their entwinement. On one hand, animal cloning based on the massive use of eggs established a model of SCNT technologies to be adopted in hESC research. On the other, easy access to a large number of cow eggs allowed the replacement of human oocytes— sometimes coded as the ethical act of saving human eggs and other times as an abominable act creating a mixture of human and animal.

Thus, the relationship between human and animal female bodies in this chain of substitution is less analogous than intersecting. Both the animals (such as egg-donor cows and dogs in cloning) and the women (such as egg donors in stem cell research) are recruited for use in biotechnology by virtue of their female reproductive organs and cells. However, these female animals are used for cloning because they are needed for cloning medical models, who will suffer for humans, and also because they share a lineage with other animals that substitute for women, such as human egg donors. Further, these women—often from socially marginalized groups—are themselves interpolated into reproductive technology and regenerative medicine by sacrificing for other humans in the name of helping people with disabilities and intractable diseases and thereby serving the nation. Thus, unlike Cooper, I suggest that the political economy does not replace but rather heightens the importance of intersectional and reflective ethics of care and responsibility toward other animals (who might not benefit so much from status as workers or from the principle of informed consent) in the chains of substitution. A situated and conditional ethics of care toward nonhuman animals that is aware of its paradoxical mobilization of depreciated feminized affective labor in neoliberal capitalism is critical for transnational and postcolonial feminist critique on biotechnology.[95]

The Chains of Substitution: A Transspecies Alliance for Postcolonial Feminism

Having established that the women egg donors for stem cell research and the egg-donor dogs for cloning are interwoven in chains of substitution in the transnational circuits of biotechnology, I suggest that the practice of substituting animals for humans in scientific and medical research offers a foil against which to reimagine transspecies alliance as a crucial task for postcolonial feminist mnemonics. There is already a long history of feminist alliance with laboratory animals in (but not limited to) the United States and Europe.[96] As Hilda Kean notes, political concerns for animal issues advanced with the emergence of feminism and socialism in the late nineteenth century, when protesters against both vivisection and wife beating saw a link between "vivisection, pornography, and the condition of women."[97]

In the late twentieth century, Andrée Collard among others criticized animal experimentation to showcase the death-oriented values of patriarchy, in line with ecofeminist critiques on patriarchal dominance over women, other animals, and nature since the 1960s.[98]

Closer to my own approach is that of Donna Haraway, who departs from an ecocritical propensity to love nature and instead reenvisions kinship in a world of techno-natural assemblages through the forceful figure of the OncoMouse™.[99] Haraway proposes sisterhood with this murine commodity transplanted with a human oncogene based on the specific embodiment of natural-cultural-technological femaleness in carrying mammary glands as a site of breast cancer (and hence, even a male mouse can be a sister). Reflecting on this human-murine kinship, Haraway rejects resting easily "with the idiom of sacrifice" as she seeks an ethics of responsibility mindful that "no balance sheet of benefit and cost will suffice."[100] She also does not evoke the general injunction of not-killing, acknowledging that humans are not outside the ecology of mortal beings.[101] Haraway instead attends to the inequality that allows humans to turn a mouse into a commodity for medical experimentation, which lies "in *the precise and changeable labor practices of the lab*, not in some transcendent excellence of the Human over Animal."[102]

As I investigate the relationship between human and other animal egg donors for cloning and hESC, Haraway's feminist ethics of responsibility merits a discussion with a postcolonial feminist perspective. The labor practices of the lab are changeable but not separable from the speciesist biopolitical order that renders (certain) animals killable for humans—which, as I discuss, is also imbricated in the racial and (post)colonial history of experimental subjects in modern science and medicine. In this light, I propose a transnational approach to the female animals entangled with women in the chains of substitution revealed in Hwang's scandal, shifting focus from the immature bioethics of cutting-edge technology in South Korea (and possibly other countries) to the globalization of bioethics that enables as much as regulates such sacrifices. Thus, my argument for the transspecies feminist alliance is a part of my effort to remember the chimeracological entanglements of these women and other animals in the face of the neoliberal imperialist and nationalist delirium, the promissory biotechnology project of which goes hand in hand with the bioethical institutionalization of human and animal research subjects on a global scale.

Charis Thompson offers an insightful analysis of the "substitute research subject" deeply engrained in current biomedical research (including hESC research) and bioethics, attending to the sociopolitical history of the scientific practice.[103] Thompson emphasizes that "non-human animals became an increasingly mandatory bioethical substitute for unethical experimentation on human subjects of research" during the post–World War II period when the use of human subjects in Nazi science emerged as a social concern.[104] After the end of the war, the Nuremberg Doctors' Trial—an American military court trying twenty-three German physicians and administrators for war crimes and crimes against humanity—resulted in the Nuremberg Code, which became the foundation of modern bioethics. In this code, animal experimentation is defined as a prerequisite for experimentation on human subjects: "3. The experiment should be so designed and based on the result of animal experimentation and a knowledge of the natural history of the disease or other problem under study that the anticipated results will justify the performance of the experiment."[105] Here, model animals do not simply substitute for humans, but also for human research subjects—who themselves would have suffered instead of other humans. In this light, Thompson notes, modern bioethics establishes experimenting on animals as an ethical substitution for experimenting on humans. However, Thompson writes, while the underlying logic that animals are "both biologically alike and ethically unlike humans" makes experimentation on animals a routine part of ethical research, this holds only so far as biological similarity legitimates the epistemological feasibility.[106]

Thompson's turn to epistemology is based on her assessment that the trope "treat someone like an animal" is "at the heart of modern biopolitics," wherein the ethical and epistemological logistics of model animals offer the means "whereby the abjection of those experimented upon *as if they were animals* was diverted onto the bodies of literal animals."[107] Nonetheless, for Thompson it would be simplistic to see the model animals as a problem of the human-centric abjection of the animal, since the matter of research subjects also concerns the status of both nonhuman and human research subjects in relation to other human beings. Furthermore, the history of animalization as a justification for dehumanizing women, slaves, and people with disability impels Thompson to find an alternative to a version of animal rights that simply adds the animal as a new subject of enfranchisement to the long list of human minority groups.[108] In respect to such political and historical complexity, Thompson does not directly examine the ethical asymmetries between human and animal but instead questions the operative feature of this paradigm—substitution—by tapping into its epistemological limitations. In other words, Thompson questions the epistemological assumption that biological similarity with humans necessarily and naturally makes animals good (or better) models for understanding humans.

Based on her observations about the field of stem cell research, Thompson argues that a move away from the scheme of substitution is not only possible but would help scientific research to advance beyond the epistemological limits of model animals (and other forms of substitute research). If the immense efforts invested into making animal models more like humans were redirected toward developing in vitro systems as an alternative, it would result in a scientifically viable and ethical research paradigm.[109] Thompson's politically and historically situated and scientifically informed argument is supported by rising ethical and epistemological concerns about the use of animals in emergent stem cell research for medical purposes, echoing more general critiques on scientific efficacy and the danger of using animal models in biomedical scientific research.[110]

Thompson's detour does circumvent the pitfall of animal-rights discourse, but it does not invalidate the question of what then makes the trope of "treating someone like an animal" paradigmatic of the beginning of modern bioethics, even (logically) before bioethics was diverted to the literal bodies of nonhuman animals. I am not suggesting that speciesism is the biopolitical ground zero, but that literal and figural animals are already there within the biopolitical order of humans. In a sense, Thompson's careful circumvention also points to the infeasibility of quarantining this trope ("treating someone like an animal") within species boundaries. As critics such as Cary Wolfe have suggested, the violence of dehumanization by way of animalization cannot be resolved simply by amending the boundary between human and animal, as this kind of effort maintains the human-animal binary that asserts the hegemonic model of humanity at the cost of abjection of animality.[111]

Here let me bring back Black feminist critiques on the hegemonic onto-epistemology (discussed more extensively in part I) to situate my point. Zakiyyah Iman Jackson has eloquently shown that "the African's humanity is not denied but appropriated, inverted and ultimately plasticized in *the methodology of abjecting animality*."[112] Jackson thus asserts the necessity for rethinking and transforming "the animal"—otherwise, "it will continue to animate antiblack discourse" that presumes the "necessity of managing, disciplining, criminalizing, and extinguishing 'the animal.'"[113] Jackson's criticism on the structure of violence against animal-African (and other marginalized human) proxies is even more persuasive considering Denise Ferreira da Silva's critique on how racialized subjects (alongside other natural beings) are relegated to the realm of the affectable—the legitimate site of intervention and regulation by reason in modern science (exclusively saved for the Anglo-European subject).[114] Jackson's and Ferreira da Silva's critiques thus not only push us to reexamine the proxy between animals and women within the chains of substitutions but also help us to consider the political status of modern bioethics in relation to the mutual legitimization between science's epistemology and the white subject's dualistic ontology (their mind and the others' bodies). In this light, as far as the resolution redirects the trope of "treating someone like an animal" from literal animals to things without questioning the structure of violence ingrained in the logic of modern science, moving to in vitro systems is a meaningful but only provisional alternative to animal models.

Thus, even when the question of ethical difference between humans and animals seems bracketed, ongoing efforts to find nonanimal models are inevitably a part of the changing biopolitical order of life, death, and suffering. And thinking from the perspective of the chain of substitution, the nature and mechanism of similarity and difference are anything but simple or evident. It is then also worth noting that assessing the epistemological soundness of particular animal species as human substitutes has hinged on the configurations of biological and ethical similarity and difference in historical and social contexts. For example, Lesley Sharp reflects on how pigs have emerged as "the other animal of transplant's future," as xenoscience moves away from nonhuman primates whose evolutionary proximity "has long shaped ideas about transspecies matches" yet repeatedly failed the hope of immunological compatibility.[115] Pigs are now valued for organ donation as "a morphologically and genetically malleable species" that also does not evoke public aversion to nonhuman primate experimentation.[116] In this light, in these chains of substitution, a transnational feminist ethics regarding animals as close to us as nonhuman primates and dogs and as far as pigs and mice is at stake.

This chapter has traced the prosthetic memories of the chain of replaceable bodies extending from animal cloning to human stem cell research. These memories endure against delirious erasure in a regime of biotechnology that on one hand aims to revamp the national economy and cure intractable diseases in South Korea and on the other normalizes a bioethics that supplements the extraction of surplus from human and nonhuman lives in the (both imperialist and nationalist) neoliberal bioeconomy on a planetary scale. The animals—who benefit less than human research subjects and tissue donors from the acknowledgment of their scientific and economic contribution and from the principle of informed consent—are crucial companions to transnational and postcolonial feminist efforts to achieve fair and just status and treatment in the biomedical complex. This is partly because animals suffer like us and on behalf of us. But it is also because their otherness helps us to reassess the reproductive and regenerative labor disproportionally performed by socially marginalized women and to renew political agency for negotiating the nationalist, patriarchal, and ableist summoning of women for biotechnological use beyond the model of the liberal subject. In the face of (and despite) the neoliberal exploitation of feminized affective labor in the name of curing other people's illnesses and recuperating the national economy, prosthetic memories from the entanglements of female animals used for cloning and human egg donors for regenerative medical research enable a postcolonial feminism to generate an ethics of care toward these lab animals—a paradoxical gift from the inhuman vision of a tentative alliance between women and animals across an abyssal difference.

Epilogue

South Korean artist Soyo Lee's *Ornamental Cactus Design* (2013–16) explores the history, bioethics, and aesthetics of the *kŏllŏ chŏmmok sŏninjang* (colorful grafted cactus), often called a moon or hibotan cactus.[1] These cacti are tiny, and each features what looks like a vibrantly colored (usually orange, red, or yellow) ball popping out of the green shaft. They first caught Lee's attention during her visit to a flower market in Amsterdam, where she was shocked to learn that these presumably desert plants came from her "less than-tropical country."[2] Based on ensuing field research in South Korea, Japan, and the Netherlands, the project's exhibition combines live cactus installations, informational displays, and cactus-grafting workshops.[3]

Lee traces the origin of these plants to the 1930s, when a Japanese cultivator cross-bred using a cactus with red spots (due to an "albino" mutation) indigenous to South America in order to produce a completely red cactus targeting European consumers.[4] After the Japanese colonial period ended, the Korean farmers who were doing the work of breeding and grafting continued developing ways to mass produce the cactus and to create more colors.[5] The variously colored moon cacti have become a major commercial export for South Korea over the past three decades and are sold as affordable and expandable ornamental plants across Europe and North America.

The story behind these eye-catching yet mundane cacti that are easily found in my neighborhood flower stores in Vienna (for only 3–5 euros each) is perhaps a trivial example of how various affects and forms of life are incorporated into planetary biocapitalism. Admittedly, these cute cacti don't evoke in me any visceral affects, like Kang Seung Lee's work on cacti propagated from Harvey Milk's does (as I discussed in the introduction).

Nonetheless, despite (or even owing to) such a sense of triviality, *Ornamental Cactus Design* offers a renewed sense of the dehumanist stakes of prosthetic memories within chimeracological entanglements. Each moon cactus is a chimera.[6] The top is a piece from a hibotan, whose "albino" lack of chlorophyll allows it to be engineered to have bright colors but also makes it incapable of photosynthesis to survive on its own. This colorful ball is thus grafted onto a rootstock cactus (usually *Hylocereus undatus*), which can photosynthesize for the grafted albino mutant as well. It isn't clear which part is prosthetic to which, but the result of such grafting is a colorful yet short-lived ornamental plant for European and American consumers. *Ornamental Cactus Design* highlights the bioethical dimension of mass producing the moon cactus through analogies of plant grafting to organ transplantation and other biomedical interventions in animals, such as Soviet medical doctor Vladimir Demikhov's notorious creation of two-headed dogs.[7] Soyo Lee's work then asks how we make sense of the contradictory affective reactions to artificially modified plants and animals (attraction or horror), and whether it is speciesism to differentiate their ethical status. The contiguous but unclosable space between the artist's analogy of plant grafting to animal organ transplantation against the technological exploitation of life forms across the globe, and recognition of the impossibility of thinking and feeling the scars of these cacti without projecting a certain degree of liberalist human subjectivity, subtends this book's search for a dehumanist feminist mnemonics of our time—a time when human and animal mind-bodies (as well as plants and other life forms) are cut, displaced, reproduced, and disposed of in the transnational circuits of advanced technology and capitalism.

Throughout this book, I have explored an emerging mode of prosthetic memory as a conceptual lens to better address both familiar and new technological assemblages of human and nonhuman mind-bodies. What if we think of prosthetic memory not in opposition to organic memory but as a reminder of chimeracological milieus, inhuman otherness, and the potential for regeneration and connection with others as the conditions of remembrance? How does this approach to memory guide us in engaging with the phantasmal and everyday entanglements of different forms of life (and non-life) in the transnational circuits of virtual and corporeal technologies? What are the gendered, racialized, and speciated contours of these entanglements, and how does the refigured concept of prosthetic memory help us enact alternative visions to counter the often isolating and debilitating forces of technological assemblages—even those that profess to cure, capacitate, and help us better master both others and the world?

Engaging with these questions while writing this book has been a two-fold commitment. On one hand, I have traced the patterns and nodes of incision, displacement, disavowal, and erasure at intersections of different relations of power and the differential norms of truth and reality that such relations generate. On the other, these differential norms of truth and reality endorse my second commitment—to engage with remembrance as a compositional practice, seeking alternative (dehumanist) visions and creating new connections—but without any promise of onto-epistemological grounds. Yet what would be the ground of my efforts to evoke the perspective of the moon cactus in Soyo Lee's photographs, or of the pebbles from Derek Jarman's cottage and Tapgol Park in Kang Seung Lee's drawing?

If there are still any grounds for the ungroundedness of my performative-speculative writing on prosthetic memories, it would be something like Sylvia Wynter's position about her theory of homo narrans, which queerly adapts the racist logics of modern science: "I would be prepared, like a Christian in a Roman imperial auditorium, to go to the lions in defense of that hypothesis."[8] My refusal to criticize tongue surgery for improving the English accent in chapter 1 (and instead searching for the other memory of the mother/tongue via theoretical and literary detours) or to track the used-up gestational surrogate-mother dogs in chapter 4 (and instead interrogating the canine affective remainders circuiting between Koreans and Western-ers) will not survive the lions' attack but is nevertheless worth a defense.

Such an ungroundable commitment to engage with the other reality that escapes taken-for-granted human reason and perception reflects my critical take on the triumphant narrative of the turn from the linguistic to the material and to the posthuman. I argue that this kind of narrative unwittingly reiterates the West's onto-epistemology that justifies violence against the others of the white/European subject (as the proper owner/user of *logos*) while dismissing any kind of language-human assemblage that opens to other realities. This book is thus a postcolonial feminist effort to approach these foreclosed realities as a site of prosthetic memory. In that sense, this book is a practice of "speaking nearby"[9]—speaking in proxy to infrahumans, animals, and machines, presenting chimeracological mutations of Gayatri Spivak's critique on how Western leftist intellectuals' disavowal of their role in representation eclipses their role in the global political economy. Thus, it explores a postcolonial feminist approach that doesn't render obsolete the biopolitical dimension of language (and representation) but instead looks at how racial, interspecies, and affective (involving shame, disgust, and love) entanglements condition the postcolonial matrix of truth, scientific knowledge, and my own writing in the transnational circuits of technology. Tracing these entanglements, the prosthetic memories in this book thus seek to move away from the exclusive majoritarian human realm of representation toward affective-discursive traces of becoming-with-others, in which this book takes part.

As a final note, I would like to reflect on my reparative efforts (in Eve K. Sedgwick's sense) to bring into the space of prosthetic memories the affective ties among what appear to be problematic or noninnocent relations— the treacherous mother-son relationship in postcolonial society (chapter 1), robot-human love (chapter 2), a former sex-exploiter's love for her deceased dog (chapter 3), supposedly dog-eating Koreans and surrogate mother dogs retired from the pet-cloning industry (chapter 4), and human and animal female bodies in biomedical research (chapter 5). This partly indicates my take on the contemporary biopolitics of technology, whose primary mode of operations has shifted from mimetic simulations and reproduction of the same (as more conventional critiques of postcolonial language and genetic technology suggest) to manipulation and incorporation of difference through displacement, fragmentation, regeneration, mutation, and cyborgization of various life forms. Moreover, as *Ornamental Cactus Design* shows, such technological governance over living forms operates through an affective capitalism that parasitizes reproductive, regenerative, and even creative processes at cellular, molecular, and technological levels—to intervene, produce, and preempt desires and aesthetics on a planetary level.[10]

Thus, this book demonstrates that prosthetic memory is an at times paradoxical but nonetheless forceful site for envisioning new forms of collectivity and alliance to counter the injurious and isolating impact of advanced technologies on the one hand and the biopolitical governance of affects and intimacy on the other—which calls for a rupture in the hegemonic human genre's monopoly on truth and reality. In this light, my most ambitious aspiration is that this book enrich the dialogue and intimacy between Black feminist critiques and East Asian and Asian American feminist discourses as we create and carry memories of embodied others in the chimeracological world that this century presents to us.

Notes

Introduction

1   The Artro, "Behind the Beauty: An Interview with Kang Seung Lee," January 20, 2023, https://www.theartro.kr/eng/features/features_view .asp?idx=5530&b_code=10&page=&searchColumn=&searchKeyword =&b_ex2=.

2   Kang Seung Lee and Jin Kwon, "QueerArch Exhibition Essay," Apexart, accessed August 2, 2023, https://apexart.org/QueerArch_E.php.

3   The Artro, "Behind the Beauty." In collaboration with Tolentino, Lee has also propagated the little plants grown from Harvey and has shared them with various people in the queer community, extending the network of care for this living archive of queer memory.

4   New Museum (@newmuseum), "An unexpected living archive, 'Julie Tolentino (Archive in Dirt)' (2019-ongoing), now on view in the 2021 Triennial, 'Soft Water Hard Stone,'" Twitter (now X), November 8, 2021, https://twitter.com/newmuseum/status/1457750539962310660.

5   Jarman, *Modern Nature*, 55; Tongsŏn An, "Kei in'gwŏn'gwa yŏksarŭl pat'angŭro chagŏp'anŭn chakka igangsŭng" [Kang Seung Lee works based on gay human rights and history], *Harper's BAZAAR Korea*, October 17, 2021, https://www.harpersbazaar.co.kr/article/59380.

6   An example of such an effort is *Garden* (2018), which involves soil, pebbles, and debris from both places—and was also exhibited at the

Triennial. For more details on the entwining of Jarman and Oh in Lee's work, see Leslie Dick's introduction to Lee's "Porous Bodies."

7 Here I borrow Rosi Braidotti's conceptualization of "transposition." With a double inspiration from both music and genetics, this term "indicates an intertextual, cross-boundary or transversal transfer, in the sense of a leap from one code, field or axis into another." Braidotti, *Transpositions*, 5.

8 New Museum (@newmuseum), "An unexpected living archive."

9 Lee, *The Exquisite Corpse of Asian America*, 140.

10 Lee, *The Exquisite Corpse of Asian America*, 140.

11 Lee, *The Exquisite Corpse of Asian America*, 140–41.

12 I borrow the phrase "an imaginary chorus" from Judith Butler's explanation about the performative force of the term *queer* as an interpellation. Through this phrase, Butler reminds us of the persistence of the power enacted in and through the repeated invocation of this term *queer* as "accusation, pathologization, [and] insult"—which conditions the possibility for subversive reclamation of the term. Butler, "Critically Queer," 18. Even though the term *prosthetic* is not an interpellation per se, its performative force evokes the social imaginaries of people with disability as the absent referent mind-bodies (i.e., the wearer of prosthetics) and groups of people associated with the supplementarity of prosthetics vis-à-vis the supposed original entity. Butler's theory of performativity helps me to reflect on the imaginary chorus of these associated ideas and affects that haunt the term *prosthetics*—even in attempts to revise and reclaim it.

13 I feel privileged to witness the recent gush of forceful Black, indigenous, and decolonial critiques on the Enlightenment and liberalist figures of the human, which also haunt the prevailing posthumanist and new materialist discourses despite (and in) their claim to go beyond the human/ism. These critiques have analyzed the onto-epistemological and political repercussions of such a tendency in understanding our species' relationship with animals, things, and the world and in comprehending what constitutes body, representation, and reality—which informs my efforts to refigure the concept of prosthetic memory. In this light, I am inspired by and aspire to converse with these critical efforts, especially Zakiyyah Iman Jackson's *Becoming Human*; Julietta Singh's *Unthinking Mastery*; Elizabeth A. Povinelli's *Geontologies*; and Denise Ferreira da Silva's *Toward a Global Idea of Race*, in addition to the works by Toni Morrison, Sylvia Wynter, and Margaret Rhee I discuss in depth in the coming chapters.

14 Plato, *Phaedrus*, 274B–277A; Heidegger, *Parmenides*, 80–81.

15 Jacques Derrida's discussion of the supplement appears in many of his works, including "Plato's Pharmacy"; "Freud and the Scene of Writing"; and "The Word Processor," all by Derrida.

16 McLuhan, *Understanding Media*, 3.

17 McLuhan, *Understanding Media*, 3–4.

18 McLuhan borrowed this idea from medical researchers like Hans Selye and Adolphe Jonas, who conceptualized "autoamputation" as a strategy to which a body resorts "when the perceptual power cannot locate or avoid the cause of irritation." McLuhan, *Understanding Media*, 42.

19 McLuhan, *Understanding Media*, 47.

20 McLuhan, *Understanding Media*, 47.

21 Landsberg, *Prosthetic Memory*.

22 Landsberg, *Prosthetic Memory*, 2

23 Landsberg, *Prosthetic Memory*, 2.

24 Landsberg, *Prosthetic Memory*, 20.

25 Landsberg, *Prosthetic Memory*, 25–28.

26 Haraway, "A Cyborg Manifesto," 157.

27 Haraway, "A Cyborg Manifesto," 151–53.

28 For discussions on the increasing and institutionalizing recruitment of humans as biological resources and experimental subjects in biomedicine in a global context, see Cooper, *Life as Surplus*; and Sunder Rajan, "Experimental Values." Richard Twine notes that biotechnology (such as genomics) has become a prevalent paradigm in treating domestic animals, arguing for the importance of biopolitical and bioethical attention to animals in this regard. Twine, *Animals as Biotechnology*.

29 Livingston and Puar, "Interspecies," 3.

30 Livingston and Puar, "Interspecies," 4–5.

31 For example, in his book *Bioinsecurities*, Ahuja offers a critical examination of racialized and gendered medical and biosecurity interventions at human-microbe interfaces in Asia and the Americas, which have shaped the US empire over the decades. In his book *The Mobile Workshop*, Mavhunga looks at encounters between African and European colonial knowledges, tracing local knowledge of the tsetse fly (*mhesvi* in the local language) that European colonizers adapted into methods to control the fly which were exploitive and destructive for indigenous people and the environment in twentieth-century Rhodesia and Zimbabwe.

32 Cooper, *Life as Surplus*, 12.

33 Haraway, "A Cyborg Manifesto," 149. According to Ronald Kline, research scientists created the cyborg techniques as means to control the bodies of

astronauts "so they could survive the harsh environment of outer space, an alternative to providing an earth-like environment for space travel." For more details about the cyborg mouse and the genealogy of cybernetics, see Kline, "Where Are the Cyborgs in Cybernetics?," 331–32 (quote on 332).

34 Rose, "Molecular Biopolitics, Somatic Ethics, and the Spirit of Biocapital," 3.

35 Franklin, "The Cyborg Embryo," 171.

36 Parisi, *Abstract Sex*, 168, 197.

37 Milburn, "Nanotechnology in the Age of Posthuman Engineering," 291–93.

38 For more postcolonial and feminist critiques on the contemporary bio-economy surrounding new genetic, regenerative, and molecular science and technologies, see Schurr, "From Biopolitics to Bioeconomies"; Braun, "Biopolitics and the Molecularization of Life"; and Foster, "Patents, Biopolitics, and Feminisms."

39 Mitchell, *Cloning Terror*, chap. 2.

40 Preciado, "Pharmaco-pornographic Politics," 108.

41 Preciado, "Pharmaco-pornographic Politics," 110.

42 *Oxford English Dictionary*, s.v. "prosthetic (n.)," September 2023, https://doi.org/10.1093/OED/5859376254.

43 Jain, "The Prosthetic Imagination," 40.

44 Jain, "The Prosthetic Imagination," 47, 48.

45 Sobchack, "A Leg to Stand On," 19.

46 Sobchack, "A Leg to Stand On," 18–19.

47 Kafer, *Feminist, Queer, Crip*, 105. Kafer's citation is from Haraway, "Cyborg Manifesto," 178.

48 Kafer argues that this kind of feminist cyborg theory often lacks any critical engagement with disability and "analysis of the material realities of disabled people's interactions with technology." Kafer, *Feminist, Queer, Crip*, 105.

49 Kafer explains that "'trach' is an abbreviation of tracheotomy, a medical procedure in which a breathing tube is inserted directly into the trachea, bypassing the mouth and nose. Someone with a trach, then, can in effect breathe through her throat, freeing her mouth for other activities." Kafer, *Feminism, Queer, Crip*, 122.

50 Puar, preface to *The Right to Maim*, xiv.

51 According to Limbs International, "only 5% of the approximate 30–40 million amputees in the developing world have access to prosthetic devices or assistance." Limbs International, "Why Limbs," accessed May 5, 2023, https://www.limbsinternational.org/why-limbs.html. In addition

to unequal access to prosthetic devices, it is also noteworthy that "while the transition from bonesetters to orthopaedic doctors took place almost concurrently in the Western world, most of the developing world was left out of these developments," such that traditional bone setting has survived "modernization" and remained an alternative source of care, especially for those who are poor and lack access to more expensive Western medicine. Ezeanya-Esiobu, *Indigenous Knowledge and Education in Africa*, 86.

52 Lorde, *The Cancer Journals*, 60–61.

53 Jeong-yeo Lim, "Herald Interview: Rethinking Amputee Status, Prosthetics Market in Korea," *Korea Herald*, April 21, 2019, http://www.koreaherald.com/view.php?ud=20190421000103. On smart skin and handcrafted prosthetics, see Harmon Leon, "Visiting Seoul's Artificial Limb District," *Vice*, March 14, 2015, https://www.vice.com/da/article/vdp5z3/visiting-the-seoul-artificial-limb-district-312.

54 Hird, "Animal Trans," 232.

55 Hird, "Animal Trans," 241.

56 Sullivan, "Somatechnics," 187.

57 Sullivan, "Somatechnics," 188.

58 Stryker and Sullivan, "King's Member, Queen's Body," 61.

59 Shildrick, *Visceral Prostheses*.

60 Shildrick, *Visceral Prostheses*.

61 Jain, "The Prosthetic Imagination," 32, emphasis added, quoting Wills, *Prosthesis*, 215.

62 For critiques on the Western model of the independent subject, see Reindal, "Independence, Dependence, Interdependence."

63 Smietana, Thompson, and Twine, "Making and Breaking Families." In this introduction, the authors offer a comprehensive and dynamic cartography of the issues raised by the development of ART and transnational surrogacy, in conversation with critical genealogies of queer reproduction, reproductive justice, and stratified reproduction.

64 Waldby and Cooper, "From Reproductive Work to Regenerative Labour," 3.

65 For critiques on invisible labor in the digital and information technology industry, see Van Doorn, "Platform Labor"; Huws, "The Hassle of Housework"; Rand, "Challenging the Invisibility of Sex Work"; and Chakraborty, *Invisible Labour*.

66 For the gendered implications of immaterial and affective labor with the rise of ICT, see Morini, "The Feminization of Labour"; Fortunati, "ICTs and Immaterial Labor"; and Hester, "Technically Female."

67   Neda Atanasoski and Kalindi Vora critically examine technoliberalism that promises a revolutionary new future, where robots and an automated labor force (as surrogate humans) will liberate humans from the drudgery of enslaved labor. Atanasoski and Vora, *Surrogate Humanity*, 4. They expose how this liberalist imaginary of human-robot interactions is entrenched in and reproduces the patriarchal, anti-Black, settler colonialist, and US and European imperialist structures of labor, exploitation, and capital accumulation (10). In a similar vein, and as I detail in chapter 2, Margaret Rhee traces the cultural associations between robots and Asians and Asian immigrants as an efficient and hard-working yet not creative labor force, and examines these associations as a site for re-envisioning the human-robot relationship. Rhee, "In Search of My Robot." Such gendered, racialized, and geopolitical investments in the concept of technology as supplement to human capacity underlie this book's efforts to rethink prosthetic memory as a postcolonial feminist mnemonic.

68   Taylor, "Interdependent Animals," 109.

69   Taylor, "Interdependent Animals," 112–13.

70   Taylor, "Interdependent Animals," 114.

71   Taylor, "Interdependent Animals," 116. Here, Taylor's citation is from Callicott, *In Defense of the Land Ethic*, 30.

72   Taylor, "Interdependent Animals," 116.

73   Taylor, "Interdependent Animals," 124.

74   They include various kinds of practices such as academic writing, testimony, autobiography, film, painting, and other genres of art, and their spectrum and depth make my attempt to chart them fragmentary at best. Since 1990, there have been immense efforts to testify to and rewrite this history through the embodied memories of former Japanese military "comfort women" against the disavowal of sexual slavery and other colonial violence and exploitation during the Japanese occupation of the Korean peninsula. To mention just a few, an English translation of comfort women's oral testimonies, *Voices of the Korean Comfort Women* (ed. and trans. Chungmoo Choi and Hyunah Yang), came out in 2023. Chi-ŏn Kim discusses how the memories of the war and its scars embodied in the former comfort women's bodies are represented through body-languages in *The Murmuring* (*Najŭn moksori*) trilogy of documentaries (directed by Young-joo Byun)—*The Murmuring* (1995), *Habitual Sadness* (1997), and *My Own Breathing* (2000). Chi-ŏn Kim, "'Najŭn moksori yŏnjak yŏn'gu," 630–31. Yundŭk Kwŏn's video "Mome saegin kiŏktŭl" (2013) shows how the scarred and sick body of a former comfort woman who suffered dissociative amnesia and aphasia carries the memories of traumatic sexual slavery.

Grace M. Cho traces the foreclosed memories of the Korean War through the figure of the *yanggongju* (a pejorative term for prostitutes at US military bases in Korea) turned military bride that haunts generations in the Korean diaspora in the United States. In this, Cho proposes a transgenerational diasporic vision of hearing the hallucinatory voices of the dead, mutilated, and sexually exploited bodies during and after the Korean War, demonstrating mnemonics for engaging with embodied memories foreclosed by physical and psychic traumas between South Korea and the United States. Cho, *Haunting the Korean Diaspora*.

75 Mbembe, *Critique of Black Reason*, 3.

76 Mbembe, *Critique of Black Reason*, 3, 21, 32.

77 Haraway, "A Cyborg Manifesto," 151–53.

78 Haraway, "A Cyborg Manifesto," 151–53.

79 Here, I refer to Lynn Randolph's painting *Cyborg* (1989), which was drawn in response to Haraway's "Manifesto for Cyborgs" (an earlier version of "A Cyborg Manifesto," published in the *Socialist Review* in 1985) and became the cover for Haraway's book *Simians, Cyborgs, and Women* (1991). In "Modest Witness," Randolph recalls how Haraway's manifesto inspired her to draw this painting during her residency at the Bunting Institute (now the Radcliffe Institute for Advanced Studies) working on her painting project "Return to Alien Roots: Painting Outside Mainstream Western Culture." Randolph also mentions that a young Chinese woman, Grace Li—one of her late husband's sociology students at the University of Houston—modeled for the painting. Lynn Randolph, "Modest Witness: A Painter's Collaboration with Donna Haraway, 2009," Lynn Randolph (artist's website), accessed August 21, 2023, http://www.lynnrandolph.com/presentations/?eid=817.

In the manifesto, Haraway makes a few direct references to Asian women, such as "the nimble fingers of 'Oriental' women," "the unnatural cyborg women making chips in Asia," and "Young *Korean* women hired in the sex industry and in electronic assembly." Haraway, "A Cyborg Manifesto," 154, 174.

80 The 2021 Atlanta spa shooting that killed eight people, of whom six were women of Asian descent (including one Korean and four Korean Americans), and the public reaction demonstrate the heightened anti-Asian sentiment and violence during the pandemic.

81 Lowe, *Immigrant Acts*, 16. Thus, Lowe presents Asian immigrants "as both symbol and allegory" for Asian Americans within the racial structure of the United States (35).

82 Nadia Y. Kim argues that the US military presence during and after the Korean War has influenced the ideology of white-Black racial hierarchy in

South Korea—which preconditions Korean immigrants' understanding of race and their identities in relation to the racial hierarchy even before entering the United States. N. Kim, *Imperial Citizens*.

83 Lowe, *The Intimacies of Four Continents*, 3. In this book, Lowe illustrates the effect of transcontinental colonial intimacies most clearly through the Chinese "coolies" brought to the British-occupied West Indies after the abolition of slavery in the Caribbean, appearing as the figure introducing the "alleged transition from slavery to freedom" (24).

84 In this book, my engagement with Black feminist critiques does not directly address the interlacing of Asian and Black racialization per se. However, in the decade since the beginning of the Black Lives Matter movement, there have been dynamic discussions on the long history of tension and solidarity between Black and Asian communities in the United States and beyond. Among other publications, *Scholar and Feminist Online* published a special issue featuring a collection of feminist and queer approaches to Afro-Asian Studies and cross-racial formations. The introduction to this special issue reviews Afro-Asian studies of the past two decades and highlights the importance of feminist and queer leadership and perspectives with the development of the Black Lives Matter movement. Sudhakar and Reddy, "Introduction."

85 Braidotti, "Affirmation versus Vulnerability."

86 Butler, *Precarious Life*, 20.

87 Butler, *Precarious Life*, 20.

88 Butler, *Precarious Life*, 42–43.

89 Butler, *Precarious Life*, 33, emphasis added.

90 Butler, *Precarious Life*, 35.

91 Butler, *Precarious Life*, 34.

92 Wolfe, *Before the Law*, 18.

93 Wolfe, *Before the Law*, 19–20.

94 Wolfe, *Before the Law*, 20–21.

95 Wolfe, *Before the Law*, 21.

96 Braidotti, "Affirmation versus Vulnerability," 242.

97 Braidotti, *Transpositions*.

98 Braidotti, *Transpositions*, 168.

99 Braidotti, *Transpositions*, 169.

100 Braidotti, *Transpositions*, 167.

101 Braidotti, "Affirmation versus Vulnerability," 242.

102 Braidotti, "Affirmation versus Vulnerability," 242, 245.

103 There have been similar criticisms of "flat ontology"—a term that has gained currency especially among the Deleuzean branch of new materialist and object-oriented ontology discourses since Manuel DeLanda's use of it in *Intensive Science and Virtual Philosophy* and its variations. Through his posthumanist question of "the animal," Cary Wolfe criticizes flat ontologies "that evacuate the radical discontinuity between qualitatively different orders," as shown in the prevalent discourse of the Anthropocene, and instead proposes a more "jagged" ontology. Wolfe, "What 'the Animal' Can Teach 'the Anthropocene,'" 132. Zakiyyah Iman Jackson's observation—"Antiblackness's arbitrary uses of power do not comply with the hierarchies presumed by critics of anthropocentricism. Furthermore, viruses, bacteria, parasites, and insects all commonly exercise dominance over human populations"—suggests that posthuman flat ontology not only fails to register racial (and other intrahuman) hierarchies but thereby undermines the efficacy of its anti-anthropocentrism. Jackson, *Becoming Human*, 15.

104 Jackson, "Outer Worlds," 215.

105 Jackson, "Outer Worlds," 216.

106 Braidotti, *Transpositions*, 50.

107 Braidotti, "Affirmation versus Vulnerability," 242.

108 Braidotti, "Affirmation versus Vulnerability," 249–50.

109 Here, decolonial and postcolonial approaches to language do not dismiss but rather put into perspective posthumanist formulations of the relationship between human and language. In this, I also heed Julietta Singh's dehumanist perspective that reflects on the colonial and neocolonial narrative of mastery in her book *Unthinking Mastery*. Singh observes that anticolonial thinkers across different geopolitical contexts such as Frantz Fanon, Albert Memmi, and Mohandas K. Gandhi "advance forms of [masculine] linguistic 'countermastery'" as a way of protesting subjectivation through colonial language (82). Nonetheless, Singh sees dehumanist potential in their thoughts as they emerge "from the position of those excluded from the status of fully imbued human" (70). Furthermore, even though postcolonial writers such as Ngũgĩ wa Thiong'o and Chinua Achebe also "rehearse the violence at stake in claiming or recrafting language in postcolony," they share "a desire for unmasterful ways of formulating the relationship between language and the postcolonial imagination" (88). Decolonial and postcolonial approaches to language are further discussed in chapter 1.

Part I. Mouth to Mouth

1   Theresa Hak Kyung Cha, *Mouth to Mouth* (1975), Electronic Arts Inter-
     mix, accessed May 18, 2023, https://www.eai.org/titles/mouth-to-mouth;
     Lewallen, "Introduction," 9, quoted from Rinder, "The Theme of Dis-
     placement," 6.

2   Min, "Narrative Chronology," 151.

3   Felman, *The Scandal of the Speaking Body*, 5. In a similar light, Rey
     Chow observes the relevance to the age of globalization of the classic
     postcolonial debate around the use of English among African writers
     of 1960–80. Chow, *Not Like a Native Speaker*. Despite different stances
     among the writers in the debate, Chow senses "a definitive epistemic
     break"—that "the colonial situation, in which one group of people is
     required to adopt and adjust to another group's language" has shat-
     tered any presumed link between a language and "those who are, for
     historical reasons, its users" (41).

4   Probyn, *Carnal Appetites*, 20.

5   Probyn, *Carnal Appetites*, 19.

6   Probyn, *Carnal Appetites*, 18.

7   Drawing on Deleuze and Guattari, Probyn looks at "the intermingling
     of the sexual and the alimentary" in "mouth machines." Probyn, *Carnal
     Appetites*, 62. The figure "mouth to mouth" extends Probyn's ideas to ad-
     dress not only the interminglings of alimentary and sexual regimes in
     mouth machines but also the articulations of multiple regimes with and
     through mouth machines.

8   For major postcolonial critiques on language concerning former French
     and British imperialism, see Fanon, "Black Man and Language," in *Black
     Skin, White Masks*; Achebe, "English and the African Writer"; Ngũgĩ,
     "Introduction"; Ngũgĩ, "The Language of African Literature"; Glissant,
     "Languages, Self-Expression."

9   My use of the term *languaging* is in line with Chow's attention to "the
     racialized scene of . . . languaging." Chow, *Not Like a Native Speaker*, 9.
     Chow borrows this term from A. L. Becker, who uses it to refer to "an
     open-ended process that combines attunement to context storing and
     retrieving memories, and communication," distinguished from the term
     language that concerns "a system of rules or structures" (125).

10   Chow, *Not Like a Native Speaker*, 14–15, emphasis added. Chow acknowl-
     edges that this proposal was inspired by Jacques Derrida's writing on
     his relationship to French, which was also a source of inspiration at
     the beginning of my own work. Derrida, *Monolingualism of the Other*.

11   Singh conceptualizes "dehumanism" as the "practice of recuperation, of stripping away the violent foundations (always structural and ideological) of colonial and neocolonial *mastery* that continue to render some beings more human than others." Singh, *Unthinking Mastery*, 4. This term thus enables us to see the traces of colonial "mastery" even within anti- and decolonialist thoughts, as we bring posthumanism and decolonial critique into critical conversation with each other.

1. A Cut in the Tongue

1   *Tongue-Tie*, directed by Park Jin-pyo, is one of six short films constituting the omnibus *If You Were Me*, commissioned by the National Human Rights Commission of the Republic of Korea.

2   Barbara Demic, "Some in S. Korea Opt for a Trim When English Trips the Tongue," *Los Angeles Times*, March 31, 2002; Chŏn-shik Ha, "Yŏngŏbarŭm ttaemune hyŏsusulkkaji?" [Tongue surgery for English pronunciation?], *Hankook Ilbo*, April 1, 2002; O-yŏn Gwŏn, "LAT, 'Yŏngŏ kyoyuk yŏlp'ung, han'guksŏ hyŏsusul yuhaeng'" [LAT, "English fever, tongue surgery is big in S. Korea"], *Hangyore*, April 1, 2002; Chin-u An, "Yŏngŏ parŭm wihae hyŏsusurŭl handaguyo?" [Tongue surgery for English pronunciation?], *Ohmynews*, April 2, 2002; Chŏl-chung Kim, "LA t'aimsŭ, 'Han'guk ŏrinidŭl yŏngŏbarŭm charharyŏ hyŏsusul'" [LA Times: "Tongue surgery on kids to improve English pronunciation"], *Chosun Ilbo*, May 2, 2002.

3   Demic, "Some in S. Korea Opt for a Trim."

4   Sŏng-ung Kang, "Han'guk ŏrini yŏngo wihe hyŏsusul" [Korean children get tongue surgery for English], *YTN*, January 2, 2004; Sŏng-hun Chin, "Yŏngŏ parŭm chok'e haryŏgo ai hyŏsusul" [Tongue surgery on kids to improve English pronunciation], *Hankook Ilbo*, January 2, 2004; Sang-Hun Choe, "S. Koreans Accent Surgery in Bid for Flawless English," *Los Angeles Times*, January 18, 2004.

5   The only article with a factual reference (among all those listed above) reports that this kind of surgery is also performed in Jinju, a relatively small city in the south. However, it still provides no evidence other than a local doctor's ambiguous comment: "I am not sure if the surgeries are done to improve English pronunciation, but recently there have been some inquiries on the surgery." Chin-u An, "Yŏngŏ parŭm wihae hyŏsusurŭl handaguyo?"

6   In a similar vein, some critics also mention this kind of tongue surgery (again, without specific evidence or reference) as emblematic of the madness of English fever, which might entail colonial submission to US

hegemony in neoliberal globalization. Y. Kim, "Yŏngyŏlp'ungŭi chiptan kwanggi," 59; K. Park, "Yŏngŏ Sinhwaŭi ŏjewa onŭl," 78. Approaching these tongue-surgery stories as a cultural repertoire allows one to ask why and how these stories keep being told and circulated (despite the lack of evidence) and how they articulate language as a dense topos of (post)colonial subjection and resistance. This approach also helps make sense of the geographical and historical iterations such as a report of Chinese using tongue surgery to improve English pronunciation and a British girl (who is a big fan of Korean pop culture) who had tongue surgery to improve Korean pronunciation. Francis Markus, "Chinese Find Learning English a Snip," *BBC News*, July 31, 2002; "British Student Has Tongue Lengthened to Speak Korean," *Telegraph*, August 11, 2011.

7   Chow, *Not Like a Native Speaker*, 14.

8   For discussion on how imperial Japan's language policy shaped assimilation and resistance in Japanese-occupied Korea, see K. Kim, "'Tonghwa'wa 'chŏhang'ŭi kiŏk." For the history of reception, education, and the social and political meaning of English in Korea, see J. Park, "Han'gugesŏ yŏngŏŭi suyonggwa chŏn'gae"; N. Kang, "Shingminjishidae yŏngŏgyoyukkwa yŏngŏŭi sahoejŏk wisang."

9   *Segyehwa* as a term was introduced by the Kim Young-sam administration (1993–98) alongside the South Korean government's development strategy to increase national competitiveness in the global market. The term came to connote a Korean way of globalization, showing the reciprocal construction of developmentalist nationalism and neoliberal globalization in South Korea. Since then, Heo and Park note, *segyehwa* discourse was widespread regardless of the political orientations of the subsequent administrations until the end of the 2010s. Heo and Park, "Han'gugŏllon'gwa segyehwa tamnon." For more discussion on *segyehwa* as a nationalist and neoliberalist project of globalization, see Lim, "Stumbling Democracy in South Korea"; and Shin, *Ethnic Nationalism in Korea*.

10   Initiated at the provocation of famous Korean writer Kŏil Pok, the debate around whether English should become an official language in South Korea unfolded for years and involved well-known writers and scholars. Pok, *Kukcheŏ shidaeŭi minjogŏ*. As Hee-sook Kim reports, advocates argued that the officialization of English would improve the nation's competence in the global market, while opponents claimed that it would injure national identity and sentiment. H. Kim, "Han'gugŏ segyehwawa yŏngŏgongyonghwaron shijangwŏllimunje," 325–26.

11   Examining the Korean exodus (T'arhan'guk) for educating children, Joon-jong Son argues that this phenomenon is not simply a matter of education but also a social and economic problem, and thus might cause social conflicts and aggravate inequality. Son, "Nuga kyoyukŭl wihae

han'gukŭl ttŏnaryŏgo hanŭn'ga?," 117. *An'gwabak* 12 (2002) focuses on how to understand the post-9/11 United States and its power in Korea. This issue features a special section titled "What English Means for Us," consisting of several articles.

12   Thus, the tongue on the operating table embodies what Hyu-Yong Park criticizes as the conjunction of neoliberal (economic) and imperialist (cultural) discourses around globalization, which underlies the English learning boom in early-2000s South Korea. H. Park, "'Segyehwashidaeŭi yŏngŏhaksŭp' yŏlgie taehan pip'anjŏk tamnonbunsŏk."

13   Another telling example in addition to the two epigraph cases is Gloria Anzaldúa's discussion of her uncontrollable tongue at the dentist as a metonym for the untamable Chicano identity/soul in face of colonial and patriarchal linguistic terrorism. Anzaldúa, "How to Tame a Wild Tongue."

14   Cliff, "Notes on Speechlessness," 8.

15   American Psychological Association, "Wild Boy of Aveyron."

16   Fanon, *Black Skin, White Masks*, 7.

17   Crystal, "A Global Language."

18   Foucault, *The Birth of Biopolitics*, 243.

19   Foucault, *The Birth of Biopolitics*, 227–28. Foucault characterizes this neoliberalist form of homo economicus as distinct from the older form of homo economicus based on the nineteenth-century traditional political economy (226).

20   Foucault, *The Birth of Biopolitics*, 229, emphasis added.

21   Foucault, *The Birth of Biopolitics*, 230.

22   Foucault, *The Birth of Biopolitics*, 227–28.

23   Such change is perhaps most evident in a fairly recent type of migration. As a number of Korean students in primary and secondary school choose to study abroad, often to learn English, a new form of transnational family—the "wild goose family"—has emerged. Often the mother and children live abroad (mostly in the United States) while the father stays in Korea and visits them only a few times each year. Through her ethnography of wild goose families in a college town in California, Cho Unh notes that this phenomenon illustrates how neoliberal globalization invades the intimacy of middle- and upper-class Korean families, where familism results in a global split (especially at the cost of the conjugal relationship) for the sake of upward social mobility. Cho, "Segyehwaŭi ch'oechŏmdane sŏn han'gugŭi kajok," 148–49.

24   Kwangyong Chŏn, *Kkŏppittan ri*. The novella revolves around Dr. Lee, who works as a physician for Japanese colonialists during the occupation and whose family is honored as "a national language-using family

[kugŏ sangyongŭi ka]." He also survives and takes advantage of the suc-
ceeding occupations by the Soviet military and then the US military with
his strategy of learning the master's language. Dr. Lee's lineage illustrates
the family as an essential institution for reproducing (post)colonial subjects in modern Korea.

25   Singh similarly attends to Gandhi's repetitive use of simile comparing
      one's native language to the mother and his portrayals of the maternal-
      ized native tongue as "pure" and "nurturing" (like mother's milk), in the
      context of the violent control of bodies marked as "impure" by their gen-
      der, caste, or sexuality in the modernization of India. Singh, *Unthinking
      Mastery*, 77.

26   S. Lee, "Chiguch'onŭi ŏnŏ chŏngch'aek," 181, 187.

27   E. Kim, *Curative Violence*, 21.

28   Park and Abelmann, "Class and Cosmopolitan Striving."

29   Park and Abelmann, "Class and Cosmopolitan Striving," 647.

30   Park and Abelmann, "Class and Cosmopolitan Striving," 647. As such, Park
      and Abelmann's approach echoes other scholars who have challenged the
      Western philosophical construct of cosmopolitanism's association with
      "the humanist idea of universalistic identifications."

31   Often considered the most privileged form of private English education,
      precollege study abroad grew rapidly in the late 1990s and early 2000s.

32   Abelmann and Kang, "Memoir/Manuals of South Korean Pre-college
      Study Abroad," 15.

33   Looking at Black writers to revisit the theory of linguistic performativ-
      ity does not mean conflating Anglo-European colonialism and slavery
      with postcoloniality in South Korea. However, it shows how linguistic
      construal of reality is already interlaced with racialized embodiment of
      being (infra)human, to open a condition for envisioning otherwise in a
      global context.

34   Cha, *Dictee*. While my discussion in this chapter focuses on the short
      piece "Calliope" from *Dictee*, I also engage with the performative force
      of Cha's writing. This work mobilizes the bare materiality of language in
      order to generate collective memories, at times even simulating ancient
      female performers and/as shamans.

35   Butler, *Excitable Speech*.

36   Butler, *Excitable Speech*, especially the introduction.

37   Henceforth, all reference to Morrison is from Morrison, "Nobel Lecture."

38   Emphasis added.

39   Butler, *Excitable Speech*, 6–7.

40 Braidotti, "Affirmation versus Vulnerability," especially 3–5.

41 The history of anti-Black biopolitics demands a careful approach to the trope that naturalizes the blind Black people with extraordinary abilities in the nonvisual sensorium, fortune-telling, and arts. In this light, my reading of blindness in Morrison's lecture is in line with Therí A. Pickens's reading of "blindness" in *Leadbelly* (poems) as "the scaffolding of the story" rather than "the prompts for Leadbelly's lesson for freedom." Pickens, "Blue Blackness, Black Blueness," 94. Another exemplary work on this subject is Terry Rowden's examination of the cultural politics around blind Black musicians, including Stevie Wonder, at the intersections of race, gender, class, and disability. Rowden, *The Songs of Blind Folk*.

42 Wynter's theory of homo narrans is developed in a few places, including the unpublished essay "Human Being as Noun?" This theory is then elaborated on in Wynter and McKittrick, "Unparalleled Catastrophe."

43 Wynter and McKittrick, "Unparalleled Catastrophe," 27.

44 Wynter and McKittrick, "Unparalleled Catastrophe," 62.

45 Wynter and McKittrick, "Unparalleled Catastrophe," 22.

46 To engage with the differential culpabilities, conditions, and impacts of the hegemonic system of production, consumption, and distribution undergirding the planetary disaster, critics have offered a variety of nomenclature alternatives to "the Anthropocene," such as the Capitalocene, Plantationocene, Anglocene, and Chthulucene. Elizabeth A. Povinelli suggests that each of these contending nomenclatures presents "a different set of ethical, political, and conceptual problems and antagonisms" concerning the dilemma of geontopower—the governance of "all specific forms of existence, whether humans or others" through the maintenance of "Life (Life v. Death) v. Nonlife" in late liberalism. Povinelli, *Geontologies*, chap. 1. Povinelli's insights into how the Western settler colonialist geontopower bears on the critical analytics of existence among her indigenous friends speak to my emphasis on chimeric vision as an important feature of the postcolonial mnemonic concerning which reality and whose world. In this vein, I read Wynter's theory of homo narrans as an instance of such a vision, an aperture to a different existence.

47 Wynter and McKittrick, "Unparalleled Catastrophe," 31, 63.

48 Wynter and McKittrick, "Unparalleled Catastrophe," 25.

49 Wynter and McKittrick, "Unparalleled Catastrophe," 25.

50 Wynter and McKittrick, "Unparalleled Catastrophe," 21.

51 Wynter and McKittrick, "Unparalleled Catastrophe," 35. Wynter argues that this reinvented model of homo economicus is the successor to

the Renaissance intelligentsia's *homo politicus* enabled by Copernican cosmogony.

52   Wynter and McKittrick, "Unparalleled Catastrophe," 27.

53   Wynter and McKittrick, "Unparalleled Catastrophe," 56.

54   Wynter and McKittrick, "Unparalleled Catastrophe," 56.

55   Wynter and McKittrick, "Unparalleled Catastrophe," 56.

56   Wynter and McKittrick, "Unparalleled Catastrophe," 25.

57   Hantel, "What Is It Like to Be a Human?," 73.

58   Hantel, "What Is It Like to Be a Human?," 77.

59   Halpern, "Schizophrenic Techniques."

60   Ferreira da Silva, "Before Man," 103.

61   Philip, "Discourse on the Logic of Language," 30.

62   Philip, "Discourse on the Logic of Language," 32.

63   Philip, "Discourse on the Logic of Language," 31.

64   Philip, "Discourse on the Logic of Language," 31.

65   This narrative is written vertically in the left margin of the main text, visualizing its distance from the rest of the poem. Philip, "Discourse on the Logic of Language," 30, 32.

66   Jackson, "Suspended Munition."

67   Jackson, *Becoming Human*, 101.

68   Cha, *Dictee*, 45–46.

2. A Song from the Cybernetic Fold

An earlier version of chapter 2 and a brief section from chapter 1 were published in "The Biopolitics of Languaging in the Cybernetic Fold," *Journal of Gender Studies* 29, no. 1 (2020), and reproduced as a chapter in C. L. Quinan and K. Thiele, eds., *Biopolitics, Necropolitics, Cosmopolitics* (New York: Routledge, 2021).

1   Sontag, "The World as India." The full text is accessible from the Susan Sontag Foundation website.

2   Sontag offers historic examples of the debate between form and content. On one side, Saint Jerome (ca. 331–420)—who translated the Bible from Hebrew and Greek into Latin—argued for keeping the sense to suit the new language at the cost of "the impoverishment of the original." On the other, German theologian Friedrich Schleiermacher (1768–1834) insisted on staying close to the source text, lest he forsake "the spirit of the language" in the original tongue.

3   A few among the many other sociological and ethnographic works on offshore call centers in India include Rajan-Rankin, "Invisible Bodies and Disembodied Voices?"; Poster, "Hidden Sides of the Credit Economy"; and Pal and Buzzanell, "The Indian Call Center Experience."

4   A similar observation has been made on the techno-Orientalist portrayal of Indian call center employees in the United States, which is "so ubiquitous as to be parodied cinematically in romantic comedies such as *Outsourced* (2006), conjuring images of Dickian androids (or *Blade Runner*'s 'replicants') who simulate human behavior and threaten the distinction between 'real' and 'fake' Americans." Roh, Huang, and Niu, "Technologizing Orientalism," 4–5. See also Turing, "Computing Machinery and Intelligence," 433–34.

5   Sedgwick and Frank, "Shame in the Cybernetic Fold," 12.

6   Sedgwick and Frank, "Shame in the Cybernetic Fold," 7, 14.

7   Ferreira da Silva, *Toward a Global Idea of Race*, 29.

8   I approach diasporic memory as that which constitutes an imagined diasporic community via what Avtah Brah calls "a confluence of narratives," wherein multiple journeys are configured into one journey "as it is lived and relived, produced, reproduced and transformed through individual as well as collective memory and rememory." Brah, "Thinking through the Concept of Diaspora," 444.

9   Greenspan, *India and the IT Revolution*, 37. In particular, Greenspan discusses the political background and implications of the explosively spreading IT industry alongside the huge pool of English-speaking engineers and the expanding middle class in India since the country implemented new policies of liberalization. See chapter 2 in *India and the IT Revolution*.

10 Susan Sontag, "The World as India," *Times Literary Supplement* 5228, June 13, 2003.

11 Harish Trivedi, "Cyber-coolies, Hindi and English," letter to the editor, *Times Literary Supplement* 5230, June 27, 2003.

12 A few weeks later, TLS published a letter from Apratim Barua confronting Trivedi's "postcolonial fury." Barua asserts that English "might have been the language of the conqueror a long time ago, but for those of us born in an independent India, that is all a past history." He says, "To us, English is the language of the Indian Constitution, the language of Nehru's 'tryst with destiny' speech. . . . We have our own accent, our own vocabulary, our own grammatical peculiarities and most importantly, our own literary canon in *English*." He adds that "the notion of a single 'national' language is derived from concepts rooted in nineteenth-century European nationalism" and that "today, standard Hindi is . . . as much an elite language

as English is." Apratim Barua, "Cyber-coolies, Hindi and English," letter to the editor, *Times Literary Supplement* 5235, August 1, 2003.

13   Gurcharan Das, "Cyber Coolies or Cyber Sahibs?," *Times of India*, September 7, 2003, https://timesofindia.indiatimes.com/home/sunday-times/all-that-matters/Cyber-coolies-or-cyber-sahibs/articleshow/169677.cms.

14   Das, "Cyber Coolies or Cyber Sahibs?," emphasis added.

15   Rhee, "In Search of My Robot."

16   Rhee, "In Search of My Robot."

17   Chun, "Race and/as Technology," 51.

18   Lowe, *Immigrant Acts*, 16, 35. Roh, Huang, and Niu, "Technologizing Orientalism," 4.

19   For further discussion on the Anglo-European imaginary of robots as the replacement for Black slaves, see Atanasoski and Vora, *Surrogate Humanity*, esp. 33–38.

20   Chun, "Race and/as Technology," 48.

21   Chun, "Race and/as Technology," 47.

22   Chun, "Race and/as Technology," 48, 49.

23   Parisi and Ferreira da Silva, "Black Feminist Tools."

24   Parisi and Ferreira da Silva, "Black Feminist Tools."

25   Parisi and Ferreira da Silva, "Black Feminist Tools."

26   Halberstam, "Automating Gender," 443.

27   Wilson, *Affect and Artificial Intelligence*. In this way, Wilson intends to displace the tendency of "paranoid reading" in critical analysis of the artificial sciences—"the tendency to read artificial agents as screens for projection (projection of masculine, late-capitalist, or heterosexual anxieties, for example)" (26).

28   Ferreira da Silva, *Toward a Global Idea of Race*.

29   Rhee, "Reflecting on Robots, Love, and Poetry," 44.

30   *The Imitation Game* (dir. Tyldum, 2014) has made well known the disgrace experienced by the British mathematician and computer scientist (who played a critical role in cracking Nazi codes during the war) due to his homosexuality.

31   M. Chen, *Animacies*, 3.

32   Rhee, "Reflecting on Robots, Love, and Poetry," 46.

33   Rhee, "BEAM, ROBOT," in *Love, Robot*, 19.

34   Menely and Ronda, "Red," 24.

35   Rhee, "BEAM, ROBOT," 17.

36 Rai, "Composite Photography," 195.

37 Rhee, "LOVE, ROBOT *for Dmitry*," in *Love, Robot*, 24.

38 Rhee, "LOVE, ROBOT *for Dmitry*," 24.

39 Bennett, "The Force of Things," 358.

40 Rhee, "MACHINE TESTIMONIAL 6," in *Love, Robot*, 52–53; O'Hara, "Having a Coke with You," 360.

41 Muñoz, *Cruising Utopia*, 6.

42 Rhee, "MACHINE TESTIMONIAL 6," 53.

43 Ferreira da Silva, *Toward a Global Idea of Race*, xv–xvi.

44 Rhee, "SLEEP, ROBOT," in *Love, Robot*, 25.

45 Rhee, "SLEEP, ROBOT," 25.

46 Rhee, "SLEEP, ROBOT," 25–26.

47 Rhee, "SLEEP, ROBOT," 26.

48 Trinh T. Minh-ha uses "elsewhere within here" in several of her works, and the meaning of the term changes each time. In *Elsewhere, Within Here*, this term points to the seemingly paradoxical forms of life at the intersection of dwelling and traveling in the age of border events, and to the imaginability of such a paradox (28). I borrow the phrase to reflect on the crossing of the normative binaries between here and there, reality and fantasy, and time and space in Rhee's poetry.

49 In this light, posthumanist critics have explored machine poetry as a site for contesting human-exclusive claims on emotive and creative qualities. See, for example, Beals, "'Do the New Poets Think?'"; Winder, "Robotic Poetics."

50 Parisi and Ferreira da Silva, "Black Feminist Tools."

51 Margaret Rhee, "Machine," *The Kimchi Poetry Project*, accessed September 9, 2023, http://kimchipoetrymachine.weebly.com/machine.html.

52 Rhee, "Machine."

53 Rhee, "Machine."

54 Rhee, "Batch One," *The Kimchi Poetry Project*, accessed September 9, 2023, http://kimchipoetrymachine.weebly.com/batch-one.html.

55 Margaret Rhee and Micha Cárdenas, "Red Bloom: Poetry Altar for Queens," The Kimchi Poetry Machine, YouTube Video, 0:20, February 25, 2015, https://www.youtube.com/watch?v=cTC2ro36rdo.

56 J. Lee, "Toward a Queer Korean American Diasporic History."

57 Stengers, "The Cosmopolitical Proposal," 995; Césaire, "Poetry and Knowledge."

58 Sontag, "The World as India." In this lecture, Sontag also acknowledges that her "pride" in the richness of English she's privileged to use is "at

odds with [her] awareness" of another privilege: "to write in a language that everyone, in principle, is obliged to—desires to—understand."

59   Sontag, "The World as India."

60   Stengers, "The Cosmopolitical Proposal," 995, 1003.

61   Ferreira da Silva, "An End to 'This' World."

62   Ferreira da Silva, *Toward a Global Idea of Race*, 154.

63   Ferreira da Silva, *Toward a Global Idea of Race*, 159.

64   Ferreira da Silva, "An End to 'This' World."

65   Ferreira da Silva, "An End to 'This' World."

66   Haraway, "A Cyborg Manifesto," 154, 174.

Part II. The Specters of Cloning

1   In this book, *cloning* refers specifically to cloning by the somatic cell nuclear transfer (SCNT) technique, in which the nucleus (with DNA) of a somatic cell is transferred into the cytoplasm of an enucleated oocyte for the creation of new organisms genetically identical to the somatic-cell donor.

2   Hawthorne, "A Project to Clone Companion Animals."

3   The epigraph from Hawthorne's presentation is quoted from Haraway, *When Species Meet*, 156. The standard price of cloning was $100,000 to $150,000 for a dog (lower for a cat) when the service first became available at BioArts International and RNL Bio, and some clients reportedly received a promotional discount for participating in media events. The price has since dropped, and as of August 2023 the US biotech company Viagen offered the service for $50,000.

4   Hawthorne would later compare the value of a clone to that of a Ferrari, appealing more explicitly to the exchange value of luxury commodities than to artistic-cultural values. See Lou Hawthorne, "Six Reasons We Are No Longer Cloning Dogs," bioartsinternational.com, September 10, 2009, http://www.bioartsinternational.com/press_release/ba09_09_09 .htm (no longer active).

5   Lippit, *Electric Animal*, 188.

6   Bourdieu, "The Forms of Capital," esp. 282.

7   Baudrillard, "The Final Solution," 3–4.

8   Mitchell, *Cloning Terror*, chaps. 2 and 3.

9   Mitchell, *Cloning Terror*, chaps. 2 and 7.

10   Stacey, *The Cinematic Life of the Gene*, chap. 4.

11   Cooper, *Life as Surplus*, 153–54.

12   Parisi, *Abstract Sex*, 34.

13   Parisi, *Abstract Sex*, 26.

14   The term *delirium* refers to Melinda Cooper's criticism of contemporary neo-imperialist capitalism's push for "reinventing life beyond the limit" through biotechnology. Cooper, *Life as Surplus*, 12.

3. "Best Friends Again"

Epigraph: "Brigitte Bardot," in Dreyer, *A Century of Sundays*, 219.

1   Fiona Macrae, "Dead Dog's Owner Creates FIVE Cloned Puppies of Her Beloved Pet," *Daily Mail*, August 5, 2008, http://www.dailymail.co.uk /sciencetech/article-1041709/Dead-dogs-owner-creates-FIVE-cloned -puppies-beloved-pet.html.

2   Although Booger was the first companion dog cloned for a paying customer, BioArts International (another biotech company, based in California with the lab in South Korea) had already successfully produced, by SCNT, several clones of companion dogs, including Missy's clones (as a part of a pilot pet-cloning project but not for a paying customer) and others produced for science and research purposes.

3   "Owner Calls Clones of Her Beloved Dog 'a Miracle,'" *Today*, August 7, 2008, http://www.today.com/news/owner-calls-clones-her-beloved-dog -miracle-wbna26073110.

4   Macrae, "Dead Dog's Owner."

5   "Owner Calls Clones."

6   "Owner Calls Clones."

7   Ian Cobain, "Now She Has Her Pit Bull Cloned. But Once She Manacled a Mormon for Sex," *Guardian*, August 8, 2008, https://www.theguardian .com/world/2008/aug/08/usa.

8   Ryan Parry and Steve Myall, "Beauty Queen Kidnapped Mormon Ex-lover and Kept Him Handcuffed as Kinky Sex Slave in Remote Cottage," *Daily Record*, April 12, 2018, https://www.dailyrecord.co.uk/news/uk-world -news/beauty-queen-kidnapped-mormon-ex-12352307. According to the *Daily Record* report, McKinney and her accomplice were charged with false imprisonment and possession of an imitation firearm, because "back then there was no provision in law for male rape or sexual assault."

9   Catherine Elsworth, "Dog Cloner Joyce McKinney Sought over Burglary to Fund Horse's Wooden Leg," *Telegraph*, August 15, 2008, http:// www.telegraph.co.uk/news/worldnews/northamerica/usa/2565925/Dog -cloner-Joyce-McKinney-sought-over-burglary-to-fund-horses-wooden -leg.html.

10   Morris, *Tabloid*. In an interview with *Vanity Fair*, Morris described how he became interested in McKinney's case in the 1970s only after her past resurfaced with the media report on the cloning of Booger. Alexandra Beggs and Bruce Handy, "Sex Bondage and Dog Cloning," *Vanity Fair*, July 12, 2011, vanityfair.com/hollywood/2011/07/sex-bondage-and-dog-cloning-errol-morris-finds-the-common-ground.

11   Amy Taubin, "Magnificent Obsessions!," *Film Comment*, July/August 2011, https://www.filmcomment.com/article/tabloid-a-crime-of-passion-and-a-tale-of-animal-loveas-related-by-errol-mor/.

12   Morris, *Tabloid*. McKinney seems to refer to French actress Brigitte Bardot's words that I also quote in the epigraph of this chapter (even though they aren't exactly the same). Bardot's animal advocacy is also addressed in chapter 4, as it stirred up nationalist sentiment against the Western-centric animal rights movement in South Korea.

13   I use the term *deviance* not to romanticize McKinney's past but to note the diminutive scandalization in media representations that presented allegedly serious abuse as a matter of sexual perversion.

14   Taubin, "Magnificent Obsessions!"

15   To mention two among many, Sam Binkley discusses how "the space of familiar, marital, and premarital intimacy has emerged as an object of work mediated by evolving technologies of government," shedding light on the dynamic and unstable assemblages of disciplinary and entrepreneurial technologies centering on "the maximization of mutuality, trust, and empathy within the bond of intimate life" in contemporary Western society. Binkley, "The Government of Intimacy," 556. Tim Dean examines how the rawness of barebacking (sex without condoms) in gay subculture is mediated by biopolitical relations, especially those of pharmacopower, with the development of an HIV treatment regime in the United States. Dean, "Mediated Intimacies."

16   M. Chen, *Animacies*, esp. chaps. 5 and 6.

17   Sullivan, "Somatechnics," 187.

18   Cubitt, *Simulation and Social Theory*, 136. Cubitt's explanation of singularity is based on Gilles Deleuze's and Jean Baudrillard's approaches to singularity as it pertains to "a difference . . . prior to the things which, in the Code or in 'generality' it appears to differentiate" (136). My research concerns the operation of this concept in the somatechnology of mourning rather than the philosophical accuracy or applicability of the concept.

19   I first encountered an abridged version of this passage in Fiester, "Ethical Issues in Animal Cloning" (340), cited from GSC, "Is Cloning Right for You?," http://www/savingsand-clone.com/services/right_for_you.php. This site is no longer available, but the article can still be accessed

via the Internet Archive, archived May 10, 2006: http://web.archive.org/web/20060510144913/https://www.savingsandclone.com/ethics/right_for_you.html.

20 GSC, "Is Cloning Right for You?"

21 GSC, "Emergencies," accessed via Internet Archive, archived May 10, 2006, http://web.archive.org/web/20060510142847/https://www.savingsandclone.com/services/pet_emergencies.html.

22 This resonates with James Stanescu's critical insights into the frequent feminization of mourning and regulation of the private sphere. See Stanescu, "Species Trouble," 578.

23 Butler, *Precarious Life*, 20.

24 Waldby, "Stem Cells," 313.

25 Waldby, "Stem Cells," 310.

26 Peter Aldhous, "Interview: It's a Dog's Life . . . Again," *New Scientist*, July 3, 2008, http://www.newscientist.com/article/dn14249-interview-its-a-dogs-life-again.html. According to his 2012 billionaire profile in *Forbes*, John Sperling left his humanities professorship at San José State University in 1976 and started the University of Phoenix, which is now part of the Apollo Group he founded with his son. Aside from adult education, his projects have "ranged from longevity research to environmental causes to cloning." "John Sperling," *Forbes*, March 12, 2012, http://www.forbes.com/profile/john-sperling/. The company announced that he was retiring at the end of 2012. Josh Brodesky, "John Sperling Retires from Apollo Group Board," *Arizona Republic*, December 14, 2012, http://www.azcentral.com/business/news/articles/20121213john-sperling-retires-from-apollo-group-board.html (no longer active).

27 Hawthorne, "A Project to Clone Companion Animals," 229.

28 Pray, "Missyplicity Goes Commercial." According to this source, by the time the partnership ceased, Texas A&M University had achieved two dog pregnancies, but neither came to term.

29 Aldhous, "Interview."

30 As I discuss in detail in chapter 4, Dr. Hwang was involved in a scandal for violating ethics laws and fabricating data in his human stem cell cloning research and was dismissed from Seoul National University.

31 James Barron, "Biotech Company to Auction Chances to Clone a Dog," *New York Times*, May 21, 2008, https://www.nytimes.com/2008/05/21/us/21dog.html.

32 GSC, "Missy: Our Inspiration," accessible via Internet Archive, archived April 27, 2006, http://web.archive.org/web/20060427111502/http://www.savingsandclone.com/about_us/missy.html.

33   GSC, "Missy," emphasis added.

34   McHugh, "Bitches from Brazil."

35   McHugh, "Bitches from Brazil," 186.

36   McHugh, "Bitches from Brazil," 187.

37   McHugh, "Bitches from Brazil," 189.

38   This kind of perception (pet cloning as reproduction of identity-less animals) is well captured in the title of the article "Bitches from Brazil," playing on Ira Levin's 1976 novel *The Boys from Brazil* (subsequently made into a movie by Franklin Schaffner) in which Hitler's clones are produced and raised in Brazil for the purpose of forming the Fourth Reich. In this sense, this perspective is also in line with the prevalent abjection of clones as aura-less copies, which I criticized earlier in the opening of part II.

39   Hawthorne's remark here refers to the pet-cloning service provided by BioArts International, a reorganized descendant of GSC. Lou Hawthorne, "Six Reasons We Are No Longer Cloning Dogs," bioartsinternational .com, September 10, 2009, http://www.bioartsinternational.com/press _release/ba09_09_09.htm (no longer active).

40   GSC, "Missy."

41   Haraway, *When Species Meet*, 46.

42   BioArts International, "BioArts Announces the Golden Clone Giveaway," press release, *Business Wire*, June 11, 2008, http://www.businesswire.com /news/home/20080611005421/en/BioArts-International-Announces -Golden-Clone-Giveaway (no longer active).

43   BioArts International, "[Correcting and Replacing] Canine Hero of 9/11 to be Cloned by BioArts International," press release, *Business Wire*, June 30, 2008, http://www.businesswire.com/news/home /20080630005821/en/CORRECTING-REPLACING-Canine-Hero-911 -Cloned-BioArts (no longer active).

44   BioArts International, "[Correcting and Replacing] Canine Hero of 9/11." According to Hayley Mick, Symington had been suspended for his unauthorized trip to New York for 9/11 rescue work while officially on sick leave, and the police department launched a criminal charge (which was eventually dropped). Symington was fired in 2005 and had relocated to Los Angeles, where he was working in the entertainment industry when he applied to the contest. Hayley Mick, "Canine Hero Wins a Chance at Immortality," *Globe and Mail*, July 3, 2008 (updated March 13, 2009), https://www.theglobeandmail.com/news/world/canine-hero-wins-a -chance-at-immortality/article656008/.

45   BioArts International, "[Correcting and Replacing] Canine Hero of 9/11." Although there are conflicting accounts of Trakr's contribution at the site

of the disaster, these controversies affirm the social semiosis of Trakr's clone worthiness. For example, *Time Magazine* named Trakr one of history's most heroic animals. See Frances Romero, "Top 10 Heroic Animals: 6. Trakr the Dog," *Time*, March 21, 2011, http://content.time.com/time/specials/packages/article/0,28804,2059858_2059863_2060232,00.html. However, Woestendiek offers a different perspective, suggesting that the heroic stories of rescue dogs after 9/11 are exaggerated. See Woestendiek, *Dog, Inc.*, 93–103.

46 CBS News, "911 Rescue Dog Cloned," *Early Show*, CBS News video, June 17, 2009, http://www.cbsnews.com/video/watch/?id=5093711n, emphasis added.

47 CBS News, "911 Rescue Dog Cloned."

48 Knowles Adkisson, "Cloned Dogs Training for Search and Rescue," *Malibu Times*, January 12, 2011, https://malibutimes.com/article_87739cc1-8d48-50bf-919f-27824c54a92e.

49 Adkisson, "Cloned Dogs."

50 Adkisson, "Cloned Dogs."

51 Marcy Darnovsky, "Cloning Canine Patriotism?," *Biopolitical Times* (blog), Center for Genetics and Society, July 11, 2008, https://www.geneticsandsociety.org/biopolitical-times/cloning-canine-patriotism.

52 Woestendiek, *Dog, Inc.*, 263.

53 All of the conversations with David cited in this chapter happened during my meeting with him in April 2013, unless otherwise noted. At that time, I interviewed him as someone who had experience with the pet-cloning service offered by Sooam. Currently (in April 2023), he is more directly involved in the pet-cloning industry. However, in this book I still call him by a pseudonym and consider our conversations to be between the researcher and a pet owner, as they include accounts of his personal experience.

54 David could not remember the title of the film, and I tried but couldn't find it myself. However, I decided to simply describe the film as he did, because what he remembered is more important than the actual content of the film. Also, while this story sounds similar to the film *Solaris* (discussed later in this chapter), it is different in details. So it remains unclear whether David was in fact talking about *Solaris* as he remembered it or was discussing a different film.

55 Hawthorne, "A Project to Clone Companion Animals," 229.

56 For Grau's inquiries into what it means to love someone as a unique individual (in terms of irreplaceability, identity, and history), see his "Irreplaceability and Unique Value"; "Love and History"; and "Love, Loss, and Identity in *Solaris*."

57   Grau, "Irreplaceability and Unique Value," 112.

58   Grau, "Irreplaceability and Unique Value," 113.

59   Grau, "Irreplaceability and Unique Value," 113.

60   Grau, "Irreplaceability and Unique Value," 126.

61   Grau, "Irreplaceability and Unique Value," 114–16.

62   Grau, "Irreplaceability and Unique Value," 127.

63   Grau, "Love and History," 264.

64   Grau, "Love, Loss, and Identity in *Solaris*."

65   To complicate things further, the replicas turn out to be only of Kelvin's own memory of Rheya.

66   Not surprisingly, he finds that his vision resonates with "a cluster of approaches that (roughly) takes the continuance of *a functioning brain* as necessary for identity." Grau, "Love and History," 269, emphasis added.

67   Nicole Perry, "Letting the Cat out of the Bag," *AV Magazine*, Spring 2007, 23, https://aavs.org/assets/uploads/2016/01/aavs_av-magazine_2007 -spring_cloning.pdf.

68   When asked if he believed it, David described how the only thing he believed is that we do not know the answer.

69   Freccero, "Carnivorous Virility," 178.

70   Nast, "Critical Pet Studies?," 896.

71   Kuzniar, *Melancholia's Dog*, 10.

72   In her book *Afro-Dog*, Boisseron also examines the subaltern and diasporic human communities' relationship with dogs, against the history of white men's claimed right to own animals through which (white) humanity is construed.

4. Disappearing Bitches

An earlier version of chapter 4 was published as "Disappearing Bitches: Canine Affect and Postcolonial Bioethics," in *Configurations: A Journal of Literature, Science and Technology* 24, no. 3 (2016).

1   Lou Hawthorne, "Six Reasons We Are No Longer Cloning Dogs," bioarts-international.com, September 10, 2009, http://www.bioartsinternational .com/press_release/ba09_09_09.htm (no longer active).

2   The biopolitical relevance of the human stem cell research scandal to the pet-cloning industry is discussed in chapter 5.

3   Hawthorne, "Six Reasons." In this announcement, Hawthorne lists six primary reasons for the cessation of the service: the tiny market, unethi-

cal black-market competition, a weak intellectual property protection, unscalable bioethics, unpredictable results, and the distraction factor (such as exhausting media attention).

4 Hawthorne, "Six Reasons."

5 I use *female dogs* not to give sex/gender identities to these dogs but to highlight their biotechnological prominence due to having female reproductive organs.

6 This chapter's approach to bioethics establishes the foundation for chapter 5's critique on bioethics as part of the biopolitical apparatus that concerns the regulation and governance of human and nonhuman lives.

7 M. Therese Lysaught argues that bioethics has become a mode of biopolitics, which creates docile bodies in developing countries for transnational biomedical research. Lysaught, "Docile Bodies," 384. Also, Aditya Bharadwaj criticizes a cartographical exercise where "maverick" science is predominantly localizable to the developing world and good science to the Euro-American world. Bharadwaj, "Experimental Subjectification," 85. While South Korea is no longer a part of the developing world, Bharadwaj's observation applies to the Anglo-Eurocentric patronizing perspectives on the country's bioethics. Chapter 5 offers a more focused critique on bioethics as a biopolitical apparatus amid neoliberal and imperialist globalization.

8 Derrida, *Specters of Marx*. Derrida's ethics of living with specters is also in line with his ethics of responsibility/hospitality toward the absolute other. See Derrida and Dufourmantelle, *Of Hospitality*.

9 Hawthorne, "Six Reasons."

10 Woo Suk Hwang, personal communication, March 19, 2013.

11 Taeyoung Shin, email message to author, September 15, 2013.

12 My Friend Again, http://myfriendagain.com. The website previously offered a promotional discount code for cell-banking company Viagen and later showed an ad for a similar company, perPETuate. The profits from these advertisements were donated to animal charities, according to the Facebook page linked to the website. When I visited it again in April 2015, the website described a cell-banking service linked directly to Sooam. As of May 2023, the website has moved to https:// clonemylove.com/ and introduces itself as My Friend Again—the Dog Cloning Company.

13 "Dog Cloning Story," My Friend Again, http://myfriendagain.com/dog _cloning_story.html. This page did not show the date of update. However, the author of this website was also unsure about Sooam's treatment of surrogates when we spoke about it in April 2013. So this page seems to have been updated between our conversation and my first access to

the page on September 28, 2013. As mentioned in note 12, this website has moved to another address, and the page is no longer available.

14   Woestendiek's comment is quoted from Michael Dhar, "Cloning Contest Seeks Worthiest UK Dog," *Live Science*, May 31, 2013, http://www .livescience.com/37020-dog-cloning-contest.html.

15   Woestendiek, email message to author, August 31, 2013.

16   Woestendiek, email message to author, August 31, 2013.

17   Matt Stevens, "Barbra Streisand Cloned Her Dog: For $50,000, You Can Clone Yours," *New York Times*, February 28, 2018, https://www.nytimes .com/2018/02/28/science/barbra-streisand-clone-dogs.html.

18   The pregnancy rate refers to the numbers of dogs pregnant over numbers of surrogate-mother dogs, which changes depending on factors such as the freshness of the somatic cell of the donor dog. On October 20, 2018, in the *Times*, Richard Lloyd Parry reported the 1,192nd puppy cloned by Sooam Biotech ("Hwang Woo-suk Interview: Inside South Korea's Sooam Dog-Cloning Facility," https://www.thetimes.co.uk/article /hwang-woo-suk-interview-inside-south-koreas-sooam-dog-cloning -facility-soknshp79). The *Times* report mentions that the rate is around 40 percent. On my visit to Sooam on March 30, 2013, I was told that the rate is between 10 percent and 50 percent (with more than five hundred puppies cloned by then). The Sooam website also describes that in 2005 the pregnancy rate had been below 2 percent, but in the five years since the average pregnancy rate rose to 30 percent ("Cloning Technology," Sooam Biotech, http://en.sooam.com/dogcn/sub03.html). For my calculation, I used 30 percent up to five hundred dogs (until 2013) and 40 percent for the remaining seven hundred dogs (until 2018). However, considering the much lower pregnancy rate at the beginning, the total number of surrogate mothers might be even higher.

19   Wolfe, *Before the Law*.

20   Deckha, "Toward a Postcolonial, Posthumanist Feminist Theory."

21   M. Chen, *Animacies*, vii–viii.

22   Rosaldo, "Imperialist Nostalgia."

23   Woestendiek, *Dog, Inc.*, esp. chaps. 20, "The Turnspit Dog," and 25, "The End of the Dog Fight."

24   Hawthorne, "A Project to Clone Companion Animals." Haraway offers an analysis of Hawthorne's ethics in her book *When Species Meet*, esp. 154–57.

25   Hawthorne, "Six Reasons."

26   Hawthorne, "Six Reasons."

27   I use the term *Western* (and *the West*) not to reconfirm the fixed binary between West and East but as a strategic misnomer to refer to criticisms

that claim a Western perspective or that construct their perspectives in opposition to Eastern, Asian, or Korean viewpoints.

28 Spivak, "Can the Subaltern Speak?," 296. "Yellow dogs" refers to *nurung-i* in Korean, a generic name for mixed-breed dogs, and the most common type for meat in Korea.

29 Spivak, "Can the Subaltern Speak?," 297.

30 Spivak, "Can the Subaltern Speak?," 272, 294.

31 Skabelund, "Can the Subaltern Bark?"; and Sunstein, "Can Animals Sue?"

32 There is a breadth of criticism on the dichotomy between discourse/ representation and affect that Massumi's theory presupposes in his book *Parables for the Virtual*. For example, Margaret Wetherell argues that human affect cannot be separated from meaning making (which is in fact the distinctiveness of human affect), and therefore examining the intertwinement of affect and discourse is a more sustainable methodological practice for analyzing social and political events. Wetherell, "Affect and Discourse," 351.

33 Jessie Yeung, Gawon Bae, Yoonjung Seo, and Marc Stewart, "South Korea Passes Bill to Ban Eating Dog Meat, Ending Controversial Practice as Consumer Habits Change," CNN, January 9, 2024, https://edition.cnn .com/2024/01/09/asia/south-korea-bill-bans-dog-meat-bill-intl-hnk /index.html.

34 Walraven, "Bardot Soup and Confucians' Meat," 109–10. Walraven refers to Chun An, "Kaegogi ŭmsikgwa kukche chŏngch'i munhwa." Chun An, a professor of sociology, studies the Korean empire (the state of Korea, which succeeded the Joseon dynasty in 1897 and was forcefully annexed to Japan in 1919) and argues for the restoration of the Korean imperial family—which is certainly heterodoxical even among nationalists in South Korea. However, I cite Walraven's reference to Chun An's work because how the history surrounding dog meat (ignored by almost all scholars in South Korea) is introduced into academic discourse by a Korean studies scholar is itself suggestive about the discursive production of dog eating in Korea.

35 Walraven, "Bardot Soup and Confucians' Meat," 109.

36 The Ministry of Health and Welfare designated dog, lizard, and worm stews as "repugnant foods." KARA, *Kaeshikyong sanŏp*, 136–37.

37 Walraven, "Bardot Soup and Confucians' Meat," 106.

38 Sonsŏk'ŭiŭi shisŏnjipchung [Sonsŏk'ŭiŭi's focus], MBC Radio, November 28 and December 3, 2001.

39 Kyŏngok Chŏn, "Chejudo 'shikyonggae t'ŭrŏk,' kyŏlguk kŭgosŭro katta" [Jeju "meat-dog" truck, ended up "there"], *OhMyNews*, July 27,

2012, http://www.ohmynews.com/nws_web/view/at_pg.aspx?CNTN _CD=A0001761491.

40 Ch'uksanbŏp [Livestock Industry Act]; and Ch'uksanmul wisaeng'gwanribŏp [Livestock Product Sanitary Control Act].

41 KARA, *Kaeshikyong sanŏp*.

42 Pyŏngsu Kim, "Kaegogi happŏp'wa pŏban chech'ul" [Bill to legalize dog meat submitted], *Yeonhap News*, August 17, 1999, http://news.naver .com/main/read.nhn?mode=LSD&mid=sec&sid1=100&oid=001&aid =0004458496.

43 The amendment was resubmitted in 2001 (when the World Cup was just around the corner) and again did not pass. J. Jo, "Tongmul onghoŭi nonŭiwa shilch'ŏnŭl t'onghae pon tongmulgwŏn tamnonŭi sahoejŏk ŭimi, " 125.

44 I. Jo, *Ch'oejongyŏn'gubogosŏ*.

45 Tongmulbohobŏp [Animal Protection Act].

46 H. Kim, "Kimhongshin ŭiwŏni pŭrijit parŭdoege ponaenŭn p'yŏnji" [Hong Shin Kim's open letter to Brigitte Bardot], Hongshin.net, August 17, 1999, http://www.hongshin.net/activity.php.

47 Pangryŏl Hwang, "Kakkye 167myŏng 'kaegogi pulgansŏp sŏnŏn'" [167 from All Walks of Life, "Declaration of Nonintervention in Dogmeat"], *Ohmynews*, December 19, 2001, http://www.ohmynews.com/NWS_Web /view/at_pg.aspx?CNTN_CD=A0000061979.

48 Y. An, *Han'gugin'gwa kaegogi*.

49 Y. An, *Han'gugin'gwa kaegogi*, 3–4. In this book, Y. An not only introduces recipes for various dog-meat dishes but also urges readers to develop recipes to fit foreigners' tastes and habits—to globalize Korean dog-meat cuisine. His position is rather eccentric even among Koreans who support dog eating, but he nonetheless hyperbolically illustrates the thoughts and sensibilities underlying popular discourses in Korea.

50 I. Jo, *Ch'oejongyŏn'gubogosŏ*, 23. The first poll was undertaken in 1997, and the second in 2000.

51 A 2021 poll showed that 48.9 percent of respondents were against legislating a ban on dog meat and 38.6 percent were in support, with the ratio of supporters rising over the past decade. Kyŏngchun Ch'oe, "Kae shikyong kŭmji ippŏp'wa 'pandae' 48.9%—'ch'ansŏng' 38.6%" [Poll finds 48.9 percent against, 38.6 percent for, the legislation of ban on dog meat], *OhMyNews*, November 3, 2021, https://omn.kr/1vu7j.

52 KARA, "Kaeshikyong FAQ 9," 106–10.

53 KARA, "Kaeshikyong FAQ 9," 113, 117–18.

54 Abu-Lughod, "Do Muslim Women Really Need Saving?"

55 Abu-Lughod, "Do Muslim Women Really Need Saving?," 787.

56 Abu-Lughod, "Do Muslim Women Really Need Saving?," 784.

57 Abu-Lughod, "Do Muslim Women Really Need Saving?," 789.

58 Walraven, "Bardot Soup and Confucians' Meat," 102.

59 For more discussion on the conflict between animal-rights discourses and nationalist/nativist discourses surrounding animals as food, see C. J. Kim, "Multiculturalism Goes Imperial"; and Gaard, "Tools for a Cross-Cultural Feminist Ethics."

60 C. J. Kim, "Slaying the Beast."

61 In South Korea, pet culture as known to Westerners took off only after the 1990s and has since become popular. As of 2022, there are about 6.02 million companion dogs in South Korea, whose population is about 50 million. Oh Seok-min, "1 in 4 S. Koreans Own Pet Animals in 2022: Data," *Yonhap News*, May 11, 2024, https://en.yna.co.kr/view/AEN20230202005000320. However, more traditional forms of keeping dogs—raised outside as guard animals, for example—also involve companionship with humans. For a detailed discussion of the history and culture of pet ownership in South Korea, see Podberscek, "Good to Pet and Eat," 624–25.

62 According to the USDA, 780,070 animals (including 59,401 dogs) were used for biomedical research in 2018 in the United States. However, this number does not include rats, mice, and other animals that are not covered by the Animal Welfare Act but constitute the majority of laboratory animals. USDA, "Annual Report Animal Usage by Fiscal Year," January 7, 2020, https://speakingofresearch.files.wordpress.com/2021/08/united-states-2018.pdf. Here, my point is not to equate the speciesism of using animals as biomedical research subjects with that of eating animals but to note how the institutionalization of laboratory animals is a backdrop to criticism on the treatment of the surrogate-mother dogs.

63 Probyn, *Carnal Appetites*, 8.

64 Probyn, *Carnal Appetites*, 131.

65 Kristeva, *Powers of Horror*, 2–3. The affects of shame and disgust have been important subjects for both queer and postcolonial literature.

66 Kristeva, *Powers of Horror*, 2.

67 Chow, "Writing in the Realm of the Senses," ii.

68 Probyn, *Carnal Appetites*, 132.

69 Probyn also questions the linear narrative that by being proud of her own body she makes those who categorize her as disgusting feel ashamed of

themselves; they would feel guilty at best, but disgust, blame, and resentment would be merely pushed under the "surface of a sanitized veneer of acceptance." Probyn, *Carnal Appetites*, 128.

70 Tomkins, "Shame-Humiliation and Contempt-Disgust," 139.

71 Podberscek's article "Good to Pet and Eat" is only one among many that examine Korea's dog-eating culture primarily through what is most shocking about it (at least to Westerners)—the idea of eating what we pet, the violation of categorization. He explains such a distinction of animals (even among the same species) through Michael Fox's concept of compartmentalization (628).

72 Herzog and Golden, "Moral Emotions and Social Activism," 487.

73 Tomkins, "Shame-Humiliation and Contempt-Disgust," 139.

74 Probyn, *Carnal Appetites*, 135.

75 Spivak, "Remembering the Limits." I have quoted this passage from Wolfe, *Animal Rites*, 7.

76 Spivak, "Can the Subaltern Speak?," 307–8.

77 Spivak, "Can the Subaltern Speak?," 308.

5. The Chains of Substitution

1 SNU Investigation Committee, *Hwangusŏk kyosu*.

2 W. Hwang et al., "Evidence of Pluripotent Human Embryonic Stem Cell Line"; W. Hwang et al., "Patient-Specific Embryonic Stem Cells."

3 Vazin and Freed, "Human Embryonic Stem Cells," 589.

4 Resnik, Shamoo, and Krimsky, "Fraudulent Human Embryonic Stem Cell Research," 101.

5 SNU Investigation Committee, *Hwangusŏk kyosu*.

6 Kye-sik Hwang, "Kŭkchŏgin 'sŭnŏp'i pokchegae kŏmjŭng' . . . ibyŏngch'ŏn kyosu 'kaeshijang' hulko tto hulko" [Dramatic proof of Snuppy the clone: Prof. Lee combed dog market, again and again], *Segye Ilbo*, January 19, 2006.

7 There are a number of cultural and political analyses of Hwang's scandal, often in relation to South Korea's nationalist and developmentalist take on science and technology. Major issues regarding the scandal have been discussed in Wu, "The Hwang Scandal and Human Embryonic Stem Cell Research," a special issue of *East Asian Science, Technology, and Society*. See also editorial preface, "Kwahakkisurhak(STS)chadŭri 'hwangusŏk sagŏn'ŭl pon'gyŏk punsŏk'ada"; G. Kim, *Hwangusŏk shinhwawa taehanmin'guk kwahak*.

8   In this light, my research attempts a postcolonial feminist understanding of the discourse of bioethics as a biopolitical institution, which subtends as much as regulates the coalescence of advanced biotechnology and neoliberal capitalism on a global scale. On the other side of the technologies that seek to optimize life at the molecular level for the future in liberal-capitalist societies (as Nikolas Rose observes in "Molecular Biopolitics"), there are lives whose biological labor and material feed these technologies under the regime of bioethics. In her book *Property in the Body*, Donna L. Dickenson alerts us to the increasing risk of all bodies (especially women's) being reduced to the status of objects for use in genomic and regenerative medicine. Similarly, in their book *Clinical Labor*, Melinda Cooper and Catherine Waldby draw our attention to the bioeconomic exploitation of tissue donors and clinical-trial subjects often drawn from the marginal pool of labor along the lines of race, gender, and class. The molecular turn in biotechnology has, as Richard Twine criticizes in *Animals as Biotechnology*, brought an intense capitalization of nonhuman animal lives in agriculture and biomedicine. And Maneesha Deckha and Yunwei Xie's "Stem Cell Debate" emphasizes the reliance of human embryonic stem cell research on animal studies and bodily materials. Their critical insights into the shortened circuits between human and animal bodily materials (and between animal science and biomedicine) help us approach bioethics in cloning technology and regenerative medicine as a fundamentally interspecies matter.

9   Cooper, *Life as Surplus*.

10   As early as May 2004, David Cyranoski reported suspicion among civil-rights activists and bioethicists in South Korea of an ethical breach in the acquisition of eggs for Hwang's research. Cyranoski, "Korea's Stem-Cell Stars Dogged." Donna Dickenson and Itziar Alkorta Idiakez note that WomenLink (a South Korean women's activist organization), in coalition with Solidarity for Biotechnology Watch, played a leading role in problematizing ethical issues in Hwang's research. Dickenson and Idiakez, "Ova Donation for Stem Cell Research," 127–28.

11   "World Stem Cell Hub Is Shut Down," *BioNews*, April 30, 2006, https://www.bionews.org.uk/page_90008.

12   "Hwangusŏk shinhwaŭi nanja ŭihok" [The suspicions over eggs in the myth of Woo Suk Hwang], PD *Such'ŏp*, Munhwa Broadcasting Company, Seoul, November 22, 2005. PD *Such'ŏp* itself was subsequently accused of violating journalism ethics because it manipulated Hwang's junior researcher and used a hidden camera to secure a recorded interview with him. Hwang's supporters staged vigils and pressured MBC TV's

prime-time advertisers to cancel their commercials, which all twelve did. This led to a formal apology from MBC.

13 SNU Investigation Committee, *Hwangusŏk kyosu*.

14 SNU Investigation Committee, *Hwangusŏk kyosu*.

15 Cyranoski, "South Korean Cloners Indicted"; Cyranoski, "Woo Suk Hwang Convicted." An appeals court reduced Hwang's prison sentence by six months (suspended for two years) in December 2010. See Vogel, "South Korean Court Reduces Hwang's Sentence."

16 Y. Lee, "Hwangusŏk sat'aenŭn ŏlmana han'gukchŏgin'ga?"; S. Kang, "Hwangusŏk sat'aerŭl t'onghan han'gugŭi kwahangmunhwa chindan"; S. Hong, "Hwangusŏk sat'aeŭi hyŏngsŏnggwa chŏn'gae."

17 Gottweis and Kim, "Explaining Hwang-Gate," 504.

18 Gottweis and Kim, "Explaining Hwang-Gate," 519, emphasis added.

19 Gottweis and Kim draw on Bob Simpson's discussion of bionationalism ("Explaining Hwang-Gate, 507), which proposes that popular understandings of new genetic and reproductive technologies have possibilities to rework "ethnic identities as imagined genetic communities" (Simpson, "Imagined Genetic Communities," 6). Different from the Icelandic Genome Project or the UK's importation of sperm from the Danish sperm bank that undergirds Simpson's argument, stem cells and oocytes in Hwang's research were rarely perceived as the biological identifier of Korean ethnicity or expected to serve Korean bodies in particular. However, I don't disagree with Gottweis and Kim's observation (presented in their earlier article) of the emergent nationalism that concerns the biological well-being and protection of Koreans in other cases—such as in the nationwide resistance against US beef imports over the perceived threat of Creutzfeldt-Jakob disease in 2008. Gottweis and Kim, "Bionationalism, Stem Cells, BSE, and Web 2.0."

20 Sŏng-ho Chŏng, "'Syup'ŏmaen' paeu, tashi hanŭl nal su issŭl kŏt'—Hwangusŏk kyosu" ["The Superman actor will be able to fly again," Prof. Woo Suk Hwang], *Yeonhap News*, March 25, 2004. Hwang frequently named Christopher Reeve and Kang Won-rae as examples of people with spinal cord injuries who would benefit from his research. E. Kim has analyzed Woo Suk Hwang syndrome through the notion of "curative violence," which "relies on the presence of disabled bodies" only to expel them from the normative prospect of the future—without questioning the assumption that "disability needs to be cured before disabled people can 'return' to society." E. Kim, *Curative Violence*, 5.

21 In South Korea and other postcolonial Asian countries, since the 1990s biotechnology has been a strategic site for strengthening the nation's status in the global economy. Aihwa Ong discusses how biotechnologies

are often "allied to nationalist efforts to restore national identity and political ambition in Asian societies." Ong, "Introduction."

22   In the Biotech 2000 program launched in 1994, the Korean government presented its plans to foster biotechnology, aiming to achieve a level competitive with the world's seven leading industrial companies by 2007. For more discussion of the development of biotech within the *segyehwa* project, see Wong et al., "South Korean Biotechnology." Also see S. Hwang, "Ch'amyŏjŏngbuŭi palchŏn'gukkajŏk BT yuksŏng chŏngch'aege kwanhan yŏn'gu."

23   Cooper, *Life as Surplus*, 4.

24   Cooper, *Life as Surplus*, esp. chaps. 5 and 6.

25   For example, in his analysis of clinical trials conducted in India, Kaushik Sunder Rajan argues that "ethics, legally enshrined and contractually enforced, are integral to the capacity-building effort around clinical research in India." From this perspective, he criticizes the habitual discussions that reduce clinical trials in the Third World to "the neo-colonial exploitation of the local population as 'guinea pigs' by rapacious multinational interests, where cutting corners is the norm and ethics is easily sacrificed." Sunder Rajan, "Experimental Values," 75–76. Twine criticizes the "business as usual approach" (mainly humane utilitarianism) to the status of animals in bioethics. He argues that this kind of approach fails to address the embeddedness of human health in animal capitalization that has intensified with the application of molecular technologies such as genomic selection and modification, transgenics, and cloning in the animal sciences. Twine, *Animals as Biotechnology*, 21.

26   Some titles of news reports and editorials at the time show how the production of Snuppy was seen as a national event: "Hwangusŏkt'im 'sŭnŏp'i'ka tŭnop'in BT han'gugŭi wisang" [Woo Suk Hwang team's Snuppy raises the status of BT Korea], editorial, *Munhwa Ilbo*, August 4, 2005; Ŭn-ji Yi, "Tongmulbokchedo 'han'gugi ch'oego' chŭngmyŏng" [Proof that "Korea is the best" in animal cloning, too], *Maeil Kyungje*, August 17, 2005.

27   Yŏng-mo Ku, "Saengmyŏngyulli pon'gyŏk'wa halttaeda" [It's time to be serious about bioethics], *JoongAng Ilbo*, August 5, 2005. Ku criticizes the government for operating like "a nation-state-corporation" that put all its eggs in the cloning-technology basket, and argues that "the dream of an advanced country at the cost of sacrificing bioethics is but a futile fantasy."

28   "Hwangusŏkt'im 'sŭnŏp'i'ka tŭnop'in BT han'gugŭi wisang."

29   "Hwangusŏkt'im 'sŭnŏp'i'ka tŭnop'in BT han'gugŭi wisang."

30   Yŏng-wan Yi, "Hwangusŏk kyosu kae pokche segye chŏt sŏnggong" [Prof. Woo Suk Hwang succeeded in the world's first dog cloning], *Chosun Ilbo*, August 4, 2005.

31 Hanwool Wu, "Kwagibu segye chŏt koyangi 100mari pokche ch'ujin" [Ministry of Science and Technology, world's first project to clone 100 cats], *Syegye Ilbo*, January 16, 2005. See also H. Wu, "Aewandongmul pokchesaŏp yŏn'gu ch'aegimja kongmo" [Contest for the chief researcher of pet animal cloning project], *Syegye Ilbo*, January 18, 2005. Korea Association for Animal Protection (KAAP) et al., "Kae koyangi pokche saŏp pandae sŏngmyŏngsŏ" [Statement against the dog and cat cloning project], January 21, 2005, http://www.kaap.or.kr/notice.html.

32 More specifically, MOST stated that the purpose of this infrastructural project was to resolve the genetic and disease anomalies that frequently occur in the cloning of disease-model animals and animals that are genetically engineered to produce medicines for humans. Myung Oh (minister of MOST), "Tappyŏn" [Response], Voice 4 Animals, February 1, 2005, http://www.voice4animals.org/new/?document_srl=7457&mid =board.

33 I. Kong, *T'ŭksu yuyong tongmul pokchesaŏp* , 2006, 16; I. Kong, *T'ŭksu yuyong tongmul pokchesaŏp*, 2011, 10. Henceforth, *Special Usefulness Animals* (2006) and *Special Usefulness Animals* (2011).

34 I. Kong, *Special Usefulness Animals* (2006), 16–22; I. Kong, *Special Usefulness Animals* (2011), 10–17.

35 Han-wool Wu, "Sŏultae suŭidae tongmulbokchet'im chŏnwŏn kujedoeltŭt" [SNU vet college cloning team likely to be saved], *Segye Ilbo*, May 12, 2006.

36 The year the SNU canine-cloning team joined the project, RNL Bio (a South Korean biotech company affiliated with SNU) announced their own plans to push forward with commercializing Snuppy technology in the fields of pet cloning and cloning dogs for clinical experiments— suggesting an increased expectation regarding the profitability of the pet-cloning industry. See Kilwŏn Kim, "Sŭnŏp'i pokche kisul sangŏp'wa toena" [Will Snuppy cloning technology be commercialized?], *Hankook Ilbo*, May 22, 2006.

37 Nationalist values under the *segyehwa* paradigm often refer to "national profit," "the nation's brand value," and "national competitiveness." I. Kong, *Special Usefulness Animals* (2011), 3.

38 I. Kong, *Special Usefulness Animals* (2011), 15.

39 I. Kong, *Special Usefulness Animals* (2011), 11, 14.

40 I. Kong, *Special Usefulness Animals* (2006), 4; *Special Usefulness Animals* (2011), 16.

41 Pyŏng-ch'an Kwak, "Tto tarŭn saengmyŏnge taehan yeŭi" [Respect for another life], *Hankyoreh*, August 16, 2005.

42 Shirhŏm tongmure kwanhan pŏmnyul [Laboratory Animal Act].

43 Stanescu, "Species Trouble," 580.

44 Sharp, "Monkey Business," 50. Sharp also notes that this unusual surgery drew severe criticism on ethical grounds in the American medical community, focused on the vulnerability of the human baby but silent on the vulnerability of the mother or the baboon (51).

45 Merleau-Ponty, "A Hierarchy of Deaths."

46 Veldkamp, "Commemoration of Dead Animals."

47 Veldkamp, "Commemoration of Dead Animals," 155–56. "Beastly and birdly living beings / Although we differ in nature our lives are the same / Your pitiful lives did not evade a virtuous death / Please do not bear a grudge against Heaven / And do not bear a grudge against us people / For the sake of human welfare and the health of your fellow birds and beasts / We pray in silence for your sad soul and wish for a happy afterlife / So that you can come into the brighter world again and live eternally." This translation is by Veldkamp except for the second line (Veldkamp's translation was "Although our looks differ we both enjoy life"), the sixth ("Because it was for the sake of human welfare and the health of your fellow beasts and birds"), and the last ("So that you can come into this world"). The changes are my own translation, in reference to the original Korean version from C. Kang, "In'gan wihae mombach'inŭn shirhŏm tongmultŭl," 398–99.

48 Veldkamp, "Commemoration of Dead Animals," 161.

49 Nishikawa and Morishita, "Current Status of Memorial Services," 180.

50 For more discussion about the Japanese Imperial Army's human experimentation, see Tsuneishi, "Unit 731 and the Human Skulls"; and Dickinson, "Biohazard."

51 For example, the supporters of the Yeonsan *ogye* (black chickens from Yeonsan Province) *wiryŏngje*, which ceased during Japanese occupation but resumed in 2003, claim that this ritual is the origin of contemporary memorials for lab animals. Kyo-yong Kwon, "Nonsan Yŏnsan ogye munhwache yisipiril kaech'oe" [Nonsan Yeonsan ogye festival to be held on 21st], *Newsis*, April 12, 2012, http://www.newsis.com/ar_detail/view.html?ar_id=NISX20120412_0011019395&cID=10807&pID=10800.

52 Iliff, "An Additional 'R.'"

53 Iliff, "An Additional 'R,'" 47.

54 The 2014 data is from Normile, "The Second Act." The 2018 data is from David Ewing Duncan, "Inside the Very Big, Very Controversial Business of Dog Cloning," *Vanity Fair*, September 2018, https://www.vanityfair.com/style/2018/08/dog-cloning-animal-sooam-hwang. Additionally, a

science article Hwang coauthored claims that they had so far produced 1,500 clones. Olsson et al., "Insights from One Thousand Cloned Dogs." It would be reasonable to conclude that the number refers to those produced at the Sooam BRF given the available information (such as the care protocol referring to Sooam BRF and the description of contributions by the international coauthors), but I can't tell whether or how many among them were cloned in commercial pet cloning.

55 Normile, "The Second Act."

56 Normile, "The Second Act."

57 For discussions on the obliteration of women's bodies and their labor in reproductive technology, genomics, and regenerative medicine, see Dickenson, *Property in the Body*, esp. chaps. 3–6; Storrow, "The Erasure of Egg Providers."

58 Artificially deriving human stem cells does not necessarily require oocytes. For example, there have been advances in creating induced pluripotent stem cells (iPSC) since Japanese Nobel laureate Shinya Yamanaka and Kazutoshi Takahashi's pioneering work in 2006. Takahashi and Yamanaka, "Induction of Pluripotent Stem Cells." Insoo Hyun defines iPSC as "fully differentiated body cells (skin, peripheral blood cells, gut cells, etc.) that have been 'reprogrammed' in the laboratory to take on the properties of embryonic stem cells (self-renewal and pluripotency)." Hyun, *Bioethics and the Future of Stem Cell Research*, 31. Nonetheless, as Hyun emphasizes, advances in iPSC technologies do not lessen the need for embryonic stem cell research for ethical and scientific reasons (31).

59 Choi and Kim, "Hwangusŏk sat'aeesŏŭi yullijŏk chaengjŏmŭi pyŏnhwa."

60 For the formation and development of ethical debates surrounding the collection of eggs for research during and after Hwang's scandal, see Choi and Kim, "Hwangusŏk sat'aeesŏŭi yullijŏk chaengjŏmŭi pyŏnhwa."

61 Woo Suk Hwang et al., "Evidence of a Pluripotent Human Embryonic Stem Cell Line," 1670.

62 Cyranoski, "Korea's Stem-Cell Stars." Cyranoski, "Crunch Time," further discusses the controversy surrounding therapeutic cloning research involving human eggs and cells.

63 Cyranoski, "Korea's Stem-Cell Stars," 3; Cyranoski, "Crunch Time," 13.

64 Hwang et al., "Patient-Specific Embryonic Stem Cells," 1779. This article also claims that all donors "were fully aware of the scope of this study, and each signed an informed consent form" and that "although expenses for public transportation and injections administered by medical personnel could have been provided, none of the donors requested this, and therefore no financial reimbursement in any form was paid" (1778).

After Hwang's second *Science* article, a South Korean NGO, Solidarity for Biotechnology Watch, held a forum on August 25, 2005, focusing on gender and bioethics issues in Hwang's research. The presented papers are available online at Shimin'gwahaksentŏ (CDST), accessed September 17, 2023, http://cdst.jinbo.net/bbs/data/data/bioact_0825.pdf.

65 SNU Investigation Committee, *Hwangusŏk kyosu*; National Bioethics Committee, *Hwangusŏk yŏn'guŭi saengmyŏngyulli munjee taehan pogosŏ*; Ministry of Health and Welfare, *Hwangusŏk yŏn'guŭi nanjasugŭpkwajŏng tŭng saengmyŏngyulli kwallyŏnsahang chosagyŏlgwa*.

66 In addition to the 2,200 eggs that were accounted for, there were also eggs retrieved from excised ovaries obtained during gynecological operations, according to reports by the Ministry of Health and Welfare and the National Bioethics Committee.

67 SNU Investigation Committee, *Hwangusŏk kyosu*.

68 J. Cho, "Nanja."

69 Choi and Kim, "Hwangusŏk sat'aeesŏŭi yullijŏk chaengjŏmŭi pyŏnhwa," 191, 195.

70 Baylis, "For Love or Money?"

71 This woman and another donor for Hwang's hESC research filed a lawsuit against the Korean government and two hospitals, requesting 32 million Korean won (US $20,000) in damages. They claimed that "they had suffered psychological and physical damages" because they were not sufficiently informed about the nature of the research and the risk of the egg-extraction procedure, but Seoul District Court in South Korea rejected the case. "Korean Egg-Donor Lawsuit Thrown Out of Court," *Nature* 458, no. 20 (2009), https://www.nature.com/articles/458020c.

72 Jeong, "Paeajulgisep'oyŏn'guwa chendŏ," 182–83.

73 In a similar vein, Charis Thompson examines 2004's Proposition 71 in California (which established a constitutional right to conduct hESC), criticizing how discourses on stem cell research have often failed to address the extensive rearticulation of conventional "women's issues" such as abortion, egg donation, and treatment of embryos that stem cell research has necessitated. Thompson, *Good Science*, 87.

74 Dickenson and Idiakez, "Ova Donation for Stem Cell Research," 129, 139.

75 Waldby, "Oocyte Markets."

76 Waldby, "Oocyte Markets," 29.

77 Cooper and Waldby, *Clinical Labor*, 107.

78 Cooper and Waldby, *Clinical Labor*, 115, emphasis added.

79 Cooper and Waldby, *Clinical Labor*, 115.

80   Cooper and Waldby, *Clinical Labor*, 14.

81   Cooper, *Life as Surplus*, 136.

82   Cooper and Waldby, *Clinical Labor*, 12.

83   Clark, "Labourers or Lab Tools?"

84   Clark, "Labourers or Lab Tools?," 157, citing Weisberg, "The Broken Promises of Monsters," 37.

85   Clark, "Labourers or Lab Tools?," 160.

86   In this vein, my research aims to put into perspective the recent posthuman emphasis on shared agency (instead of shared vulnerability), such as Lynda Birke, Mette Bryld, and Nina Lykke's proposition to consider laboratory rats "both in terms of materialization of specific scientific practices and as active participants" in science. Birke, Bryld, and Lykke, "Animal Performances," 167.

87   G. Kim, "Tongmulbokcheesŏ."

88   G. Kim, "Tongmulbokcheesŏ," 25.

89   G. Kim, "Tongmulbokcheesŏ," 33–34. However, Hwang's plan to apply this technology to the mass reproduction of cows was ultimately not successful, and the Ministry of Agriculture and Forestry's Plan to Supply Premium Cows by Cloning Technology ended with unsatisfactory results (31–32).

90   G. Kim, "Tongmulbokcheesŏ," 35.

91   G. Kim, "Tongmulbokcheesŏ," 38.

92   G. Kim, "Tongmulbokcheesŏ," 38–39.

93   G. Kim, "Tongmulbokcheesŏ," 46–47.

94   Cyranoski, "Crunch Time," 12.

95   This kind of feminist ethics is also illustrated by Julietta Hua and Neel Ahuja's examination of the politics of care, based on their interviews with caregivers at a small sanctuary in the United States "for chimpanzees declared 'surplus' or 'retired' from biomedical research." Hua and Ahuja, "Chimpanzee Sanctuary," 619. They portray modest ethics of care "framed primarily in terms of providing a limited form of the 'good life' for the [captive] chimps," enabled and compromised by the imperial conscription of chimps during the Cold War, the public understanding of animal ethics, and the coupling of neoliberal austerity that mobilizes cheap feminized affective labor (635).

96   In South Korea, critiques on the use and treatment of lab animals from a stated or explicit feminist perspective are rare. However, I do not necessarily see this as an absence compared with Anglo-European feminist theories and activisms. Instead, I suggest the possibility that there are

feminist engagements with lab animals in Korea that are not described as feminist or do not necessarily conform to the existing discourses of feminisms (thus evading my search). Examining such a possibility within historical and social contexts would be a subject of research on its own. Critical discourses on the relationship between women and animals (or feminism and animal advocacy) in general are also rare. Ju-young Hwang has written on the intersection of gender and speciesism, which interweaves existing (mainly Anglo-European) ecofeminist discourses on the relationship between women and nonhuman animals with several cultural and political examples. J. Hwang, "Yŏjain tongmulgwa tongmurin yŏja."

97   Quoted from Adams and Gruen, "Groundwork," 8.

98   Collard and Contrucci, *Rape of the Wild*.

99   Haraway, *Modest_Witness*, 52.

100   Haraway, *When Species Meet*, 76.

101   Haraway, *When Species Meet*, 79.

102   Haraway, *When Species Meet*, 77, emphasis added.

103   Thompson, *Good Science*, 189.

104   Thompson, *Good Science*, 191.

105   Thompson, *Good Science*, 192. "Nuremberg Code: Directives for Human Experimentation" is available at Office of Research Integrity, accessed March 25, 2024, https://ori.hhs.gov/content/chapter-3-The-Protection-of -Human-Subjects-nuremberg-code-directives-human-experimentation.

106   Thompson, *Good Science*, 192–93.

107   Thompson, *Good Science*, 214.

108   Thompson, *Good Science*, 214–16.

109   Thompson, *Good Science*, 220–22.

110   For example, Andrew Fenton and Frederic Gilbert examine how critical issues in the use of animals in spinal cord injury stem cell research in the United States motivate reassessment of the moral feasibility of this kind of research. Fenton and Gilbert, "On the Use of Animals." Andrew Knight points out the methodological and applicability issues of animal models based on systemic reviews of animal experimentation in toxicological and clinical research in EU countries (the implications of which I believe extend to other parts of the world). Knight, "Critically Evaluating Animal Research." He argues that the benefits (mostly) humans get from such research do not offset the harm incurred by the animal subjected to scientific procedure, and demands that resources and efforts be "directed into more promising and justifiable fields of research and healthcare" (335).

111 Cary Wolfe warns that "as long as the automatic exclusion of animals from [ethical] standing remains . . . dehumanization by means of . . . 'animalization' will be readily available for deployment against whatever body happens to fall outside the ethnocentric 'we.'" Wolfe, *Before the Law*, 21.

112 Jackson, *Becoming Human*, 23, emphasis added. Reflecting on the historical bestialization of blackness, Jackson argues that "what is commonly deemed dehumanization is . . . the violence of humanization or the burden of inclusion into a racially hierarchized universal Humanity" (18). Thus, to counter the abjection of animality "that constantly rebounds on marginalized humans," we need a nonbinaristic model of humans-animals that challenges the hegemonic notion of humanity (18).

113 Jackson, *Becoming Human*, 53.

114 Ferreira da Silva, *Toward a Global Idea of Race*.

115 Sharp, "The Other Animal of Transplant's Future," s63.

116 Sharp, "The Other Animal of Transplant's Future," s63.

Epilogue

1 Research-based artist Soyo Lee works at the intersections of biology and media arts and runs the one-person publisher Saengmulgwa Munhwa (Lifeforms in Culture) dedicated to artistic work on biology.

2 Maxine Builder, "Bioart Ethics and the Weird History of Korea's Mutant Cacti," *Medium*, January 11, 2016, https://medium.com/the -establishment/bioart-ethics-and-the-weird-history-of-koreas-mutant -cacti-30a849a5c87c.

3 Soyo Lee's *Ornamental Cactus Design* has been exhibited in various places, including *New Romance: Art and the Posthuman*, held at both the National Museum of Modern and Contemporary Art (NMMC, Seoul) in Korea and the Museum of Contemporary Art Australia (MCA, Sydney) in 2015–16. More information on the Sydney exhibition is accessible on MCA's website: https://www.mca.com.au/artists-works/exhibitions /new-romance-art-and-the-posthuman/soyo-lee/ (accessed October 22, 2023). The project also resulted in a hand-sized artistic documentary book: S. Lee, *Kwansangyong sŏninjang tijain*.

4 S. Lee, *Kwansangyong sŏninjang tijain*, 62, 65.

5 Builder, "Bioart Ethics."

6 S. Lee, *Kwansangyong sŏninjang tijain*, 15.

7 S. Lee, *Kwansangyong sŏninjang tijain*, 53–55.

8 Wynter and McKittrick, "Unparalleled Catastrophe for Our Species?," 31.

9   Here I borrow Trinh T. Minh-ha's term "speaking nearby." Using this term, Trinh proposes a mode of speaking "that does not objectify, does not point to an object as if it is distant from the speaking subject or absent from the speaking place" and "that reflects on itself and can come very close to a subject without, however, seizing or claiming it." N. Chen, "'Speaking Nearby,'" 87.

10   Here, my approach echoes Luciana Parisi and Steve Goodman's portrayal of affective capitalism as "a parasite on the feelings, movements, and becomings of bodies," through which it preemptively abducts memory from potential futurity. Parisi and Goodman, "Mnemonic Control," 164.

Bibliography

Abelmann, Nancy, and Jiyeon Kang. "Memoir/Manuals of South Korean Precollege Study Abroad: Defending Mothers and Humanizing Children." *Global Networks* 14, no. 1 (2014): 1–22.

Abu-Lughod, Lila. "Do Muslim Women Really Need Saving? Anthropological Reflections on Cultural Relativism and Its Others." *American Anthropologist* 104, no. 3 (2002): 783–90.

Achebe, Chinua. "English and the African Writer." *Transition*, no. 75/76 (1997): 342–49.

Adams, Carol J., and Lori Gruen. "Groundwork." In *Ecofeminism: Feminist Intersections with Other Animals and the Earth*, edited by Carol J. Adams and Lori Gruen, 7–36. London: Bloomsbury, 2014.

Ahuja, Neel. *Bioinsecurities: Disease Interventions, Empire, and the Government of Species*. Durham, NC: Duke University Press, 2016.

American Psychological Association. "Wild Boy of Aveyron." APA *Dictionary of Psychology*, April 19, 2018. https://dictionary.apa.org/wild-boy-of-aveyron.

An Chun. "Kaegogi ŭmsikgwa kukche chŏngch'i munhwa" [Dog-meat food and international political culture]. In *Yŏsŏng chŏngch'i munhwaron* [Women's political culture]. Seoul: Karasani, 1991.

An Yongkŭn. *Han'gugin'gwa kaegogi* [Koreans and dog meat]. Seoul: Hyoil, 2000.

Anzaldúa, Gloria. "How to Tame a Wild Tongue." In *Borderlands/La Frontera: The New Mestiza*, 4th ed., 53–64. San Francisco: Aunt Lute, 1987.

Atanasoski, Neda, and Kalindi Vora. *Surrogate Humanity: Race, Robots, and the Politics of Technological Futures*. Durham, NC: Duke University Press, 2019.

Barthes, Roland. *Camera Lucida: Reflections on Photography*. Translated by Richard Howard. New York: Hill and Wang, 1981.

Baudrillard, Jean. "The Final Solution: Cloning beyond the Human and Inhuman." In *The Vital Illusion*, edited by Julia Witwer, 1–30. New York: Columbia University Press, 2000.

Baylis, Françoise. "For Love or Money? The Saga of Korean Women Who Provided Eggs for Embryonic Stem Cell Research." *Theoretical Medicine and Bioethics* 30, no. 5 (2009): 385–96.

Beals, Kurt. "'Do the New Poets Think? It's Possible': Computer Poetry and Cyborg Subjectivity." *Configurations* 26, no. 2 (2018): 149–77.

Bennett, Jane. "The Force of Things: Steps toward an Ecology of Matter." *Political Theory* 32, no. 3 (2004): 347–72.

Bharadwaj, Aditya. "Experimental Subjectification: The Pursuit of Human Embryonic Stem Cells in India." *Ethnos* 79, no. 1 (2014): 84–107.

Binkley, Sam. "The Government of Intimacy: Satiation, Intensification, and the Space of Emotional Reciprocity." *Rethinking Marxism* 24, no. 4 (2012): 556–73.

Birke, Lynda, Mette Bryld, and Nina Lykke. "Animal Performances: An Exploration of Intersections between Feminist Science Studies and Studies of Human/Animal Relationships." *Feminist Theory* 5, no. 2 (2004): 167–83.

Boisseron, Bénédicte. *Afro-Dog: Blackness and the Animal Question*. New York: Columbia University Press, 2018.

Bourdieu, Pierre. "The Forms of Capital." In *Readings in Economic Sociology*, edited by Nicole Woolsey Biggart, 280–91. Malden, MA: Blackwell, 2002.

Brah, Avtah. "Thinking through the Concept of Diaspora." In *The Post-colonial Studies Reader*, 2nd ed., edited by Bill Ashcroft, Gareth Griffiths, and Helen Tiffin, 443–46. London: Routledge, 2006.

Braidotti, Rosi. "Affirmation versus Vulnerability: On Contemporary Ethical Debates." *Symposium: Canadian Journal of Continental Philosophy* 1, no. 1 (2006): 235–54.

Braidotti, Rosi. *Transpositions: On Nomadic Ethics*. Cambridge, UK: Polity, 2006.

Braun, Bruce. "Biopolitics and the Molecularization of Life." *Cultural Geographies* 14, no. 1 (2007): 6–28.

Butler, Judith. "Critically Queer." *GLQ: A Journal of Lesbian and Gay Studies* 1, no. 1 (1993): 17–32.

Butler, Judith. *Excitable Speech: A Politics of the Performative*. New York: Routledge, 1997.

Butler, Judith. *Precarious Life: The Powers of Mourning and Violence*. London: Verso, 2006.

Byun Young-joo, dir. *Habitual Sadness (Najŭn moksori 2)*. Docu Factory Vista, 1997. Film, 90 min.

Byun Young-joo, dir. *The Murmuring (Najŭn moksori)*. Docu Factory Vista, 1995. Film, 93 min.

Byun Young-joo, dir. *My Own Breathing* (*Sumgyŏl*). Docu Factory Vista, 1999. Film, 96 min.

Callicott, J. Baird. *In Defense of the Land Ethic: Essays in Environmental Philosophy*. Albany: State University of New York Press, 1989.

Césaire, Aimé. "Poetry and Knowledge." In *Lyric and Dramatic Poetry, 1946–82*, translated by Clayton Eshleman and Annette Smith, xlii–lvi. Charlottesville: University of Virginia Press, 1990. Originally published 1945 in *Tropiques*.

Cha, Theresa Hak Kyung. *Dictee*. Berkeley: University of California Press, 2001.

Cha, Theresa Hak Kyung, dir. *Mouth to Mouth*. 1975. Video, 8 min.

Chakraborty, Indranil. *Invisible Labour: Support Service in India's Information Technology Industry*. London: Routledge, 2021.

Chen, Mel Y. *Animacies: Biopolitics, Racial Mattering, and Queer Affect*. Durham, NC: Duke University Press, 2012.

Chen, Nancy N. "'Speaking Nearby': A Conversation with Trinh T. Minh-ha." *Visual Anthropology Review* 8, no. 1 (1992): 82–91.

Cho, Grace M. *Haunting the Korean Diaspora: Shame, Secrecy, and the Forgotten War*. Minneapolis: University of Minnesota Press, 2008.

Cho Joo-hyun. "Nanja: Saengmyŏnggisurŭi shisŏn'gwa yŏsŏng mom ch'ehŏmŭi chŏngch'isŏng" [Eggs: The vision of biotechnology and the politics of women's embodied experience]. *Han'guk yŏsŏnghak* 22, no. 2 (2006): 5–40.

Cho Uhn. "Segyehwaŭi ch'oech'ŏmdane sŏn han'gugŭi kajok: Shin'gŭllobŏl mojanyŏ kajok sarye yŏn'gu" [Korean families on the forefront of globalization: A case study on neo-global mother-child families]. *Kyŏngjewa Sahoe* 64 (2004): 148–71.

Choi Eun kyung and Ock-joo Kim. "Hwangusŏk sat'aeesŏŭi yullijŏk chaengjŏmŭi pyŏnhwa" [The shift of ethical debates caused by Woo Suk Hwang's scandal]. *Saengmyŏng yullri* 7, no. 2 (2006): 81–97.

Chŏn Kwangyong. *Kkŏppittan ri* [Kapitan Lee]. Sejong: Myŏnghyŏn, 2010. E-book. Originally published 1962.

Chow, Rey. *Not Like a Native Speaker: On Languaging as a Postcolonial Experience*. New York: Columbia University Press, 2014.

Chow, Rey. "Writing in the Realm of the Senses: Introduction." *differences: A Journal of Feminist Cultural Studies* 11, no. 2 (1999): i–ii.

Ch'uksanbŏp [Livestock Industry Act]. *Statutes of Republic of Korea*. 2021 (1963).

Ch'uksanmul wisaeng'gwanribŏp [Livestock Product Sanitary Control Act]. *Statutes of Republic of Korea*. 2021 (1962).

Chun, Wendy Hui Kyong. "Race and/as Technology, or How to Do Things to Race." In *Race after the Internet*, edited by Lisa Nakamura and Peter Chow-White, 38–60. New York: Routledge, 2011.

Clark, Jonathan L. "Labourers or Lab Tools? Rethinking the Role of Lab Animals." In *The Rise of Critical Animal Studies: From the Margins to the Center*, edited by Nik Taylor and Richard Twine, 139–64. New York: Routledge, 2014.

Cliff, Michelle. "Notes on Speechlessness." *Sinister Wisdom: A Journal of Words and Pictures for the Lesbian Imagination in All Women* 5 (1978): 5–9.

Collard, Andrée, and Joyce Contrucci. *Rape of the Wild: Man's Violence against Animals and the Earth*. Bloomington: Indiana University Press, 1989.

Cooper, Melinda. *Life as Surplus: Biotechnology and Capitalism in the Neoliberal Era*. Seattle: University of Washington Press, 2008.

Cooper, Melinda, and Catherine Waldby. *Clinical Labor: Tissue Donors and Research Subjects in the Global Bioeconomy*. Durham, NC: Duke University Press, 2014.

Crystal, David. "A Global Language." In *English in the World: History, Diversity, Change*, edited by Philip Seargeant and Joan Swann, 151–77. New York: Routledge, 2012.

Cubitt, Sean. *Simulation and Social Theory*. London: Sage, 2001.

Cyranoski, David. "Crunch Time for Korea's Cloners." *Nature* 429, no. 6987 (May 2004): 12–14. https://doi.org/10.1038/429012a.

Cyranoski, David. "Korea's Stem-Cell Stars Dogged by Suspicion of Ethical Breach." *Nature* 429, no. 6987 (May 2004): 3. https://doi.org/10.1038/429003a.

Cyranoski, David. "South Korean Cloners Indicted." *Nature*, May 12, 2006. https://doi.org/10.1038/news060508-15.

Cyranoski, David. "Woo Suk Hwang Convicted, but Not of Fraud." *Nature* 461, no. 7268 (October 2009): 1181. https://doi.org/10.1038/4611181a.

Dean, Tim. "Mediated Intimacies: Raw Sex, Truvada, and the Biopolitics of Chemoprophylaxis." *Sexualities* 18, no. 1–2 (2015): 224–46.

Deckha, Maneesha. "Toward a Postcolonial, Posthumanist Feminist Theory: Centralizing Race and Culture in Feminist Work on Nonhuman Animals." *Hypatia* 27, no. 3 (2012): 527–45.

Deckha, Maneesha, and Yunwei Xie. "The Stem Cell Debate: Why Should It Matter to Animal Advocates?" *Stanford Journal of Animal Law and Policy* 1 (2008): 71–100.

DeLanda, Manuel. *Intensive Science and Virtual Philosophy*. London: Continuum, 2002.

Derrida, Jacques. "Freud and the Scene of Writing." In *Writing and Difference*, translated by Alan Bass, 196–231. Chicago: University of Chicago Press, 1978.

Derrida, Jacques. *Monolingualism of the Other: Or, The Prosthesis of Origin*. Translated by Patrick Mensah. Stanford, CA: Stanford University Press, 1998.

Derrida, Jacques. "Plato's Pharmacy." In *Dissemination*, translated by Barbara Johnson, 61–171. London: Athlone, 1981.

Derrida, Jacques. *Specters of Marx: The State of the Debt, the Work of Mourning, and the New International*. Translated by Peggy Kamuf. New York: Routledge, 2006.

Derrida, Jacques. "The Word Processor." In *Paper Machine*, translated by Rachel Bowlby, 19–32. Stanford, CA: Stanford University Press, 2005.

Derrida, Jacques, and Anne Dufourmantelle. *Of Hospitality*. Translated by Rachel Bowlby. Stanford, CA: Stanford University Press, 2000.

Dick, Leslie. Introduction to "Porous Bodies," by Kang Seung Lee. *X-tra: Contemporary Art Journal* 22, no. 4 (2020). https://www.x-traonline.org/article/porous-bodies.

Dickenson, Donna. *Property in the Body: Feminist Perspectives*. 2nd ed. Cambridge: Cambridge University Press, 2017.

Dickenson, Donna, and Itziar Alkorta Idiakez. "Ova Donation for Stem Cell Research: An International Perspective." *IJFAB: International Journal of Feminist Approaches to Bioethics* 1, no. 2 (2008): 125–44.

Dickinson, Frederick R. "Biohazard: Unit 731 Postwar Japanese Politics of National 'Forgetfulness.'" In *Dark Medicine: Rationalizing Unethical Medical Research*, edited by William R. LaFleur, Gernot Böhme, and Susumu Shimazono, 85–104. Bloomington: Indiana University Press, 2008.

Dreyer, Nadine, ed. *A Century of Sundays: 100 Years of Breaking News in the Sunday Times, 1906–2006*. Cape Town: Zebra Press, 2006.

Editorial preface. "Kwahakkisurhak(STS)chaduri 'hwangusŏk sagŏn'ŭl pon'gyŏk punsŏk'ada" [STS scholars analyzing the Woo Suk Hwang scandal to the root]. Special issue, *Yŏksa pip'yŏng* 74 (2006): 19–21.

Ezeanya-Esiobu, Chika. *Indigenous Knowledge and Education in Africa*. Singapore: Springer, 2019.

Fanon, Frantz. *Black Skin, White Masks*. Translated by Richard Philcox. New York: Grove Press, 2008. Originally published 1952 in French by Éditions du Seuil (Paris).

Felman, Shoshana. *The Scandal of the Speaking Body: Don Juan with J. L. Austin, or Seduction in Two Languages*. Stanford, CA: Stanford University Press, 2003.

Fenton, Andrew, and Frederic Gilbert. "On the Use of Animals in Emergent Embryonic Stem Cell Research for Spinal Cord Injuries." *Journal of Animal Ethics* 1, no. 1 (2011): 37–45.

Ferreira da Silva, Denise. "Before Man: Sylvia Wynter's Rewriting of the Modern Episteme." In *Sylvia Wynter: On Being Human as Praxis*, edited by Katherine McKittrick, 90–105. Durham, NC: Duke University Press, 2015.

Ferreira da Silva, Denise. "An End to 'This' World: Denise Ferreira da Silva Interviewed by Susanne Leeb and Kerstin Stakemeier." *Texte Zur Kunst*, April 12, 2019. https://www.textezurkunst.de/en/articles/interview-ferreira-da-silva/.

Ferreira da Silva, Denise. *Toward a Global Idea of Race*. Minneapolis: University of Minnesota Press, 2007.

Fiester, Autumn. "Ethical Issues in Animal Cloning." *Perspectives in Biology and Medicine* 48, no. 3 (2005): 328–43.

Fortunati, Leopoldina. "ICTs and Immaterial Labor from a Feminist Perspective." *Journal of Communication Inquiry* 35, no. 4 (2011): 426–32.

Foster, Laura A. "Patents, Biopolitics, and Feminisms: Locating Patent Law Struggles over Breast Cancer Genes and the *Hoodia* Plant." *International Journal of Cultural Property* 19, no. 3 (2012): 371–400.

Foucault, Michel. *The Birth of Biopolitics: Lectures at the Collège de France, 1978–1979.* Edited by Michel Senellart. Translated by Graham Burchell. Hampshire: Palgrave Macmillan UK, 2008.

Foucault, Michel. *"Society Must Be Defended": Lectures at the Collège de France, 1975–1976.* Edited by Mauro Bertani and Alessandro Fontana. Translated by David Macey. New York: Picador, 2003.

Franklin, Sarah. "The Cyborg Embryo: Our Path to Transbiology." *Theory, Culture and Society* 23, no. 7–8 (2006): 167–87.

Freccero, Carla. "Carnivorous Virility; or, Becoming-Dog." *Social Text* 29, no. 1 (106) (2011): 177–95.

Gaard, Greta. "Tools for a Cross-Cultural Feminist Ethics: Exploring Ethical Contexts and Contents in the Makah Whale Hunt." *Hypatia* 16, no. 1 (2001): 1–26.

Glissant, Édouard. "Languages, Self-Expression." In *Caribbean Discourse: Selected Essays*, translated by J. Michael Dash, 171–94. Charlottesville: University Press of Virginia, 1989.

Gottweis, Herbert, and Byoungsoo Kim. "Bionationalism, Stem Cells, BSE, and Web 2.0 in South Korea: Toward the Reconfiguration of Biopolitics." *New Genetics and Society* 28, no. 3 (2009): 223–39.

Gottweis, Herbert, and Byoungsoo Kim. "Explaining Hwang-Gate: South Korean Identity Politics between Bionationalism and Globalization." *Science, Technology, and Human Values* 35, no. 4 (2010): 501–24.

Grau, Christopher. "Irreplaceability and Unique Value." *Philosophical Topics* 32, no. 1/2 (2004): 111–29.

Grau, Christopher. "Love and History." *Southern Journal of Philosophy* 48, no. 3 (2010): 246–71.

Grau, Christopher. "Love, Loss, and Identity in *Solaris*." In *Understanding Love*, 97–122. Oxford: Oxford University Press, 2014.

Greenspan, Anna. In *India and the IT Revolution: Networks of Global Culture.* Houndmills, UK: Palgrave Macmillan, 2004.

Halberstam, Jack. "Automating Gender: Postmodern Feminism in the Age of the Intelligent Machine." *Feminist Studies* 17, no. 3 (1991): 439–60.

Halpern, Orit. "Schizophrenic Techniques: Cybernetics, the Human Sciences, and the Double Bind." *Scholar and Feminist Online* 10, no. 3 (2012). https://sfonline.barnard.edu/schizophrenic-techniques-cybernetics-the-human-sciences-and-the-double-bind/.

Hantel, Max. "What Is It Like to Be a Human? Sylvia Wynter on Autopoiesis." *PhiloSOPHIA: A Journal of Continental Feminism* 8, no. 1 (2018): 61–79.

Haraway, Donna J. "A Cyborg Manifesto: Science, Technology, and Socialist-Feminism in the Late Twentieth Century." In *Simians, Cyborgs, and Women: The Reinvention of Nature*, 149–81. New York: Routledge, 1991.

Haraway, Donna J. *Modest_Witness@Second_Millennium. FemaleMan_Meets_OncoMouse: Feminism and Technoscience*. New York: Routledge, 1997.

Haraway, Donna J. *Staying with the Trouble: Making Kin in the Chthulucene*. Durham, NC: Duke University Press, 2016.

Haraway, Donna J. *When Species Meet*. Minneapolis: University of Minnesota Press, 2007.

Hawthorne, Lou. "A Project to Clone Companion Animals." *Journal of Applied Animal Welfare Science* 5, no. 3 (July 2002): 229–31.

Heidegger, Martin. *Parmenides*. Translated by Andrè Schuwer and Richard Rojcewitcz. Bloomington: Indiana University Press, 1998. Originally published 1982 in German by Vittono Klostermann (Frankfurt am Main).

Heo Yun Cheol and Hong Won Park. "Han'gugŏllon'gwa segyehwa tamnon: Chosŏnilbowa han'gyŏreŭi segyehwa podo pigyo yŏn'gu" [Segyehwa discourses in Korean media: Comparison of news coverage in Chosun Ilbo and the Hankyoreh]. *Ŏllon'gwahakyŏn'gu* 10, no. 4 (2010): 562–602.

Herzog, Harold A., and Lauren L. Golden. "Moral Emotions and Social Activism: The Case of Animal Rights." *Journal of Social Issues* 65, no. 3 (2009): 485–98.

Hester, Helen. "Technically Female: Women, Machines, and Hyperemployment." *Salvage*, August 8, 2016. https://salvage.zone/in-print/technically-female-women-machines-and-hyperemployment/.

Hird, Myra J. "Animal Trans." In *Queering the Non/Human*, edited by Myra J. Hird and Noreen Giffney, 227–47. London: Routledge, 2016.

Hong Seong-tai. "Hwangusŏk sat'aeŭi hyŏngsŏnggwa chŏn'gae" [The formation and development of the Woo Suk Hwang scandal]. In *Hwangusŏk sat'aewa han'guksahoe* [The Woo Suk Hwang scandal and Korean society], edited by Se-kyun Kim, Kapsoo Choi, and Seong-Tai Hong, 15–46. Seoul: Nanam, 2006.

Hua, Julietta, and Neel Ahuja. "Chimpanzee Sanctuary: 'Surplus' Life and the Politics of Transspecies Care." *American Quarterly* 65, no. 3 (2013): 619–37.

Huws, Ursula. "The Hassle of Housework: Digitalisation and the Commodification of Domestic Labour." *Feminist Review* 123, no. 1 (2019): 8–23.

Hwang Joo-young. "Yŏjain tongmulgwa tongmurin yŏja: Chongch'abyŏlchuŭirŭl nŏmŏ kyoch'asŏnguro" [Animals that are women and women who are animals: Beyond speciesism toward intersectionality]. *Kyoch'asŏng × p'eminijŭm* [Intersectionality × feminism], edited by Misook Sa, 139–87. Seoul: Tosŏch'ulp'an yŏiyŏn, 2019.

Hwang Soyoung. "Ch'amyŏjŏngbu'uŭi palchŏn'gukkajŏk BT yuksŏng chŏngch'aege kwanhan yŏn'gu: Hwangusŏk yŏn'gut'im chiwŏn chŏngch'aegŭi shilp'aerŭl chungshimŭro" [A study on the national-developmentalist BT promotion policy in Korea: Focusing on the failure of Dr. Hwang Woo Suk's research promotion policy]. Master's thesis, Yeonsei University, 2006.

Hwang, Woo Suk, Sung Il Roh, Byeong Chun Lee, Sung Keun Kang, Dae Kee Kwon, Sue Kim, Sun Jong Kim, et al. "Patient-Specific Embryonic Stem Cells Derived from Human SCNT Blastocysts." *Science* 308, no. 5729 (2005): 1777–83. Retracted.

Hwang, Woo Suk, Young June Ryu, Jong Hyuk Park, Eul Soon Park, Eu Gene Lee, Ja Min Koo, Hyun Yong Jeon, et al. "Evidence of a Pluripotent Human Embryonic Stem Cell Line Derived from a Cloned Blastocyst." *Science* 303, no. 5664 (2004): 1669–74. Retracted.

Hyun, Insoo. *Bioethics and the Future of Stem Cell Research.* Cambridge: Cambridge University Press, 2013.

Iliff, Susan. "An Additional 'R': Remembering the Animals." *Institute for Laboratory Animal Research Journal* 43, no. 1 (2002): 38–47.

Jackson, Zakiyyah Iman. *Becoming Human: Matter and Meaning in an Antiblack World.* New York: New York University Press, 2020.

Jackson, Zakiyyah Iman. "Outer Worlds: The Persistence of Race in Movement 'beyond the Human.'" *GLQ: A Journal of Lesbian and Gay Studies* 21, no. 2–3 (2015): 215–18.

Jackson, Zakiyyah Iman. "Suspended Munition: Mereology, Morphology, and the Mammary Biopolitics of Transmission in Simone Leigh's *Trophallaxis.*" *e-flux* 105 (December 2019). https://www.e-flux.com/journal/105 /305272/suspended-munition-mereology-morphology-and-the-mammary -biopolitics-of-transmission-in-simone-leigh-s-trophallaxis/.

Jain, Sarah S. "The Prosthetic Imagination: Enabling and Disabling the Prosthesis Trope." *Science, Technology, and Human Values* 24, no. 1 (1999): 31–54.

Jarman, Derek. *Modern Nature.* Minneapolis: University of Minnesota Press, 2009. Originally published 1994 by Overlook Press (Woodstock, NY).

Jeong Yeon-Bo. "Paeajulgisep'oyŏn'guwa chendŏ: Nanjajegonggwa yŏsŏngŭi nodong mit ch'amyŏrŭl chungshimŭro" [Human embryonic stem cell research and gender: Focusing on egg donation and women's labor and participation]. *P'eminijŭm yŏn'gu* 7, no. 1 (2007): 177–209.

Jo Im-gon. *Ch'oejongyŏn'gubogosŏ: Shikyonggyŏn wisaengch'ŏrirŭl wihan chŏngch'aek yŏn'gu* [Final report: Research on policies for the hygienic treatment of meat dogs]. Seoul: Hankuk chjeongch'aek hakhoe, 2012.

Jo Jung-Heon. "Tongmul onghoŭi nonŭiwa shilch'ŏnŭl t'onghae pon tongmulgwŏn tamnonŭi sahoejŏk ŭimi" [A study of animal rights discourse through the social discussion and practice of animal advocacy]. *Pŏp'hangnonch'ong* 30, no. 1 (2013): 111–32.

Jonze, Spike, dir. *Her.* Warner Bros, 2013. Film, 126 min.

Kafer, Alison. *Feminist, Queer, Crip.* Bloomington: Indiana University Press, 2013.

Kang Chi-nam. "In'gan wihae mombach'inŭn shirhŏm tongmultŭl" [Lab animals sacrificed for humans]. *Shindong-A* 531 (2003): 398–99.

Kang Naehee. "Shingminjishidae yŏngŏgyoyukkwa yŏngŏŭi sahoejŏk wisang" [English education and its social importance in colonial Korea]. An'gwabak 18 (2005): 262–91.

Kang Shin-ik. "Hwangusŏk sat'aerŭl t'onghan han'gugŭi kwahangmunhwa chindan" [A diagnosis of Korean science culture through the Woo Suk Hwang scandal]. Yŏksa pip'yŏng 74 (2006): 115–43.

KARA (Korean Animal Rights Advocates). "Kaeshikyong FAQ 9" [Dog-eating FAQ 9]. Sum 1, emended and enlarged edition (2010): 90–139.

KARA (Korean Animal Rights Advocates). Kaeshikyong sanŏp shilt'aejosawa kŭmjibangan maryŏnŭl wihan yŏn'gu pogo [Report on the dog-consumption industry and measures for prohibition]. Seoul, 2012.

Kim Chi-ŏn. "'Najŭn moksori yŏnjak yŏn'gu: Chŏngch'ijŏk chuch'erosŏŭi ilbon'gun 'wianbu'" [A study on the "Nazeon Moksori" trilogy: Japanese "comfort woman" as political subject]. Sanghŏ hakpo 59 (2020): 603–38.

Kim, Claire Jean. "Multiculturalism Goes Imperial: Immigrants, Animals, and the Suppression of Moral Dialogue." Du Bois Review: Social Science Research on Race 4, no. 1 (2007): 233–49.

Kim, Claire Jean. "Slaying the Beast: Reflections on Race, Culture, and Species." Kalfou: A Journal of Comparative and Relational Ethnic Studies (Spring 2010): 57–74.

Kim, Eunjung. Curative Violence: Rehabilitating Disability, Gender, and Sexuality in Modern Korea. Durham, NC: Duke University Press, 2017.

Kim Geun Bae. Hwangusŏk shinhwawa taehanmin'guk kwahak [The myth of Woo Suk Hwang and the science of South Korea]. Seoul: Yŏksabip'yŏngsa, 2007.

Kim Geun Bae. "Tongmulbokcheesŏ in'ganbaeabokchero: Hwangusŏk yŏn'gut'imŭi pokchegisul chinhwa" [From animal cloning to human embryo cloning: Evolution of clone technology in Woo Suk Hwang's research team]. Yŏksa pip'yŏng 74 (2006): 22–54.

Kim Hee-sook. "Han'gugŏ segyehwawa yŏngŏgongyonghwaron shijang wŏllimunje" [Problems with the Internationalization of Korean versus English officialization from the perspective of market economy principles]. Han'gugŏ ŭimihak 8 (2001): 323–58.

Kim Kwon-jung. "'Tonghwa'wa 'chŏhang'ŭi kiŏk: Shingminji chosŏnŭi irŏ" [Memory of "assimilation" and "resistance": Japanese language in colonial Chosŏn]. Han'gungminjogundongsayŏn'gu 45 (2005): 123–59.

Kim, Nadia Y. Imperial Citizens: Koreans and Race from Seoul to LA. Stanford, CA: Stanford University Press, 2008.

Kim Yŏng-myŏng. "Yŏngyŏlp'ungŭi chiptan kwanggi" [English fever, a collective madness]. Kyoyuk pip'yŏng 9 (2002): 56–64.

Kline, Ronald. "Where Are the Cyborgs in Cybernetics?" Social Studies of Science 39, no. 3 (2009): 331–62.

Knight, Andrew. "Critically Evaluating Animal Research." In Animal Experimentation: Working towards a Paradigm Change, edited by Kathrin Herrmann and Kimberley Jayne, 321–40. Leiden: Brill, 2019. http://www.jstor.org/stable /10.1163/j.ctvjhzqof.21.

Kong Il-keun. *T'ŭksu yuyong tongmul pokchesaŏp* [Development of somatic-cell nuclear transfer technology in special-usefulness animals]. Seoul: Ministry of Science and Technology, 2006.

Kong Il-keun. *T'ŭksu yuyong tongmul pokchesaŏp* [Development of somatic-cell nuclear transfer technology in special-usefulness animals]. Seoul: Ministry of Education and Science Technology, 2011.

Kristeva, Julia. *Powers of Horror: An Essay on Abjection*. Translated by Leon S. Roudiez. New York: Columbia University Press, 1982.

Kuzniar, Alice A. *Melancholia's Dog: Reflections on Our Animal Kinship*. Chicago: University of Chicago Press, 2006.

Kwŏn Yundŭk, dir. "Mome saegin kiŏktŭl" [Memories engraved on the body]. 2013. Single-channel video, 13 min.

Landsberg, Alison. *Prosthetic Memory: The Transformation of American Remembrance in the Age of Mass Culture*. New York: Columbia University Press, 2004.

Lee, JeeYeun. "Toward a Queer Korean American Diasporic History." In *Q&A: Queer in Asian America*, edited by David L. Eng and Alice Y. Hom, 185–209. Philadelphia: Temple University Press, 1998.

Lee, Rachel C. *The Exquisite Corpse of Asian America: Biopolitics, Biosociality, and Posthuman Ecologies*. New York: New York University Press, 2014.

Lee Soyo. *Kwansangyong sŏninjang tijain* [Ornamental cactus design]. Seoul: Saengmulgwa Munhwa, 2017.

Lee Suk-ho. "Chiguch'onŭi ŏnŏ chŏngch'aek: Chegukchuŭi shijŏrŭi yŏngŏjŏngch'aekkwa yŏngŏ kongyonghwae puch'inŭn myŏt kaji tansangdŭl" [Language policy of the global village: English policy during the imperial era and thoughts on English officialization]. *Silch'on munhak* (2000): 179–95.

Lee Young-hee. "Hwangusŏk sat'aenŭn ŏlmana han'gukchŏgin'ga? Hwangusŏk sat'aeŭi pop'yŏnsŏnggwa t'ŭksusŏng ikki" [To what extent is Woo Suk Hwang's scandal specific to Korea? Reading the universality and specificity of Woo Suk Hwang's case]. *Kwahakkisurhak yŏn'gu* 7, no. 2 (2007): 23–46.

Leem, So Yeon, and Jin Hee Park. "Rethinking Women and Their Bodies in the Age of Biotechnology: Feminist Commentaries on the Hwang Affair." *East Asian Science, Technology and Society: An International Journal* 2, no. 1 (March 2008): 9–26.

Lewallen, Constance. "Introduction: Theresa Hak Kyung Cha—Her Time and Place." In *The Dream of the Audience: Theresa Hak Kyung Cha (1951–1982)*, 1–14. Berkeley: University of California Press, 2001.

Lim, Hyun-chin. "Stumbling Democracy in South Korea: The Impacts of Globalization and Restructuring." In *Korea Confronts Globalization*, edited by Yunshik Chang, Hyun-ho Seok, and Donald Baker, 139–66. New York: Routledge, 2008.

Lippit, Akira Mizuta. *Electric Animal: Toward a Rhetoric of Wildlife.* Minneapolis: University of Minnesota Press, 2000.

Livingston, Julie, and Jasbir K. Puar. "Interspecies." *Social Text* 29, no. 1 (106) (2011): 3–14.

Lorde, Audre. *The Cancer Journals.* San Francisco: Aunt Lute, 1980.

Lowe, Lisa. *Immigrant Acts: On Asian American Cultural Politics.* Durham, NC: Duke University Press, 1996.

Lowe, Lisa. *The Intimacies of Four Continents.* Durham, NC: Duke University Press, 2015.

Lysaught, M. Therese. "Docile Bodies: Transnational Research Ethics as Biopolitics." *Journal of Medicine and Philosophy* 34, no. 4 (August 2009): 384–408.

Margulis, Lynn, and Dorion Sagan. *What Is Sex?* New York: Simon and Schuster, 1997.

Massumi, Brian. *Parables for the Virtual: Movement, Affect, Sensation.* Durham, NC: Duke University Press, 2002.

Mavhunga, Clapperton Chakanetsa. *The Mobile Workshop: The Tsetse Fly and African Knowledge Production.* Cambridge, MA: MIT Press, 2018.

Mbembe, Achille. *Critique of Black Reason.* Translated by Laurent Dubois. Durham, NC: Duke University Press, 2017.

McHugh, Susan. "Bitches from Brazil." In *Representing Animals*, edited by Nigel Rothfels, 180–98. Bloomington: Indiana University Press, 2002.

McLuhan, Marshall. *Understanding Media: The Extensions of Man.* Cambridge, MA: MIT Press, 1994. Originally published 1964 by McGraw-Hill (New York).

Menely, Tobias, and Margaret Ronda. "Red." In *Prismatic Ecology: Ecotheory beyond Green*, edited by Jeffrey Cohen, 22–41. Minneapolis: University of Minnesota Press, 2013.

Merleau-Ponty, Noémie. "A Hierarchy of Deaths: Stem Cells, Animals and Humans Understood by Developmental Biologists." *Science as Culture* 28, no. 4 (2019): 492–512.

Milburn, Colin. "Nanotechnology in the Age of Posthuman Engineering: Science Fiction as Science." *Configurations* 10, no. 2 (2002): 261–95.

Min, Susette. "Narrative Chronology." In *The Dream of the Audience: Theresa Hak Kyung Cha (1951–1982)*, 151–54. Berkeley: University of California Press, 2001.

Ministry of Health and Welfare. *Hwangusŏk yŏn'guŭi nanjasugŭpkwajŏng tŭng saengmyŏngyulli kwallyŏnsahang chosagyŏlgwa* [Report of investigation of the bioethical issues, including procurement of eggs, in Woo Suk Hwang's research]. Seoul, 2006.

Mitchell, W. J. T. *Cloning Terror: The War of Images, 9/11 to the Present.* Chicago: University of Chicago Press, 2011. Kindle ed.

Morini, Cristina. "The Feminization of Labour in Cognitive Capitalism." *Feminist Review* 87 (2007): 40–59.

Morris, Errol, dir. *Tabloid.* Sundance Selects, 2011. Film, 87 min.

Morrison, Toni. "Nobel Lecture." Lecture, Nobel Prize in Literature, December 7, 1993. https://www.nobelprize.org/prizes/literature/1993/morrison/lecture/.

Muñoz, José Esteban. *Cruising Utopia: The Then and There of Queer Futurity.* New York: New York University Press, 2009.

Nast, Heidi J. "Critical Pet Studies?" *Antipode* 38, no. 5 (2006): 894–906.

National Bioethics Committee. *Hwangusŏk yŏn'guŭi saengmyŏngyulli munjee taehan pogosŏ* [Report on bioethical problems in Woo Suk Hwang's research]. Seoul, November 2006.

Ngũgĩ wa Thiong'o. "Introduction: Toward the Universal Language of Struggle." In *Decolonising the Mind: The Politics of Language in African Literature,* 1–3. Oxford: James Currey, 1986.

Ngũgĩ wa Thiong'o. "The Language of African Literature." In *Decolonising the Mind: The Politics of Language in African Literature,* 4–33. Oxford: James Currey, 1986.

Nishikawa, Tetsu, and Naoki Morishita. "Current Status of Memorial Services for Laboratory Animals in Japan: A Questionnaire Survey." *Experimental Animals* 61, no. 2 (2012): 177–81.

Normile, Dennis. "The Second Act." *Science* 343, no. 6168 (January 17, 2014): 244–47.

O'Hara, Frank. "Having a Coke with You." In *The Collected Poems of Frank O'Hara,* edited by Donald Allen, 360. Berkeley: University of California Press, 1995.

Olsson, P. Olof, Yeon Woo Jeong, Yeonik Jeong, Mina Kang, Gang Bae Park, Eunji Choi, Sun Kim, Mohammed Shamim Hossein, Young-Bum Son, and Woo Suk Hwang. "Insights from One Thousand Cloned Dogs." *Scientific Reports* 12, no. 1 (2022). https://doi.org/10.1038/s41598-022-15097-7.

Ong, Aihwa. "Introduction: An Analytics of Biotechnology and Ethics at Multiple Scales." In *Asian Biotech: Ethics and Communities of Fate,* edited by Aihwa Ong and Nancy N. Chen, 1–54. Durham, NC: Duke University Press, 2010. Kindle ed.

Pal, Mahuya, and Patrice Buzzanell. "The Indian Call Center Experience: A Case Study in Changing Discourses of Identity, Identification, and Career in a Global Context." *Journal of Business Communication* 45, no. 1 (2008): 31–60.

Parisi, Luciana. *Abstract Sex: Philosophy, Bio-technology, and the Mutations of Desire.* London: Continuum, 2004.

Parisi, Luciana, and Denise Ferreira da Silva. "Black Feminist Tools, Critique, and Techno-poethics." *e-flux* 123 (December 2021). https://www.e-flux.com/journal/123/436929/black-feminist-tools-critique-and-techno-poethics/.

Parisi, Luciana, and Steve Goodman. "Mnemonic Control." In *Beyond Biopolitics: Essays on the Governance of Life and Death,* edited by Patricia Ticineto Clough and Craig Willse, 163–76. Durham, NC: Duke University Press, 2011.

Park Hyu-Yong. "'Segyehwashidaeŭi yŏngŏhaksŭp' yŏlgie taehan pip'anjŏk tamnonbunsŏk: Sahoejŏk kihohwagwajŏngŭi t'amsaek" [Critical discourse analysis of the "English-learning" boom: In the lens of social symbolization]. *Sahoeŏnŏhak* 14, no. 2 (2006): 169–96.

Park Jin-pyo, dir. *Tongue-Tie (Shinbihan yŏngŏnara)*. Short film, 12 min. In *If You Were Me (Yŏsŏt kaeŭi shisŏn)*, directed by Kyun-dong Yeo et al. Chungeorahm Film, 2003. Omnibus film, 110 min.

Park Jong Seong. "Han'gugesŏ yŏngŏŭi suyonggwa chŏn'gae, 1883–2002" [English-language education in Korea from 1883 to 2002]. *An'gwabak* 12 (2002): 49–65.

Park Kŏ-yong. "Yŏngŏ Sinhwaŭi ŏjewa onŭl" [The past and present of the myth of English]. *Naeirŭl yŏnŭn yŏksa* 32 (2008): 77–88.

Park, So Jin, and Nancy Abelmann. "Class and Cosmopolitan Striving: Mothers' Management of English Education in South Korea." *Anthropological Quarterly* 77, no. 4 (2004): 645–72.

Philip, M. NourbeSe. "Discourse on the Logic of Language." In *She Tries Her Tongue, Her Silence Softly Breaks*, 29–34. Middletown, CT: Wesleyan University Press, 2015.

Pickens, Therí A. "Blue Blackness, Black Blueness: Making Sense of Blackness and Disability." *African American Review* 50, no. 2 (2017): 93–103.

Plato. *Phaedrus*. Translated by Alexander Nehamas and Paul Woodruff. Indianapolis: Hackett, 1995.

Podberscek, Anthony L. "Good to Pet and Eat: The Keeping and Consuming of Dogs and Cats in South Korea." *Journal of Social Issues* 65, no. 3 (2009): 615–32.

Pok Kŏil. *Kukcheŏ shidaeŭi minjogŏ* [National language in the age of international language]. Seoul: Munhakkwa chisŏngsa, 1998.

Poster, Winifred R. "Hidden Sides of the Credit Economy: Emotions, Outsourcing, and Indian Call Centers." *International Journal of Comparative Sociology* 54, no. 3 (2013): 205–27.

Povinelli, Elizabeth A. *Geontologies: A Requiem to Late Liberalism*. Durham, NC: Duke University Press, 2016.

Pray, Leslie. "Missyplicity Goes Commercial." *Scientist*, November 26, 2002. https://www.the-scientist.com/missyplicity-goes-commercial-52440.

Preciado, Paul B. "Pharmaco-pornographic Politics: Towards a New Gender Ecology." *Parallax* 14, no. 1 (2008): 105–17.

Probyn, Elspeth. *Carnal Appetites: FoodSexIdentities*. London: Routledge, 2000.

Puar, Jasbir K. *The Right to Maim: Debility, Capacity, Disability*. Durham, NC: Duke University Press, 2017.

Rai, Amit. "Composite Photography." *South Asian Popular Culture* 8, no. 2 (July 2010): 195–201.

Rajan-Rankin, Sweta. "Invisible Bodies and Disembodied Voices? Identity Work, the Body and Embodiment in Transnational Service Work." *Gender, Work and Organization* 25, no. 1 (2017): 9–23.

Rand, Helen M. "Challenging the Invisibility of Sex Work in Digital Labour Politics." *Feminist Review* 123, no. 1 (2019): 40–55.

Reindal, Solveig Magnus. "Independence, Dependence, Interdependence: Some Reflections on the Subject and Personal Autonomy." *Disability and Society* 14, no. 3 (1999): 353–67.

Resnik, David B., Adil Shamoo, and Sheldon Krimsky. "Fraudulent Human Embryonic Stem Cell Research in South Korea: Lessons Learned." *Accountability in Research* 13, no. 1 (2006): 101–9.

Rhee, Margaret. "In Search of My Robot: Race, Technology, and the Asian American Body." *Scholar and Feminist Online* 13.3–14.1 (2016). https://sfonline.barnard.edu/margaret-rhee-in-search-of-my-robot-race-technology-and-the-asian-american-body/.

Rhee, Margaret. *Love, Robot*. New York: Operating System, 2017.

Rhee, Margaret. "Reflecting on Robots, Love, and Poetry: Finding the Poetry in Programming and the Algorithms in Poems." *XRDS: Crossroads, the ACM Magazine for Students* 24, no. 2 (2017): 44–46.

Rinder, Lawrence R. "The Theme of Displacement in the Art of Theresa Hak Kyung Cha and a Catalogue of the Artist's Oeuvre." Master's thesis, Hunter College, 1990.

Roh, David S., Betsy Huang, and Greta A. Niu. "Technologizing Orientalism: An Introduction." In *Techno-Orientalism: Imagining Asia in Speculative Fiction, History, and Media*, edited by David S. Roh, Betsy Huang, and Greta A. Niu, 1–22. London: Rutgers University Press, 2015.

Rosaldo, Renato. "Imperialist Nostalgia." *Representations* 26 (Spring 1989): 107–22. https://doi.org/10.2307/2928525.

Rose, Nikolas. "Molecular Biopolitics, Somatic Ethics and the Spirit of Biocapital." *Social Theory and Health* 5, no. 1 (2007): 3–29.

Rowden, Terry. *The Songs of Blind Folk: African American Musicians and the Cultures of Blindness*. Ann Arbor: University of Michigan Press, 2009.

Schurr, Carolin. "From Biopolitics to Bioeconomies: The ART of (Re-)producing White Futures in Mexico's Surrogacy Market." *Environment and Planning D: Society and Space* 35, no. 2 (2017): 241–62.

Scott, Ridley, dir. *Blade Runner*. Warner Bros, 1982. Film, 117 min.

Sedgwick, Eve Kosofsky, and Adam Frank. "Shame in the Cybernetic Fold: Reading Silvan Tomkins." In *Shame and Its Sisters: A Silvan Tomkins Reader*, edited by Eve Kosofsky Sedgwick and Adam Frank, 1–28. Durham, NC: Duke University Press, 1995.

Sharp, Lesley A. "Monkey Business." *Social Text* 29, no. 1 (106) (2011): 43–69.

Sharp, Lesley A. "The Other Animal of Transplant's Future." *Hastings Center Report* 48, no. S4 (2018): S63–66.

Shildrick, Margrit. *Visceral Prostheses: Somatechnics and Posthuman Embodiment*. London: Bloomsbury, 2022.

Shin, Gi-Wook. *Ethnic Nationalism in Korea: Genealogy, Politics, and Legacy.* Stanford, CA: Stanford University Press, 2006.

Shin, Taeyoung, Duane Kraemer, Jane Pryor, Ling Liu, James Rugila, Lisa Howe, Sandra Buck, Keith Murphy, Leslie Lyons, and Mark Westhusin. "A Cat Cloned by Nuclear Transplantation: This Kitten's Coat-Coloration Pattern Is Not a Carbon Copy of Its Genome Donor's." *Nature* 415, no. 6874 (February 2002): 859–59. https://doi.org/10.1038/nature723.

Shirhŏm tongmure kwanhan pŏmnyul [Laboratory Animal Act]. *Statutes of Republic of Korea.* 2022 (2008).

Simpson, Bob. "Imagined Genetic Communities: Ethnicity and Essentialism in the Twenty-First Century." *Anthropology Today* 16, no. 3 (2000): 3–6.

Singh, Julietta. *Unthinking Mastery: Dehumanism and Decolonial Entanglements.* Durham, NC: Duke University Press, 2018.

Skabelund, Aaron. "Can the Subaltern Bark? Imperialism, Civilization, and Canine Cultures in Nineteenth-Century Japan." In *JAPANimals: History and Culture in Japan's Animal Life*, edited by Gregory M. Pflugfelder and Brett L. Walker, 194–243. Ann Arbor: Center for Japanese Studies, University of Michigan, 2005.

Smietana, Marcin, Charis Thompson, and France Winddance Twine. "Making and Breaking Families: Reading Queer Reproductions, Stratified Reproduction and Reproductive Justice Together." *Reproductive Biomedicine and Society Online* 7 (November 2018): 1–18. https://www.ncbi.nlm.nih.gov/pmc/articles/PMC6491795/.

SNU Investigation Committee. *Hwangusŏk kyosu yŏn'guŭihok kwallyŏn chosa kyŏlgwa pogosŏ* [Final report on Professor Woo Suk Hwang's research allegations]. Seoul: Seoul National University, January 10, 2006.

Sobchack, Vivian. "A Leg to Stand On: Prosthetics, Metaphor, and Materiality." In *The Prosthetic Impulse: From a Posthuman Present to a Biocultural Future*, edited by Marquard Smith and Joanne Morra, 17–41. Cambridge, MA: MIT Press, 2005.

Son Joon-jong. "Nuga kyoyukŭl wihae han'gukŭl ttŏnaryŏgo hanŭn'ga?" [Who leaves Korea for the sake of education?] *Kyoyuksahoyhakyŏn'gu* 15, no. 2 (2005): 95–120.

Sontag, Susan. "The World as India: The St. Jerome Lecture on Literary Translation." Susan Sontag Foundation, 2007. http://www.susansontag.com/prize/onTranslation.shtml.

Spivak, Gayatri. "Can the Subaltern Speak?" In *Marxism and the Interpretation of Culture*, edited by Cary Nelson and Lawrence Grossberg, 267–310. Urbana: University of Illinois Press, 1988.

Spivak, Gayatri. "Remembering the Limits: Differences, Identity and Practice." In *Socialism and the Limits of Liberalism*, edited by Peter Osborne, 227–39. London: Verso, 1991.

Stacey, Jackie. *The Cinematic Life of the Gene*. Durham, NC: Duke University Press, 2010.

Stanescu, James. "Species Trouble: Judith Butler, Mourning, and the Precarious Lives of Animals." *Hypatia* 27, no. 3 (2012): 567–82.

Stengers, Isabelle. "The Cosmopolitical Proposal." In *Making Things Public: Atmospheres of Democracy*, edited by Bruno Latour and Peter Weibel, 994–1003. Cambridge, MA: MIT Press, 2005.

Storrow, Richard F. "The Erasure of Egg Providers in Stem Cell Science." *Frontiers: A Journal of Women Studies* 34, no. 3 (2013): 189–212.

Stryker, Susan, and Nikki Sullivan. "King's Member, Queen's Body: Transsexual Surgery, Self-Demand Amputation and the Somatechnics of Sovereign Power." In *Somatechnics: Queering the Technologisation of Bodies*, edited by Nikki Sullivan and Samantha Murray, 49–63. London: Ashgate, 2009. e-book.

Sudhakar, Anantha, and Vanita Reddy. "Introduction: Feminist and Queer Afro-Asian Formations." *Scholar and Feminist Online* 14, no. 3 (2018). https://sfonline.barnard.edu/introduction-feminist-and-queer-afro-asian-formations/.

Sullivan, Nikki. "Somatechnics." *TSQ: Transgender Studies Quarterly* 1, no. 1–2 (2014): 187–90.

Sunder Rajan, Kaushik. "Experimental Values: Indian Clinical Trials and Surplus Health." *New Left Review* 45 (May/June 2007): 67–88.

Sunstein, Cass R. "Can Animals Sue?" In *Animal Rights: Current Debates and New Directions*, edited by Cass R. Sunstein and Martha Craven Nussbaum, 251–62. Oxford: Oxford University Press, 2004.

Takahashi, Kazutoshi, and Shinya Yamanaka. "Induction of Pluripotent Stem Cells from Mouse Embryonic and Adult Fibroblast Cultures by Defined Factors." *Cell* 126, no. 4 (2006): 663–76.

Taylor, Sunaura. "Interdependent Animals: A Feminist Disability Ethic-of-Care." In *Ecofeminism: Feminist Intersections with Other Animals and the Earth*, edited by Carol J. Adams and Lori Gruen, 141–60. New York: Bloomsbury, 2014.

Thompson, Charis. "Asian Regeneration? Nationalism and Internationalism in Stem Cell Research in South Korea and Singapore." In *Asian Biotech: Ethics and Communities of Fate*, edited by Aihwa Ong and Nancy N. Chen, 95–117. Durham, NC: Duke University Press, 2010.

Thompson, Charis. *Good Science: The Ethical Choreography of Stem Cell Research*. Cambridge, MA: MIT Press, 2013.

Thompson, Charis. *Making Parents: The Ontological Choreography of Reproductive Technologies*. Cambridge, MA: MIT Press, 2005.

Tomkins, Silvan. "Shame-Humiliation and Contempt-Disgust." In *Shame and Its Sisters: A Silvan Tomkins Reader*, edited by Eve Kosofsky Sedgwick and Adam Frank, 133–78. Durham, NC: Duke University Press, 1995.

Tongmulbohobŏp [Animal Protection Act]. *Statutes of Republic of Korea.* Amended April 26, 2022. https://elaw.klri.re.kr/kor_service/lawView.do ?hseq=60704&lang=ENG.

Trinh T. Minh-ha. *Elsewhere, Within Here: Immigration, Refugeeism and the Boundary Event.* New York: Routledge, 2011.

Tsuneishi, Kei-chi. "Unit 731 and the Human Skulls Discovered in 1989: Physicians Carrying Out Organized Crimes." In *Dark Medicine: Rationalizing Unethical Medical Research,* edited by William R. LaFleur, Gernot Böhme, and Susumu Shimazono, 73–84. Bloomington: Indiana University Press, 2008.

Turing, A. M. "Computing Machinery and Intelligence." *Mind* 59, no. 236 (1950): 433–60.

Twine, Richard. *Animals as Biotechnology: Ethics, Sustainability and Critical Animal Studies.* London: Earthscan, 2010.

Tyldum, Morten, dir. *The Imitation Game.* Weinstein Company, 2014. Film, 115 min.

Van Doorn, Niels. "Platform Labor: On the Gendered and Racialized Exploitation of Low-Income Service Work in the 'On-Demand' Economy." *Information, Communication and Society* 20, no. 6 (2017): 898–914.

Vazin, Tandis, and William J. Freed. "Human Embryonic Stem Cells: Derivation, Culture, and Differentiation: A Review." *Restorative Neurology and Neuroscience* 28, no. 4 (2010): 589–603.

Veldkamp, Elmer. "Commemoration of Dead Animals in Contemporary Korea." *Review of Korean Studies* 11, no. 3 (2008): 149–69.

Verhoeven, Paul, dir. *Total Recall.* TriStar Pictures, 1990. Film, 113 min.

Vogel, Gretchen. "South Korean Court Reduces Hwang's Sentence." *Science,* December 16, 2010. https://www.science.org/content/article/south-korean -court-reduces-hwangs-sentence.

Waldby, Catherine. "Oocyte Markets: Women's Reproductive Work in Embryonic Stem Cell Research." *New Genetics and Society* 27, no. 1 (2008): 19–31.

Waldby, Catherine. "Stem Cells, Tissue Cultures and the Production of Biovalue." *Health* 6, no. 3 (2002): 305–23.

Waldby, Catherine, and Melinda Cooper. "From Reproductive Work to Regenerative Labour: The Female Body and the Stem Cell Industries." *Feminist Theory* 11, no. 1 (2010): 3–22.

Walraven, Boudewijn C. A. "Bardot Soup and Confucians' Meat: Food and Korean Identity in Global Context." In *Asian Food,* edited by Katarzyna J. Cwiertka and Boudewijn C. A. Walraven, 95–115. Honolulu: University of Hawai'i Press, 2001.

Weisberg, Zipporah. "The Broken Promises of Monsters: Haraway, Animals and the Humanist Legacy." *Journal for Critical Animal Studies* 7, no. 2 (2009): 22–62.

Wetherell, Margaret. "Affect and Discourse: What's the Problem? From Affect as Excess to Affective/Discursive Practice." *Subjectivity* 6, no. 4 (2013): 349–68.

Wills, David. *Prosthesis*. Stanford, CA: Stanford University Press, 1995.

Wilson, Elizabeth A. *Affect and Artificial Intelligence*. Seattle: University of Washington Press, 2010.

Winder, William. "Robotic Poetics." In *A Companion to Digital Humanities*, edited by Susan Schreibman, Raymond George Siemens, and John Unsworth. Malden, MA: Blackwell, 2004. https://companions.digitalhumanities.org/DH/?chapter=content/9781405103213_chapter_30.html.

Woestendiek, John. *Dog, Inc.: How a Collection of Visionaries, Rebels, Eccentrics, and Their Pets Launched the Commercial Dog Cloning Industry*. New York: Penguin, 2012.

Wolfe, Cary. *Animal Rites: American Culture, the Discourse of Species, and Posthumanist Theory*. Chicago: University of Chicago Press, 2003.

Wolfe, Cary. *Before the Law: Humans and Other Animals in a Biopolitical Frame*. Chicago: University of Chicago Press, 2013.

Wolfe, Cary. "What 'the Animal' Can Teach 'the Anthropocene.'" *Angelaki: Journal of the Theoretical Humanities* 25, no. 3 (2020): 131–45.

Wong, Joseph, Uyen Quach, Halla Thorsteinsdóttir, Peter A. Singer, and Abdallah S. Daar. "South Korean Biotechnology: A Rising Industrial and Scientific Powerhouse." *Nature Biotechnology* 22, no. 12 (December 2004): DC42–47.

Wu, Chia-Ling, ed. "The Hwang Scandal and Human Embryonic Stem Cell Research." Special issue, *East Asian Science, Technology, and Society* 2, no. 1 (2008).

Wynter, Sylvia. "Human Being as Noun? Or Being Human as Praxis? Towards the Autopoetic Turn/Overturn: A Manifesto." Unpublished manuscript, 2007.

Wynter, Sylvia, and Katherine McKittrick. "Unparalleled Catastrophe for Our Species? Or, To Give Humanness a Different Future." In *Sylvia Wynter: On Being Human as Praxis*, edited by Katherine McKittrick, 9–89. Durham, NC: Duke University Press, 2015.

Index

ecology of sensation, 66, 71
egg donors, 79, 140, 144; dog, 103,
    105–7, 122, 127–28, 132–33, 136,
    139; human, 122, 139, 144
embodiment, 16–17, 28; Black, 45;
    cloning and, 79, 84, 93, 96–97;
    racialized, 162n33; of technology
    of memory, 7; women's, 136, 140
embryos, 132–33, 187n73; cloning of,
    121, 123, 137; human, 19, 86, 125,
    138; mammalian, 3; recipients of,
    102, 107; Snuppy and, 132; in stem
    cell research, 86, 121, 133, 187n73
empathy, 9, 93, 170n15
encounter value, 89–90, 93
English (language), 17, 38–40, 42–43, 53,
    55, 58–61, 133, 158n3, 159n6, 160n8,
    160n10, 161n12, 161n23, 165n9,
    165–66n12, 167n58; accent, 28, 35,
    38, 43, 57, 60, 147; education, 38–39,
    44, 162n31; hegemony of, 33; pro-
    nunciation, 5, 28, 34, 38–39, 41, 53,
    159–60nn5–6. *See also* call centers
epistemology, 141; onto-, 35, 49, 142,
    147; of science, 143
erasure, 89, 126, 133, 143, 147; biopo-
    litical, 30; of memories, 5; of
    mother tongue, 55; necropolitical,
    4; of otherness, 130
ethics, 89, 109, 183n25; affirmative,
    25–27; animal, 188n95; blue-collar,
    116; of care, 18–20, 137, 139, 144;
    Derrida's, 103, 120, 175n8; feminist,
    27, 98, 138, 140, 143, 188n95; of griev-
    able life, 24; Hawthorne's, 176n24;
    of human embodiment, 17; journal-
    ism, 181n12; laws, 171n30; of mourn-
    ing, 23, 83, 98, 130; postcolonial, 131;
    of responsibility, 140, 175n8; univer-
    sal, 113; of vulnerability, 48
evolution, 89; Darwinian, 51; human,
    50; interspecies, 3

Fanon, Frantz, 41–42, 50–51, 62, 74,
    157n109, 158n8
feminisms, 15, 139, 189n96; cyborgian,
    20; decolonial, 13; postcolonial,
    30, 33, 144; socialist, 10

feminist mnemonics, 30, 133; dehu-
    manist, 146; postcolonial, 4–6, 13,
    23, 45, 80, 139, 154n67
feminist politics, 122, 136
Ferreira da Silva, Denise, 52, 59, 63,
    67, 72–73, 142–43, 150n13
Foucault, Michel, 25, 42–43, 108,
    161n19

gender, 5, 19, 35, 54, 63, 79–80, 126,
    162n25, 163n41; bioethics and,
    187n64; dog eating and, 102;
    identity, 175n5; intimacy and, 83;
    labor and, 181n8; mourning and,
    29; norms, 44; speciesism and,
    189n98
gene, 4–5, 12, 28; gene banking, 85
genealogies, 26; anticolonial, 42; of
    cybernetics, 152n33; feminist, 73,
    137; of linguistic performativity,
    38; postcolonial, 7, 73; of pros-
    thetic memory, 5, 13; queer, 64,
    70–72; of reproduction, 153n63; of
    wiryŏngje, 131
Genetic Savings and Clone (GSC), 75,
    84–87, 90, 93, 107, 172n39. *See also*
    BioArts International
globalization, 29, 58, 60, 124, 158n3,
    161n12; of bioethics, 140; of
    Black Lives Matter movement,
    22; Korean way of, 160n9; of
    markets, 21; neoliberal, 5, 33, 38,
    58, 63, 160n6, 161n23, 175n7; poli-
    cies, 44
Gottweis, Herbert, 123–25, 182n19
governance, 123, 125; biopolitical, 83,
    148; of life, 10, 29, 163n46, 175n6;
    necropolitical, 54; postcolonial,
    21, 39; technological, 148
grafting, 9, 145–46
Grau, Christopher, 93–95, 97, 173n56
grief, 2, 82–83, 85–86, 91–93, 95.
    See also mourning
grievable life, 86; ethics of, 24.
    See also Butler, Judith

Haraway, Donna, 10–11, 15, 21–22, 73,
    89, 140, 155n79, 176n24

mourning, 23, 26–27, 29, 84, 86, 92, 95, 129, 170n18; biopolitics of, 25; ethics of, 23, 83, 98, 130; feminization of, 171n22; pet cloning and, 17, 76, 79, 82–85, 93, 98–99, 102
My Friend Again, 104, 175n12

nationalism, 112, 124–25, 128; bionationalism, 123–24, 182n19; developmentalist, 160n9; European, 165n12; Korean, 103; postcolonial, 129
normativity: emotional, 99; nonnormativity, 65; Western, 108

Oh, Joon-Soo, 2, 150n6
oikos, 90–91
ontology, 23–25, 27, 157n103; dualistic, 143
oocytes, 19, 124, 133, 135, 137, 139, 182n19, 186n58; enucleated, 121, 168n1; markets for, 135, 137
other, the, 7, 24, 118, 120, 130; language of, 34; of white/European subject, 73, 147
Other, the, 52, 108, 116
otherness, 3–4, 109, 130, 144, 146

Parisi, Luciana, 11, 62–63, 73, 78, 191n10
Park, Jin-pyo, 37, 159n1
Park, So Jin, 43–44, 162n30
patriarchy, 20–21, 140
performativity, 48, 150n12; cosmogonic, 71; linguistic, 28, 34, 38, 45–47, 162n33; techno-linguistic, 35
pet cloning, 11, 17, 29, 86, 88–89, 91–93, 95, 98–99, 107, 127–28, 148, 169n2, 172nn38–39; industry, 10, 173n53, 174n2, 184n36; mourning and, 76, 82–85, 99; surrogates in, 103; transnational, 29, 79, 84, 102, 105, 115–16, 120. *See also* commercial pet cloning; Missyplicity Project; Sooam Biotech Research Foundation (BRF)
Philip, M. NourbeSe, 35, 45, 53–54, 56

plants, 4, 10, 145–46, 149n3; grafting of, 9, 145–46 (*see also* cacti)
Plato, 7, 13
poetry, 55, 59, 64–65, 68–69, 72, 74; human-machine, 5; machine, 6, 17, 69–71, 167n49; thinking and, 62. *See also* Cha, Theresa Hak Kyung; Rhee, Margaret
poiesis, 62–63, 69, 73–74. *See also* autopoiesis
polis, 90–92
postcoloniality, 6, 39, 116, 120, 162n33
precarity, 47–48, 79; biopolitical, 27; of Black people in the United States, 46; human, 23; of life, 24, 46
Probyn, Elspeth, 33, 115, 118, 158n7, 179n69
prostheticity, 33; of cloning, 84; of language, 48, 53; of languaging, 40, 45, 49, 52, 64, 74; of the self, 7; of tongues, 28, 45
prosthetic memory, 1–11, 13–14, 16, 18, 20, 25, 27, 30, 33, 146–48, 150n13; as form of collective memory, 28; postcolonial feminist approach to, 23; as postcolonial feminist mnemonic, 154n67; postcolonial transspecies feminist approach to, 126
prosthetics, 6, 8, 14–18, 150n12; handcrafted, 153n53; micro-prosthetics, 12; supplementarity of, 20
Puar, Jasbir K., 10, 15

race, 5, 19, 26, 29, 35, 49, 54, 62–63, 72, 163n41; bioeconomic exploitation and, 181n8; hierarchies of, 117; knowledges of, 59; Korean immigrants and, 156n82; norms, 83; transnationalization of bioethics and, 102
racialization, 22, 61, 156n84
racism, 21, 23, 42
Reeve, Christopher, 124, 182n20
regenerative medicine, 78, 80, 122, 181n8, 186n57; industry, 19; reproductive technology and, 10, 134–35, 137, 139

relationality, 88, 92; heteronormative, 95; queer, 67

representation, 6, 26, 30, 77, 109, 116, 118, 150n13; affect and, 177n32; human, 27; media, 24; Western leftist intellectuals' role in, 147–48

reproduction, 42, 45, 52, 56, 77, 79, 135; of animals, 107, 137; artificial, 76; asexual, 106, 132; biocybernetics, 12, 77; of biological materials, 89; biotechnological, 138; of copies, 75; of cows, 188n89; of dogs, 88, 90; genetic, 83, 91; of homo economicus, 43; pet cloning as, 88, 172n38; queer, 153n63; of the same, 148; self-reproduction, 78; sexual, 11

resistance, 21, 33, 35, 111, 160n6, 160n8

Rhee, Margaret, 28, 59, 61, 65–66, 74, 150n13, 154n67, 167n48; *Kimchi Poetry Machine*, 34–35, 64, 69–70, 72; *Love, Robot*, 35, 64–66, 68, 71–72

RNL Bio, 81, 102–4, 107, 168n3, 184n36

Rose, Nikolas, 11, 181n8

sacrifice, 80, 129–30, 140; of animals, 127, 129, 131–32; spirit of, 134; widow, 108

Sedgwick, Eve Kosofsky, 58, 148

segyehwa, 39–40, 124–25, 127–28, 132, 160n9, 183n22, 184n37

self-amputation, 8, 14

Seoul National University (SNU), 16, 87, 101, 121, 123, 126, 130, 134, 171n30. *See also* RNL Bio

sex industry, 21, 155n79

sexual difference, 16, 72

sexuality, 15, 29, 35, 79, 83, 162n25; canine, 89–90; feminine, 71

shame, 103, 109, 115–18, 120, 148, 179n65

Sharp, Lesley, 129, 143, 185n44

singularity, 76, 84, 86, 89, 92–95, 97–98, 170n18

slavery, 8, 20, 26, 49, 162n33; abolition of, 156n83; sexual, 154n74

Sobchack, Vivian, 14, 17

somatechnics, 16, 98

somatechnology, 40–42, 72, 74, 77, 83–84; of mourning, 93, 99, 107n18

somatic cell nuclear transfer (SCNT), 81, 87, 95, 121–22, 127, 132, 137–38, 168–69nn1–2

Sontag, Susan, 28, 35, 57–61, 64, 71–73, 164n2, 167n58

Sooam Biotech Research Foundation (BRF), 87, 93, 104–5, 127, 132, 173n53, 175nn12–13, 176n18, 186n54; BioArts International and, 90, 101, 107. *See also* dog cloning

South Korea, 1, 12, 22, 31, 42–44, 78–79, 93, 101–3, 105–10, 114–15, 121, 128, 130, 132, 135, 145, 160n9, 169n2, 175n7; Animal Protection Act, 111; animal rights movement in, 170n12; bioethics and, 29, 80, 103, 109, 140, 181n10; biomedicine in, 124; biotechnology in, 30, 125, 182n21; diseases in, 143; English and, 38–39, 160n10, 161n12; lab animals in, 106, 188n96; Livestock Product Processing Act, 111–12; memory and, 6, 9, 28; nationalists in, 177n34; pet culture in, 179n61; postcoloniality in, 162n33; prosthetic memories and, 4, 76; racial hierarchy in, 155–56n82; United States and, 155n74. *See also* dog meat; pet cloning; Seoul National University (SNU); Sooam Biotech Research Foundation (BRF); stem cell research; tongue surgery

sovereignty, 20, 112, 114–15

Special-Usefulness Animal Cloning Project, 127–28

species, 17, 29, 54, 68–69, 72, 79–80, 83, 98, 126; animal, 92, 143, 180n71; bioethics and, 102; boundaries, 3, 142; difference, 94; encounters, 97; endangered, 127–28; extinction of, 76; hierarchies, 78, 117; human, 49–52, 77; kinship, 5; meat, 115; nonhuman, 109; order, 65; replaceability between, 138